Shadow Prices for Project Appraisal

To Alba and Elio, for the education.
To Mirta, for the understanding.
To Lucía and Pablo, for the hope.

Shadow Prices for Project Appraisal

Theory and Practice

Elio H. Londero
Inter-American Development Bank, Washington, DC, USA

with a contribution from

Héctor Cervini
Universidad Autónoma Metropolitana, Azcapotzalco, Mexico DF

Edward Elgar
Cheltenham, UK • Northampton, MA, USA

Published by
Edward Elgar Publishing Limited
Glensanda House
Montpellier Parade
Cheltenham
Glos GL50 1UA
UK

Edward Elgar Publishing, Inc.
136 West Street
Suite 202
Northampton
Massachusetts 01060
USA

A catalogue record for this book
is available from the British Library

Library of Congress Cataloguing in Publication Data

Londero, Elio H.
    Shadow prices for project appraisal: theory and practice/
Elio H. Londero with a contribution from Héctor Cervini.
        p. cm.
    Includes bibliographical references and indexes.
    1. Shadow prices. 2. Economic development projects—
Evaluation. I. Cervini, Héctor. II. Title.
HB143.L66   2003
338.9—dc21

                                        2003049036

ISBN 1 84376 357 5

Printed and bound in Great Britain by MPG Books Ltd, Bodmin, Cornwall

Contents

Figures

Tables

Preface

This book aims at explaining what are shadow (or accounting) prices, how they can be estimated, and how they should be used. It is based on the author's experience in conducting field estimates, directing multicountry studies, applying the resulting prices, and supervising their use. It is also rooted in the conviction regarding the importance of understanding the theoretical foundations for interpreting the results, and the importance of knowing the reasoning leading to the formulae for their proper application.

The book is addressed to economists interested in estimating shadow prices, as well as those students and practitioners of cost–benefit analysis interested in going beyond the intuitive treatment of the subject. Thus it falls between purely theoretical work, often removed from the needs of practitioners, and intuitive approaches frequently lacking a satisfactory grounding in welfare economics and step by step demonstrations of the formulae used in practice. It is intended to be accessible to anyone who has completed an intermediate course in microeconomics. No special mathematical knowledge or ability is required, since only elementary mathematics are employed, and mostly in appendices.

The author would like to thank *El Trimestre Económico, Desarrollo y Sociedad, Project Appraisal*, and the Inter-American Development Bank for the authorization to use materials previously published by them.

Comments provided by Héctor Cervini, Joan Pasqual, David Potts, and John Weiss, and perceptive questions by Guadalupe Souto, contributed to improving the book, and are gratefully acknowledged. Opinions expressed in this book, as well as remaining errors and omissions, are the responsibility of the authors, and are not intended to represent views of the institutions with which they are or were associated, nor of those that helped make this book possible.

Elio H. Londero
Vienna, Virginia

Acknowledgments

The publishers wish to thank the following who have kindly given permission for the use of copyright material.

Inter-American Development Bank for books *Precios de Cuenta* (Accounting Prices),Washington DC: Inter-American Development Bank, 1992, and *Benefits and Beneficiaries*, Washington DC: Inter-American Development Bank, 1987, 1996.

Beech Tree Publishing for article 'Shadow Pricing Rules for Partially Traded Goods', *Project Appraisal*, **11** (3), 169-82.

Fondo de Cultura Económica, for article 'Los fundamentos del análisis costo beneficio y su reflejo en las principales versiones operativas' (The Foundations of Cost–benefit Analysis and their Reflection in the Most Important Operational Versions), *El Trimestre Económico*, **58** (1), 73-99.

Centro de Estudios sobre Desarrollo Económico, Universidad de Los Andes, for article 'Sobre el uso de técnicas de insumo-producto para la estimación de precios de cuenta' (On the Use of Input–Output Techniques for Estimating Accounting Prices), *Desarrollo y Sociedad*, (24), 131-58.

Every effort has been made to trace all the copyright holders but if any have been inadvertently overlooked the publishers will be pleased to make the necessary arrangements at the first opportunity.

1. Basic Concepts

1.1 INTRODUCTION

The appraisal of an investment project consists of estimating the project flows of costs and benefits in order to determine whether the flow of benefits is at least enough to compensate for the flow of costs. In the case of a private or financial appraisal of an investment, the objective is to determine whether the investor's will gain or lose money with the project and how much. The focus is on the investor's gains and loses. Cost–benefit analysis (CBA), instead, takes a societal point of view. Oversimplifying, such a point of view translates into two main differences between a financial appraisal and a CBA. First, a CBA is interested in the gains and losses of all affected by the project. Second, CBA is not only interested in the monetary gains and losses, but also in the nonmonetary ones, and refers to all these effects as those on the economic welfare of the individual. In order to make these objectives operational, CBA has developed criteria to estimate money measures of all the effects on the individual's welfare, and has devised alternative ways for aggregating these effects into a total.

Financial analyses are based on market prices of goods and services demanded or supplied by the project, since these prices indicate the changes in income associated with buying or selling one unit. CBA uses prices that aim at capturing the money-measures of the effects attributable to an additional demand or supply of goods and services on all individuals affected. These prices are normally called shadow or accounting prices. Intuition suggests that while market prices may be observed in market transactions, shadow prices would need to be estimated.

This book aims at explaining what shadow prices are and how they can be estimated. It emerged from the conviction that the proper estimation and use of shadow prices require a minimum knowledge of the ethical and theoretical foundations of these alternative price systems. Such knowledge is necessary for understanding and then for being able to explain the nature of the information provided by a cost–benefit analysis, its differences from a financial analysis, and its limitations. Greater familiarity with the underlying principles also facilitates recognizing the common foundations of alternative CBA proposals and the identification of their main differences. For these reasons, building on Londero (1987, 1991), the remainder of this chapter

1

provides a brief introduction to applied welfare economics as the foundation of cost–benefit analysis in general and of shadow prices in particular.

Traditional applied welfare economics starts at the level of the individual, trying to obtain money measures of his/her welfare changes. It then proceeds to aggregating these money measures into one 'total' welfare change. In following this approach, this chapter emphasizes the reasoning underlying the measurement of changes in individuals' welfare and the judgements required to obtain aggregate measures of 'total' welfare change. In doing so, it also provides a preview of the method that will be used to derive familiar formulae for estimating specific shadow prices. Finally, it places the rest of the book in the context of the most significant literature on the subject. This step-by-step approach of building from the more general principles to specific shadow prices may require some extra patience from the applied economist interested exclusively in finding answers to specific situations. This book is based on the idea that it is impossible to provide recipes for all possible situations, and that it is a better investment to become knowledgeable in the more general approach, and then adapt it to particular cases.

The analytical method is fundamentally partial equilibrium. It allows a step by step tracing of the effects resulting from the additional demands and supplies generated by a project, and facilitates discussion of the approximations that are often needed in practice. There is a loss of rigor as a result, but there are also gains in greater proximity to real situations and greater adaptability to specific cases. Some simple general equilibrium derivations of the formulae are presented in appendixes only as an introductory step. The reader interested in general equilibrium approaches may consult Drèze and Stern (1987), Squire (1989) and Dinwiddy and Teal (1996).

Starting with measuring welfare changes at the level of the individual or groups of individuals, and then moving to the aggregation of such measures is also the preferred approach to understanding and measuring the distributional effects of projects in the context of cost–benefit analysis. This subject has been explored in detail by the author elsewhere (Londero, 1987, 1996a), and the arguments will not be reiterated here. Nevertheless, the derivations of the algebraic expressions for estimating shadow prices devote special attention to the needs of estimating distributional effects. The reader should have no problem in connecting the contents of this book with the approach of the above-mentioned publications.

Based on the general method described in Chapter 1, Chapters 2 to 6 present the derivation of the familiar formulae frequently used in practice, and thus provide the assumptions and reasoning underlying these formulae. It is expected that a more detailed, albeit simple presentation of the analytics will facilitate adapting the reasoning to different situations, thus discouraging the mechanical application of familiar formulae to situations in which conditions often differ from those assumed in the derivation of these simple formulae.

Chapter 6, building on Londero (1989), provides a detailed presentation on the use of input–output techniques for estimating shadow prices for marginally produced goods, considering both the preparation of specific tables and the use of existing ones. A solid understanding of this more complex method facilitates identifying the limitations of the simpler alternatives presented at the end of the chapter.

Chapter 7 starts with a presentation on how to apply existing shadow prices, followed by suggestions on how to use them for calculating new ones. The project analyst cannot be expected to produce his or her own estimates, and would normally rely on existing ones. For that reason, this chapter also discusses how to update existing estimates, including the price-updating of input–output tables for that purpose.

In order to help bridge theory and practice, Chapter 8 provides a case study extracted from a real estimation conducted by Héctor Cervini et al. (1990) as part of an applied research project directed by the author (Londero, 1992). The numerical results are outdated, but the detailed and comprehensive approach makes this study useful for methodological purposes.

The analytical chapters, as well as the case study, deal with important and often neglected subjects in applied studies. Examples are the use of long-run marginal cost estimates, specification and treatment of goods in fixed supply, identification and treatment of price discrimination, and the correspondence between prevailing and long-run equilibrium relative prices and the possible need to price-update the data due to relative price misalignment.

1.2 FOUNDATIONS OF COST–BENEFIT ANALYSIS

CBA stems from an interest in comparing alternative resource allocations, in order to determine which one is better. Since those alternatives are the result of actions that carry diverse effects, CBA includes the criteria for defining those affected, characterizing the effects, measuring the effects on those affected (gainers and losers) and comparing the resulting measures. It will be shown that these criteria are based on value judgements that distinctly characterize this type of analysis, as well as the proper use of its results.

The first criterion is the one to determine who have been affected. From a theoretical point of view, each person determines whether he or she has been affected or not. In practice, however, it is the analyst's responsibility to trace the effects of the project in order to identify those affected. The theoretical criterion acts as a control on the analyst's decision, for it provides the basis for contesting the original identification.

The second criterion, used for defining *who* characterizes the effects, states that it is each person affected who defines whether the effects of an action are beneficial or harmful to him or her. In other words, if someone says that something is good (bad) for him or her, that is the way it is considered in the analysis. Mishan (1981b) has proposed three interpretations of this criterion:

1. it is a 'judgement of fact: – a belief that each person ... generally knows what he wants better than other persons';
2. it is a 'judgement of morality: – a belief that the good society is one that ought to act *as if* each man knows his own interests better than any other person'; and
3. it is a 'principle of political expediency: – a belief that in a Western type democracy, at least, it is politically expedient to act on the assumption that each person knows his own interest better than others do'.

Political expediency does not seem to be a foundation that would be consistent with the remaining criteria used by CBA. If political expediency means the compliance with both ease of implementation and consistency with other methods used in the political process, it is apparent that it would be more 'expedient' to use the decision of an elected institution (e.g. a legislative body) instead. If political expediency means expediency for the social group in power, this criterion (as well as others) should be derived from the objectives of such a group. Political expediency is a matter of degree, according to which several criteria could be ranked, and it is not clear in what sense the CBA criterion would be the most politically expedient. Also, political expediency should manifest itself in other criteria, such as those for measuring the effects and comparing the resulting measures. Thus, effects could be measured by their expected impact on electoral results (e.g. through contributions to electoral campaigns), or be based on a fundamental principle proclaimed by western democracies: one person, one vote. However, it will be shown that the measurement criterion is not consistent with the 'one person, one vote' principle, and that comparison criteria are not in line with an electoral results criterion, although it is well known that this latter criterion is in fact used by political institutions to select investment projects.

Consider now the criterion to characterize the effects as a judgement of fact: what the individual wants is beneficial to him, what he or she rejects is harmful, and what is indifferent to him or her has no effect (on balance). All these considerations underlie the use of indifference curves in welfare economics. This interpretation requires another criterion that determines whether the affected person's judgement coincides or not with what the effects 'actually are' for him or her, or a verification criterion of the former. This verification criterion should allow a determination of whether the effects judged by the person as good (bad) for him or her actually are good (bad), implying the existence of a nonnormative criterion for judging goodness or badness, a clear contradiction.

Finally there is the 'judgement of morality'. It is based on the belief of how a good society should act, and provides a foundation to welfare economics for all who share such a judgement. It is a judgement that may carry a wider or narrower consensus, but it is one that frequently clashes with those used for resource allocation decisions; for example, mandatory primary education and the appointment of public defendants.

Another related criterion is the one defining if *all* those affected are included, or only a subset. For example, military expenditures affect the citizens of the spending country as well as those of other countries. By the same token, foreign direct investment affects inhabitants of both the investing and the recipient countries. The solution cannot be anything but another value judgement, which is reflected in CBA conventions. In analyzing the allocation of resources to an investment project, only costs and benefits to residents of the country carrying out the analysis are taken into account. A common market institution, instead, should take into account costs and benefits to residents of all member countries. It should be noted that there exists no generally accepted criterion to define, according to the electoral result, the subset of those affected and included in the analysis. In other words, voting rights are not used to distinguish the included from the not included. Such an omission suggests that the contribution to the electoral result is not considered a valid criterion for identifying the effects, or those affected.

CBA's measurement criterion, known as the compensating variation (CV), comes from traditional neoclassical welfare economics.[1] This criterion consists of comparing the situation resulting from the action being analyzed (the with-project situation) with the situation that would exist if such an action would not be carried out (the without-project situation) in order to formulate the following question: what is the change in the monetary income of the affected person that is required for him or her to consider that he is enjoying the same welfare that he or she would have enjoyed if such an action had not been carried out? Such an amount is the compensating variation of the action being analyzed for that person, and it is used as a monetary measure of the individual's welfare change. For example, if access to a park would increase someone's welfare, his or her CV of free access to the park would be the reduction in his or her monetary income in the with-access situation that would be required for him or her to return to the welfare level he or she would have enjoyed without free access to the park. Such a reduction in his or her income would be the money-measure of his or her welfare change attributable to gaining access to the park. Note that the criterion is based on the value judgement establishing who determines whether someone has been affected, and implies that the affected individual is able to determine the overall effect

---

1. There exists a second, closely related measurement criterion known as the equivalent variation. Meade (1972) and Mishan (1988, Part IV) analyze the implications of using one or the other. For an advanced treatment of measures of welfare change, see McKenzie (1983).

of the action and translate it into a sum of money. It then becomes apparent that the measurement criterion is not consistent with the 'one person, one vote' principle, but it intends to capture the intensity of the effect for the affected individual relative to the effects that he or she would be able to obtain by disposing of a sum of money.

If the action consists of increasing the individual's monetary income, the measurement problem is a simple one: if the person receives a $100 transfer, the corresponding CV is obviously $100.[2] When the action consists of changes in the demand for consumption goods that are commodities, the measurement criterion uses the theoretical framework known as the 'theory of consumer behavior'. Within this framework it is possible to demonstrate that the CV may be quantified with reasonable approximation using the individual's preferences as revealed by his or her demand function for the good in question.[3] In the case of changes in the demand or supply of intermediate goods, the measurement criterion relies on the ability attributed to markets to reflect in the demand for such goods the consumers' valuations of consumption changes attributable to those demand or supply changes. If goods are not traded in conventional markets (e.g. pollution), measurement is more difficult due to the absence of data that would allow measurement of CV directly.[4]

Measurement takes place in a partial equilibrium context. In other words, it is assumed that all prices other than that of the good being studied remain unchanged. Individual markets are studied in isolation, as if they were independent from other markets, reflecting the expectation that a price change in one market does not have significant repercussions in other markets.

This book will not deal with the measurement of costs and benefits for specific projects, and will concentrate on the effects of changes in the demand or supply of commodities under the implicit assumption that there are no external effects. To that effect, a simple example will illustrate the type of reasoning involved when measurement is based on demand functions. This example will facilitate the introduction later on of the concept of shadow (or accounting) prices.

Consider the case of a consumption good in fixed supply, represented in Figure 1.1(a). The additional supply would reduce price and induce an increase in consumption by the individuals whose demand functions are aggregated in the market demand function D. Such is the case of individual e,

---

2. The $ sign is used to designate any unspecified national currency, while US dollars will be denoted by US$.

3. Sen (1973, 1977, 1987) criticizes these assumptions.

4. See Mishan (1988, Parts III and VI), and *Journal of Economic Perspectives* (1994).

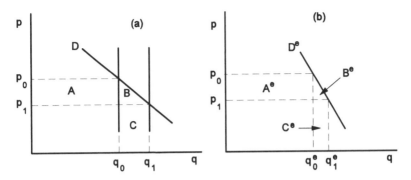

Figure 1.1 An increase in the supply of q

whose demand function is represented in Figure 1.1(b). The 'theory of consumer behavior' allows for the CV of price reduction $p_0 - p_1$ to be approximated by the area $A^e + B^e$ in Figure 1.1.(b) – area known as the change in the consumer's surplus.[5] This measure may in turn be broken down into what the consumer no longer pays for the quantity consumed without the price reduction (area A^e), plus his or her willingness to pay for quantity $q_1^e - q_0^e$ (area $B^e + C^e$), minus the amount actually paid for that additional quantity (area C^e). These income changes, as well as those of other persons, all attributable to the change being analyzed, are presented in Table 1.1. The consumer gains area A^e, equal to the price reduction multiplied by his or her consumption in the without-change situation. This gain for the consumer is a loss for those no longer receiving that amount. Since in this simple example the consumption good is in fixed supply, this consumer's income gain is loss of revenue for the producers of q, excluding the project. The consumer is also willing to pay $B^e + C^e$, but only pays C^e, which is additional project revenue for the sale of $q_1^e - q_0^e$. Summing up, the project receives additional revenue C^e, the consumer gains $A^e + B^e$, and the other producers lose revenue for an amount equivalent to A^e. The 'Total' column of the table brings the analysis to the subject of the interpersonal comparison criteria.

Once the set of all persons to be considered for the analysis has been defined (say all residents of a country), all affected members of the set have been identified, and all corresponding CVs have been estimated, it is still necessary to define a criterion for coming up with a judgement based on those measures. A well-known criterion is the (strict) Pareto improvement, named in recognition of Vilfredo Pareto, who formulated it. According to this

---

5. Winch (1975, Ch. 7), Mishan (1981b, Ch. 23) and Londero (1987, Appendix A) provide simple demonstrations.

Shadow Prices for Project Appraisal

*Table 1.1   Consumer e's compensating variation of the project's additional
supply*

	Project	Consumers	Other producers	Total
Expenditure in q_0^e	—	A^e	$-A^e$	—
Willingness to pay for $q_1^e - q_0^e$	—	$B^e + C^e$	—	$B^e + C^e$
Paid for $q_1^e - q_0^e$	C^e	$-C^e$	—	—
Total	C^e	$A^e + B^e$	$-A^e$	$B^e + C^e$

Source: Figure 1.1.

criterion, an action will be considered an improvement in 'social welfare' for
the subset of those considered in the analysis if at least one of them gains and
no other member loses. For example, if the rich gain $1 without any other
member losing there would be an improvement in social welfare. Instead, if
for the poor to gain $100 the rich have to lose $1 it cannot be said that social
welfare has been improved. Regardless of the consensus that could be built
around the value judgement supporting the criterion, its use would result in a
majority of cases being rejected, since there are very few cases for which
following one course of action instead of the alternative would not result in at
least one loser. Why is it then that such a limited criterion has commanded so
much attention in the literature? One of the reasons may be that it does not
require 'interpersonal welfare comparisons'; that is, it does not require a
judgement on whether one additional unit of income for one person is more or
less valued than one additional unit for another person.[6]

Given the fact that very few cases will qualify as Pareto improvements,
which would not include some that seem to carry a wide consensus (e.g. poor
+$100, rich -$1), it has been proposed that economists should restrict
themselves to showing the CVs attributable to the project by beneficiary, and
leave the decision to 'others'. This proposal, which seems to be that of Mishan
(1988, Ch. 29, Section 2), only prevents the economist from making the
interpersonal comparisons, but does not remove the need to make them. Others
have tried to extend the Pareto improvement criterion to the cases where there
are losers.[7] If in the preceding example it would be possible to take $1.1 from
the poor's gain, transfer $1 to the rich and use the remaining 0.1 to finance the

6. Sen (1987) provides a more detailed treatment.

7. See Hicks (1939, Section 7; 1975, Section 1) and Mishan (1988, Ch. 29, Section 2).

costs of effecting the transfer or compensation, a compensated Pareto improvement would be obtained. But, this approach raises more questions than it answers: (1) why compensate exactly instead of over or under-compensating?; (2) what is the maximum cost that can be paid to effect the transfer? Once paying a compensation and the cost to effect it have been accepted, determining the optimum transfer requires knowing that cost and the 'total welfare function' to be used, which requires the adoption of an interpersonal welfare comparison criterion (Ray, 1984, Ch. 2).

CBA intends to provide information on the contribution to 'total' or 'social welfare' also when there are losers. For that reason it is based on a family of criteria where interpersonal welfare comparisons do take place. These comparisons allow the contribution to total welfare to be expressed as a function of individual welfare changes measured by the corresponding CVs. The measure of total welfare change, or *net benefits* (*NB*), may be expressed as

$$NB = f[CV_t^e(\Delta q)] \tag{1.1}$$

where CV_t^e is the CV of individual e at moment t attributable to change Δq. These criteria for comparison may be analytically classified into two closely related groups. The first one deals with comparisons of CVs that refer to the same point in time; the second refers to comparing CVs over time. Both criteria consist of a weighted sum of the CVs of those affected, for which they could also be considered as aggregation criteria that allow the move from a set of individual welfare changes to a measure of 'total welfare'.

Consider, for example, the marginal allocation J affecting only two individuals, P and R, with CVs $CV^P(J)$ and $CV^r(J)$, respectively. Doing J implies forgoing K, which also affects only P and R in the amounts $CV^P(K)$ and $CV^r(K)$. Welfare changes attributable to follow the course of action J instead of K would be

$$\Delta W(J - K) = w^P [CV^P(J) - CV^P(K)] + w^r [CV^r(J) - CV^r(K)] \tag{1.2}$$

or, more simply,

$$\Delta W(J - K) = w^P CV^P(J - K) + w^r CV^r(J - K) \tag{1.3}$$

where w^P and w^r represent the valuations that P and R CVs are given in total welfare function W. The change in total welfare expressed in the numeraire may be presented using the valuation given to individual i, w^i, as unit of account or numeraire

$$NB(J - K) = \frac{\Delta W(J - K)}{w^j}$$

This expression provides the *net benefits* attributable to following the course of action J instead of K. If w^r is used as the numeraire the expression for the net benefits would be

$$NB(J - K) = (w^p/w^r)\, CV^p(J - K) + CV^r(J - K)$$

If, for example, the course of action J reduces the price of bread, K reduces that of jewelry, both use the same resources, and P does not consume jewelry and R does not consume bread, the course of action $J - K$ would benefit P and R would be the loser. Consequently, $CV^p(J - K)$ would be positive and $C^{rr}(J - K)$ would be negative. If the corresponding CVs are

$$CV^p(J - K) = 50 \tag{1.4}$$

$$CV^r(J - K) = -70 \tag{1.5}$$

net benefits of doing J, and consequently not doing K, would be

$$NB(J - K) = (w^p/w^r)\, 50 - 70 \tag{1.6}$$

and the result in terms of total welfare would depend on the interpersonal welfare comparison criterion implicit in w^p and w^r.[8]

In practice, it is possible to define *distributional weights u* expressing how many times as valuable in the welfare function is \$1 of additional consumption of an individual (i.e. $CV = 1$) in comparison with an equal amount of additional consumption for the individual selected to define the numeraire. In the case of the preceding example,

$$u^p = w^p / w^r \tag{1.7}$$

would be the distributional weight of individual p. Thus, in the example of Table 1.1, the 'Total' column, which is simply the algebraic sum of the CVs of those affected by the additional supply $q_1 - q_0$, may be interpreted as the total benefits attributable to that additional supply only if the interpersonal aggregation criterion assigns equal weights w^i to all affected.

CBA also has to solve an intertemporal comparison problem, that is, how to compare a \$1 gain (loss) today with a \$1 gain (loss) a year from now. It

---

8. Sen (1979) and Mishan (1988) provide a more detailed presentation of the subjects discussed thus far.

allows the aggregation of CVs of effects that take place at different points in time, and leads to the concept of *discount rate*. In the preceding example of course of action $J - K$, say that effects on individual R take place at two different points in time called years zero and one. In year zero, and valued with the perspective of that year, R is affected by $CV_0(J - K)$. In year one, and also with the perspective of that year, R is affected by $CV_1(J - K)$. Note that CVs reflect the person's valuation at the moment the effect takes place, requiring the person to have certainty about the future.

The analysis conducted thus far has been based on two principles: each affected individual determines how he or she has been affected, and the money-measure of those effects is based on individual preferences. Therefore, it seems consistent with these value judgements to accept individual intertemporal preferences as the basis for the intertemporal comparison. In such a case, R's net benefits may be expressed as

$$NB^r(J - K) = v_0^r\, CV_0(J - K) + v_1^r\, CV_1(J - K) \tag{1.8}$$

where weights v_t^r represent R's (different) valuation of two identical effects taking place at different points in time. These are the weights that allow the aggregation of CVs corresponding to different moments.

A judgement of fact regarding individual preferences and a simplifying assumption are required in order to deduce the individual discount rate. The judgement of fact says that weights v_t^r decrease over time. Sometimes this is presented by saying that one additional unit of consumption is more valuable today than tomorrow. The simplifying assumption states that weights v_t^r decrease at a constant rate d^r, that is

$$v_0^r = v_1^r\,(1 + d^r) = v_2^r\,(1 + d^r)^2 = \ldots = v_t^r(1 + d^r)^t$$

Following the convention of using the equivalent contribution to 'economic welfare' in year zero as the numeraire, these relationships among intertemporal weights v_t^r may be presented as

$$\frac{v_t^r}{v_0^r} = \frac{1}{(1 + d^r)^t} \tag{1.9}$$

where d^r is R's *individual discount rate*.

1.3   SHADOW PRICES AND THE DISCOUNT RATE

This section is devoted to the analysis of two crucial concepts in CBA: those of shadow (or accounting) price, and the discount rate. Such an analysis will later on permit a brief discussion of the differences among the most important proposals for making CBA operational.

A shadow price is a measure of the welfare effects of marginal changes in the supply or demand of goods and services. If a project were to increase the availability (increase supply or reduce demand) of a certain good, that increase would affect people and the corresponding effects could be measured by the respective CVs. Thus, if Δq is the increase in the availability of good q at a certain point in time, $CV^e(\Delta q)$ could represent the CV of individual e attributable to the increase in q. Once all CVs attributable to Δq are known and the interpersonal comparison criterion has been defined, the contribution of Δq to 'total welfare' at such a point in time may be presented as the weighted sums of the CVs

$$\Delta W(\Delta q) = w^1\, CV^1(\Delta q) + w^2\, CV^2(\Delta q) + \ldots + w^n\, CV^n(\Delta q) \quad (1.10)$$

where w^e is the weight that individual e's CV receives in the welfare function; that is, the result of the interpersonal aggregation criterion. By selecting individual k's valuation w^k as numeraire, net benefits attributable to Δq would be

$$NB(\Delta q) = \Delta W(\Delta q) \,/\, w^k$$

$$NB(\Delta q) = u^1\, CV^1(\Delta q) + u^2\, CV^2(\Delta q) + \ldots + u^n\, CV^n(\Delta q) \quad (1.11)$$

where u^i is the distribution weight defined in (1.7). The *shadow price* of q for a change Δq is the amount of net benefits attributable to Δq expressed per unit of Δq

$$sp_q = \frac{\Delta W(\Delta q)}{w^k\, \Delta q} = \frac{NB(\Delta q)}{\Delta q}$$

that is,

$$sp_q = \frac{u^1\, CV^1(\Delta q) + u^2\, CV^2(\Delta q) + \ldots + u^n\, CV^n(\Delta q)}{\Delta q} \quad (1.12)$$

The shadow price so defined will be a function of Δq. In practice, however, for small changes in q it is assumed that the shadow price is the change in total economic welfare attributable to a unit change in the availability of q.[9] It is

---

9. Sen (1975, Ch. 11, 12 and 13) analyzes different definitions of shadow price.

important to highlight that the quantitative expression of a shadow price requires *making the interpersonal aggregation criterion explicit*. This subject will be reconsidered in the following section when discussing alternative interpersonal aggregation criteria proposed in the literature.

Project inputs and outputs are normally valued at market prices ($q_j \times p_j$), making it useful to know the ratios of shadow to market prices, or shadow price ratios $spr_j = sp_j / p_j$. Then, values at shadow prices may be obtained by multiplying values at market prices by the corresponding *spr*. Shadow price ratios have the additional advantage of not being affected by inflation as long as inflation does not affect relative prices.

With regard to the individual's discount rate, strict adherence to value judgements defining the set of those affected and included, as well as whether effects are harmful or beneficial, coupled with the measurement criterion seem to have solved the main conceptual problems. Once individuals' discount rates are known, intertemporal aggregation of individual CVs is possible. However, two practical problems remain. First, knowing the individuals' discount rates; second, once individual discount rates are known, effecting the intertemporal aggregation when individual discount rates are different for different individuals.

In theoretical models attempting to represent 'perfect', 'undistorted' financial markets (e.g. no income taxes on interest), and making certain additional assumptions regarding individuals' behavior in disposing of their incomes over time, it is shown that all individual discount rates would be equal to the (risk free) market interest rate, and consequently equal among themselves.[10] Under perfect certainty on future prices and income, a person would be willing to reduce his or her present consumption (save) in one unit if in the next period he or she can obtain at least $(1 + d^e)$ through the financial system. It is also assumed that additional units of saving (reductions in consumption) require increasing compensation (i.e. the individual supply of savings is an increasing function of the interest rate). Thus the individual would reduce his or her present consumption (save) until his or her individual discount rate for the resulting level of savings equals the financial market interest rate. In other words, if for interest rate r the individual saves $100, it is because saving an additional unit would require a higher interest rate, and saving one less would mean losing the difference between what he or she can obtain in the financial market $(1 + r)$ and the minimum compensation he or she requires to forgo that extra unit $(1 + d^e)$. Thus, the individual would save until reaching a point where

---

10. Frederick, Loewenstein and O'Donoghue (2002) provide a critical survey of the traditional theoretical approach to the individual discount rate.

$$1 + d^e = 1 + r \tag{1.13}$$

The result is that the financial market would allow the individual discount rates and the interest rate to be equalized. Since this result is assumed to hold for all individuals, everyone's discount rate would be equal to the market interest rate. Consequently, individual discount rates would not differ if perfect, 'undistorted' financial markets would exist. These markets would allow the simultaneous observation of everyone's discount rate.

This approach has been the subject of several criticisms.[11] First, the behavioral assumption is challenged, i.e. that individuals optimize over time. Second, no certainty exists about future income and prices; moreover, uncertainty about future incomes and expenses is seen as a fundamental reason for saving. Also, such uncertainty should not affect investment decisions, which should be limited to the uncertainty of the project itself. In particular, since the discount rate is real (net of inflation) while the market interest rate is nominal, compliance with the model's assumptions would require certainty regarding future inflation. Finally, if interest income is taxed, individuals would equate their discount rate to the after tax interest rate, that is

$$d^e = r \left(1 - t^e\right) \tag{1.14}$$

where t^e is the tax rate for individual e. Since normally tax rates are different for different people, there would be different individual discount rates underlying a unique before-tax interest rate. Moreover, since the market interest rate depends on the savings function, which in turn depends on income distribution, accepting the market interest rate for a normative analysis would imply acceptance of the existing income distribution, and this value judgement may or may not be consistent with the interpersonal comparison criterion. For all of the above reasons, it can be safely concluded that the foundations for using the market interest rate as a normative discount rate are shaky.

There is a second important internal criticism to the approach of using the individuals' discount rate. It is based on the impossibility of applying to intertemporal comparisons, the basic principle that it is each person who determines whether he or she has been affected and by how much.[12] The reason is obvious. Many of those who have to reduce their present consumption may not be alive by the time that benefits are received. Similarly, many of those who would receive the benefits have not yet been born. The problems of using this generation's intertemporal preferences become apparent

---

11. For a more detailed analysis of the rest of this section, see Sen (1961), Dobb (1960), Layard (1978a), Mishan (1981a, Ch. 18), and Arrow (1995).

12. See Mishan (1981a, Ch. 18; 1988, Ch. 41).

in the case of a nuclear plant. The present generation would bear the investment costs, benefits would be received by only some of them, and it would be the future generation, whose CVs count less due to discounting, that would have to deal with the radioactive residuals.

If the intertemporal preferences of the present generation are not accepted as the basis for discounting future consumption, what is the foundation for discounting? One answer has been based on the following assertion: an additional unit of consumption is less valuable the higher the consumption level of the person receiving it. Since consumption grows over time, the future generation would be richer than the present. It then follows that an additional unit of consumption for a member of the future generation should be valued less (discounted) than one for the present generation.

Logical consistency demands that the same principle be applied to members of the present generation. In such a case, an additional unit of consumption for a poor person should be more valuable than an additional unit of consumption for a rich person, both units accruing at the same time. It follows that under this line of argument there should be a clear connection between the interpersonal and intertemporal aggregation criteria.

Mishan (1981b, Ch. 42) proposed two alternative interpretations of assertions such as 'the value of an additional unit of consumption is higher the lower the income level of the recipient'. If the 'preference' for a more egalitarian income distribution is what is meant, then the proposition is clearly a value judgement. It could be considered a judgement of fact if it refers to what is believed to actually happen, based on 'observation, experience, introspection, and imagination' (p. 317). Both interpretations have been used as a basis for interpersonal and intertemporal comparison criteria.

1.4   DIFFERENT METHODS

When approached for the first time, CBA appears to offer several, seemingly different methodologies. Without expert guidance, the newcomer would have the impression that they are radically different approaches and it may not be easy to identify what they have in common and where they differ. A closer look will show that almost all methods share the value judgement that underlies the criterion to determine whether a person has been affected and how, and almost all methods use the CV as the measurement criterion.[13] It will also show that differences concentrate on interpersonal and intertemporal criteria.

---

13. UNIDO's (1972) 'merit wants' and the rejection of the private valuation of additional work (Lal, 1973) are among the few exceptions. For arguments opposing these exceptions see Harberger (1977) and Hamilton (1977), as well as Sen's (1979) more general approach.

Consider the so-called 'efficiency analysis', probably most clearly presented by Mishan (1988). The crudest but clearest version of efficiency analysis is based on an interpersonal value judgement stating that an additional unit of consumption is equally valuable regardless of the income level of the recipient ($u^i = u^j = u$). Thus, if CV^e_t is the CV of person e at time t, from (1.11) the net benefits attributable to Δq at time t would be

$$NB_t(\Delta q_t) = u \left[CV^1_t(\Delta q_t) + CV^2_t(\Delta q_t) + \ldots + CV^n_t(\Delta q_t)\right] \qquad (1.15)$$

An investment project may be conceived of as a flow of inputs and outputs i over time t; that is, a flow Δq_{it}, where some Δq_{it} are positive (outputs) and others are negative (inputs). Consequently, the project would lead to a welfare increase if

$$NB(\Delta q_{it}) = u \left(v_0 \, \Sigma_i \, NB_{i0} + v_1 \, \Sigma_i \, NB_{i1} + \ldots + v_m \, \Sigma_i \, NB_{im}\right) > 0 \quad (1.16)$$

where NB_{it} are the net benefits attributable to Δq_{it}, and v_t are the intertemporal weights, assumed here to be equal for all persons to simplify the presentation. Since the sign of $NB(\Delta q_{it})$ is the same as that of $NB(\Delta q_{it})/u$, the interpersonal aggregation criterion may also be expressed as the sum of the CVs. This criterion allows for the horizontal sum along the rows of Table 1.1 and for its *Total* column to be interpreted as the efficiency benefits attributable to $q_1 - q_0$ in a given year.

Similar tables could be prepared for each of the persons affected, and then 'total' benefits could be obtained by summing each person's benefits. Fortunately, that can be avoided, since it can be easily demonstrated that areas below the market demand function are the aggregation of the corresponding areas below the individual demand functions. That is, with reference to Figures 1.1(a) and 1.1(b),

$$A = A^1 + A^2 + \ldots + A^n$$
$$B = B^1 + B^2 + \ldots + B^n$$
$$C = C^1 + C^2 + \ldots + C^n$$

In words, efficiency benefits of the additional supply may be measured from market price and quantity data. In the example of Table 1.1, those benefits are the algebraic sum of: (1) project revenue, (2) the sum of CV of the consumers of q, and (3) the reduction in revenue for other producers. The result, area $B + C$, is known as *willingness to pay* for the additional consumption. That explains why in some cases the efficiency value of small additions to the availability of a *consumption* good may be approximated by the value of sales at market prices.[14]

With regard to shadow prices, the use of equal weights allows for the distributional weight u to be ignored in (1.12), since the same weight would multiply all shadow prices, and consequently it would not alter the ranking or the sign of total net benefits. As a result, the expression for an efficiency price becomes

$$sp_i = \frac{CV^1(\varDelta q_i) + CV^2(\varDelta q_i) + \ldots + CV^n(\varDelta q_i)}{\varDelta q_i} \tag{1.17}$$

the sum of the compensating variations attributable to $\varDelta q_i$ per unit thereof.

This same criterion is sometimes presented in a different form under the name of the *potential Pareto improvement*, a name derived from the (strict) Pareto improvement presented in section 1.2. This criterion states that there would be one of these 'improvements' if as a result of an action it is *possible* for the winners to compensate the losers by a hypothetical costless transfer and still gain something.[15] Thus, if the sum of the CVs of all affected is positive, the action would constitute a potential Pareto improvement, since it implies that the winners' sum of CV exceeds that of the losers, making a costless compensatory transfer *possible*. However, losers will remain such and winners would not transfer anything, because the compensation is only *potential*.

By only requiring that the compensation is *possible*, the criterion becomes useless unless something can be said about the desirability of following a course of action that complies with it. On the other hand, if it states, as it seems to, that a potential Pareto improvement is desirable, then it is identical to the sum of the CVs, implying the equal valuation of marginal income changes for all affected, regardless of their income levels, as the interpersonal aggregation criterion (or distributional value judgement). Finally, if the principle is not to say anything about the desirability of one of these 'improvements', the analyst should indicate *who* win and *who* lose, and by *how much*, so someone else may apply a distributional value judgement. The problem is not solved. It is transferred to someone else.[16]

---

14. Londero (1987) provides a simple demonstration of the links between areas below the individual demand curves and areas below the market demand curve, as well as a discussion of the valuation of intermediate and traded goods.

15. Effecting transfers at a cost implies abandoning the equal valuation of marginal income changes. See Ray (1984).

16. Mishan (1980, 1981b and 1988) gives excellent presentations of the potential Pareto improvement by a proponent. Also see Hicks (1975), Meade (1972) and Sen (1987).

With regard to the intertemporal aggregation criterion, the principle that those affected determine the nature and magnitude of the effects must be abandoned, since the future generation is not present. In practice the principle gives way to another: only revealed preferences by the present generation are taken into account. Then, if it exists, the rate of interest of the perfect financial market is accepted as the discount rate, as presented in section 1.3. If interest income is subject to income taxes, some corrections are required resulting in different discount rates for different individuals according to their (marginal) tax rates. Since the tax rate is frequently related to the income level, an estimate of the distribution of costs and benefits by year and income bracket would be required to discount each flow by the corresponding rate. Since this is not practical, the use of an average marginal tax rate has been proposed. However, such an approach is difficult to accept, since different marginal tax rates – and consequently different individual discount rates – make the 'equivalent average' discount rate project specific and dependent on the interpersonal and intertemporal distribution of costs and benefits.[17]

The preceding presentation may be called strict 'efficiency' analysis. It is consistent with giving equal valuation to the marginal income changes of all affected, and in accepting the intertemporal preferences of the present generation. If marginal income changes are equally valuable regardless of the income level of the recipient, income distribution has to be deemed acceptable. Similarly, using the intertemporal preference of this generation allegedly 'revealed' by the market is, as previously pointed out, to accept a result largely affected by income distribution through the savings function.

Taxes on interest income create an additional problem. In the absence of these taxes (or other interferences generating similar effects) a perfect market would not only equalize the discount rates among individuals, but also the discount rate with the profitability of the marginal investment. Income taxes would make the interest rate equal to the *after tax* rate of return, and differences between the rate of discount and the marginal rate of return on investment[18] require the use of shadow (accounting) prices of investment (Marglin, 1963b; UNIDO, 1972; Londero, 1987). Their use makes it necessary to distinguish additional units of consumption from additional units of savings.[19] The changes required in applied CBA by this approach have led to

---

17. An exchange with Professor Mishan led to clarification of this issue.

18. Strictly speaking, it is the rate of return at 'efficiency' prices.

19. Harberger (1973) has proposed the use a weighted average of the individuals' discount rate and the marginal return on investment. Feldstein (1978) demonstrated that the approach is not generally correct, but it is curiously widespread. Also see UNIDO (1972, Section 13.4), Ray (1984, Ch. 2), and Sjaastad and Wisecarver (1977).

calling it 'extended efficiency analysis', although traditional efficiency analysis is a particular case of the former (where the individuals' rate of discount equals the marginal rate of return on investment). This more general approach may be based on a discount rate derived from individuals' preferences or – abandoning an important principle of efficiency analysis – on a discount rate that expresses an intertemporal value judgement (Marglin, 1963a). When in subsequent chapters reference is made to efficiency prices, it is implicitly assumed that the discount rate equals the marginal rate of return on investment.

Efficiency analysis is characterized by its interpersonal aggregation (comparison) criterion assigning equal weights to the marginal income changes of all affected, regardless of their income levels. Another approach, whose best-known representatives include UNIDO (1972), Little and Mirrlees (1974), and Squire and van der Tak (1975), is based on a different distributional value judgement that may be summarized as follows: additional consumption for all those affected who have the same income level receives the same valuation in the welfare function, but one additional unit of consumption is more valuable the lower the consumption level of the recipient. The discount rate is based on the same distributional value judgement, and as a result depends on the expected growth of consumption. With the exception of UNIDO (1972), consistency between interpersonal and intertemporal weights is attained by defining a functional relation between individuals' consumption levels and 'total economic welfare'. Interpersonal and intertemporal aggregation criteria are then derived from this function. An example will illustrate the case.[20]

Since additional consumption for individuals with different consumption levels would be valued differently in the welfare function, a consumption level would have to be designated as a unit of account or numeraire, say per capita consumption in year zero $\bar{c}_0$. The valuation for the additional consumption of a person with this per capita consumption level would then be $w(\bar{c}_0)$. Since these valuations decrease (increase) with increases (reductions) in consumption, they may be represented as in Figure 1.2, where additional consumption for the person with a consumption level $c_0^r > \bar{c}_0$ is valued at $w(c_0^r) < w(\bar{c}_0)$. When aggregating within each year, per capita consumption in each year would be the logical numeraire, on the basis of which distributional weights for all people could be defined. Then, an additional unit of consumption for a person with a consumption level c_p^r would be u_t' more valuable than the same unit for the person with the per capita level in that year $\bar{c}_t$, where

20. Ray (1984) discusses the alternatives. Also see Appendix 1.1.

$$u'_t = \frac{w(c'_t)}{w(\bar{c}_t)} \qquad (1.18)$$

It follows that the distributional weight will be one for the person with the per capita level, and that efficiency analysis is a particular case of Figure 1.2 where function $w(c)$ is a horizontal line.

Note that distributional weights carry a subscript t indicating the point in time at which the interpersonal comparison is taking place. In practice, the comparison of income levels is carried out in only one year, normally the project's base year, and the resulting weights are used for the whole analysis period.

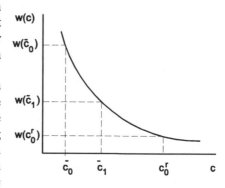

Figure 1.2 Welfare values at different consumption levels

The attention now turns to the relation between the rate of discount and distributional weights when the justification for discounting is based on the growth of consumption over time. In Figure 1.2, per capita consumption levels in years zero and one are denoted by $\bar{c}_0$ and $\bar{c}_1$, and the contribution to total welfare of an additional unit for consumption by a person with those levels would be $w(\bar{c}_0)$ and $w(\bar{c}_1)$, respectively. It is apparent that as long as the growth in per capita consumption is the only reason for discounting, these valuations are conceptually equivalent to the intertemporal valuations v^e_t discussed in section 1.2 in analyzing the individual's discount rate. The difference is that the v^e_t reflect any motives that the individuals may have for discounting future consumption, while the $w(\bar{c}_t)$ only take additional consumption into account.

Consider a project generating consumption changes whose CVs are CV^e_t, where e is the individual and t the moment when those effects take place. From (1.11), the aggregation of CVs at any moment t would be

$$B_t = \Sigma_e u^e_t CV^e_t \qquad (1.19)$$

where the u^e_t are the interpersonal distributional weights of individuals e, expressing consumption changes of each individual in terms of equivalent changes for the individual at the per capita level. Since 'total welfare' is a function of per capita consumption, the change in total welfare in year t would be $w_t (B_t / N_t)$, where $w_t = w(\bar{c}_t)$ is the valuation of additional consumption for the hypothetical individual receiving the per capita consumption level, and N_t

is total population in year t. Thus the change in 'total welfare' corresponding to flow B_t would be

$$\Delta W = \Sigma_{t=0} \, w_t \, (B_t \, / \, N_t) \tag{1.20}$$

and the present value of net benefits would be

$$\Delta W/w_0 = \Sigma_{t=0} \, (w_t \, / \, w_0)(B_t \, / \, N_t) \tag{1.21}$$

From (1.21) it can be demonstrated (see Appendix 1.1) that the discount rate would be

$$d = (1 - \mu \, \dot{c})(1 + n) - 1 \tag{1.22}$$

where n is the population growth rate, $\dot{c}$ is the rate of growth of per capita consumption, and $\mu = (c/w)(\Delta w/\Delta c)$ is the so-called 'elasticity of the marginal utility of per capita consumption'.

Therefore, the discount rate may be expressed as a function of two parameters for which acceptable estimates may be available ($\dot{c}$ and n), and a third (μ) representing the assumed functional relationship between changes in the per capita consumption of the individual and the corresponding changes in 'total welfare' W. The approaches then may differ in their positions regarding parameter μ.[21]

All these approaches, however, share the problem of considering the consumption rate of growth as exogenous. If investment is to be expanded until the efficiency marginal rate of return equals the rate of discount, the future rate of growth of per capita consumption would be a function of the discount rate through the level of investment. To avoid this inconsistency, Marglin (1963a) proposed to start by setting the (feasible and) desired growth rate in order to derive the required investment rate from that target. Since for the policymaker that investment rate would be optimal by definition, the rate of return of the marginal investment *would be* equal to the rate of discount. If that were not the case, present consumption would be reduced in order to increase investment (future consumption). It may be thus inferred that when, in traditional efficiency analysis, the rate of return of the marginal investment is used as a discount rate, the investment rate is assumed to be optimal in a normative sense; that is, it is not different because the policymaker considers it optimal. This assumption will be implicit in future references to efficiency prices.

This book will consider primarily efficiency prices. The presentation,

---

21. Ray (1984) and Londero (1991) analyze operational proposals on the subject.

however, allows for an easy transition to estimating distributional effects and thus considering distributional aspects in an applied manner. The reader interested in those topics may wish to consult UNIDO (1972) and Londero (1987), where approaches essentially similar to that presented in this book are used to address in detail interpersonal and intertemporal distributional considerations. The importance of estimating distributional effects is also discussed in Londero (1996a) and Potts (1999).

APPENDIX 1.1   INTERPERSONAL AND INTERTEMPORAL WEIGHTS

This appendix provides a more formal presentation of the interpersonal and intertemporal welfare comparisons, and a derivation of formulae for the distributional weights and the discount rate.[22] Let the total welfare derived from consumption at time t be represented by the aggregation of individual welfare levels in that period expressed on a per capita basis:

$$W_t = W_t\left(\Sigma_e \frac{U_t^e(q_{it}^e)}{N_t}\right) \tag{1.A1}$$

Welfare from consumption at time t would increase if consumption increases for a given population, and would decrease if the population increases for a given level of consumption. A change in W_t would be

$$dW_t = \frac{1}{N_t}\Sigma_e \frac{\partial W_t}{\partial U_t^e} \Sigma_i \frac{\partial U_t^e}{\partial q_{it}^e} dq_{it}^e \tag{1.A2}$$

In equilibrium $\partial U_t^e / \partial q_{it}^e = \lambda^e p_{it}$, where p is the price and λ the marginal utility of consumption expenditure. Replacing $\partial U_t^e / \partial q_{it}^e$ in (1.A2) results in

$$dW_t = \frac{1}{N_t}\Sigma_e \frac{\partial W_t}{\partial U_t^e} \lambda^e \Sigma_i p_{it} dq_{it}^e \tag{1.A3}$$

Total welfare would be a function of welfare derived from consumption at each moment t; that is, $W = W(W_t)$, from where

$$dW = \Sigma_t \frac{\partial W}{\partial W_t} dW_t \tag{1.A4}$$

Replacing (1.A3) in (1.A4), an increase in total welfare would be

22. The reader may also wish to consult Drèze and Stern (1987), Squire (1989), and Dinwiddy and Teal (1996).

$$dW = \Sigma_t \frac{\partial W}{\partial W_t} \Sigma_e \frac{1}{N_t} \frac{\partial W_t}{\partial U^e_t} \lambda^e_t \Sigma_i p_{it} \, dq^e_{it} \qquad (1.A5)$$

The intertemporal distribution weight of individual e would be the increase in total welfare resulting from a unit increase in the individual's consumption expenditure expressed relative to the same measure for individual k whose marginal welfare increase is used as numeraire

$$u^e_t = \left(\frac{\partial W_t}{\partial U^e_t} \Big/ \frac{\partial W_t}{\partial U^k_t} \right) \frac{\lambda^e_t}{\lambda^k_t} \qquad (1.A6)$$

If these weights do not change along time; that is, if

$$u^e_t = \left(\frac{\partial W_t}{\partial U^e_t} \Big/ \frac{\partial W_t}{\partial U^k_t} \right) \frac{\lambda^e_t}{\lambda^k_t} = \ldots = \left(\frac{\partial W_0}{\partial U^e_0} \Big/ \frac{\partial W_0}{\partial U^k_0} \right) \frac{\lambda^e_0}{\lambda^k_0} \qquad (1.A7)$$

multiplying and dividing the right-hand side of (1.A6) by $\partial W_t / \partial U^k_t = \lambda^k_t$ yields

$$dW = \Sigma_t \frac{\partial W}{\partial W_t} \frac{\partial W_t}{\partial U^k_t} \lambda^k_t \frac{1}{N_t} \Sigma_e u^e \Sigma_e p_{it} \, dq^e_{it} \qquad (1.A8)$$

Expressing dW relative to the changes in the individual k's welfare in the initial period results in

$$\frac{dW}{\dfrac{\partial W}{\partial W_0} \dfrac{\partial W_0}{\partial U^k_0} \lambda^k_0} = \Sigma_t \frac{\dfrac{\partial W}{\partial W_t} \dfrac{\partial W_t}{\partial U^k_t} \lambda^k_t}{\dfrac{\partial W}{\partial W_0} \dfrac{\partial W_0}{\partial U^k_0} \lambda^k_0} \frac{1}{N_t} \Sigma_e u^e \Sigma_i p_{it} \, dq^e_{it} \qquad (1.A9)$$

The notation may be now simplified by recalling that λ^k_t is the marginal utility of k's consumption expenditure in period t, and defining

$$\frac{\partial W}{\partial W_t} \frac{\partial W_t}{\partial U^k_t} \lambda^k_t = \frac{\partial W}{\partial W_t} \frac{\partial W_t}{\partial U^k_t} \frac{\partial U^k_t}{\partial c^k_t} = w(c^k_t) = w^k_t$$

where c_t^k is k's consumption in period t. Since the welfare function only considers individuals' consumption levels, unit changes to the consumption of two individuals with the same consumption levels would get the same valuation in the welfare function, that is $w_t^k = w_t^r$ for all $c_t^k = c_t^r$. Therefore, the w_t^k for a hypothetical individual may be used as a numeraire. If the individual at the per capita consumption level is selected, equation (1.A9) may be written as[23]

$$\frac{dW}{w_0} = \Sigma_t \, \frac{w_t}{w_0} \, \frac{1}{N_t} \, \Sigma_e \, u^e \, \Sigma_i \, p_{it} \, dq_{it}^e \qquad (1.A10)$$

A series of changes over time dq_{jt} would increase total welfare if

$$\frac{dW}{w_0} = \Sigma_t \, \frac{w_t}{w_0} \, \frac{1}{N_t} \, \Sigma_e \, u^e \, \Sigma_i \, p_{it} \, \frac{\partial q_{it}^e}{\partial q_j} \, dq_{jt}^e > 0 \qquad (1.A11)$$

If dW/w_0 is positive, $N_0 \, dW/w_0$ would also be. Therefore, in practice analysts would calculate

$$\frac{N_0}{w_0} \frac{dW}{\partial q_{jt}} = \Sigma_t \, \frac{w_t}{w_0} \, \frac{N_0}{N_t} \, \Sigma_e \, u^e \, \Sigma_i \, p_{it} \, \frac{\partial q_{it}^e}{\partial q_{jt}} \qquad (1.A12)$$

The first summation (over t) indicates the intertemporal aggregation, where

$$\frac{w_{t+1} \, N_0}{w_t \, N_{t+1}} = \frac{1}{1 + d_t} \qquad (1.A13)$$

is the discount rate. The second summation (over e) indicates the interpersonal aggregation, and the third summation (over i) is the aggregation of the consumption changes. In practice, expression (1.A12) is called the present value of the net benefits attributable to the flow dq_{jt}; that is

$$NB(dq_{jt}) = \Sigma_t \, \frac{w_t}{w_0} \, \frac{N_0}{N_t} \, \Sigma_e \, u^e \, \Sigma_i \, p_{it} \, \frac{\partial q_{it}^e}{\partial q_{jt}} \, dq_{jt} \qquad (1.A14)$$

---

23. Little and Mirrlees (1974) selected what they called the 'critical consumption level'.

Interpersonal and intertemporal aggregation will now be considered separately. Starting with the interpersonal aggregation, in any period t, total benefits attributable to a unit change in q_j, or shadow price of q_j, would be

$$sp_{jt} = \Sigma_e \, u^e \, \Sigma_i \, p_{it} \, \frac{\partial q^e_{it}}{\partial q_{jt}} \qquad (1.A15)$$

That is, the aggregation of the value of the changes in the individuals' consumption baskets originating in the additional supply or demand of good j.[24] Finally, the 'efficiency' price of j would be the one that corresponds to unitary weights u^e for all affected individuals. Care should be exercised in interpreting equation (1.A15), since partial derivatives represent the changes to restore full equilibrium, and *not* the *ceteris paribus* partial equilibrium changes normally used in practice.

With regard to the intertemporal aggregation, an operational formula requires a few assumptions. First, that population grows a constant rate n; therefore, total population in year t would be $N_t = N_0 \, (1 + n)^t$. Second, it is customary in cost–benefit analysis to assume that the discount factor decreases at a constant rate. Thus (1A.13) may be presented as follows:

$$1/(1 + d) = w_1 / [w_0 \, (1 + n)]$$

$$1/(1 + d)^2 = w_2 / [w_0 \, (1 + n)^2]$$

$$\vdots \qquad (1.A16)$$

$$1/(1 + d)^t = w_t / [w_0 \, (1 + n)^t]$$

Equations (1A.16) allow for (1.A14) to be expressed as

$$NB(dq_{jt}) = \Sigma_t \, \frac{1}{(1 + d)^t} \, \Sigma_e \, u^e \, \Sigma_i \, p_{it} \, dq^e_{it} \qquad (1.A17)$$

which is the traditional formula for the present value.

As for the relationship of the discount rate with weights w_t and the population growth rate, from (1.A16) the discount rate would be

---

24. This equation is equivalent to Squire's (1989, p. 1101, equation (2)). If dq_{jt} had effects beyond period t, the present value of the change in the basket would have to be used.

$$1 + d = \frac{w_t}{w_{t+1}} (1 + n) \qquad (1.\text{A}18)$$

Substituting for $w_t = w_{t+1} - dw$, (1.A18) becomes

$$1 + d = [1 - (dw/w)] (1 + n) \qquad (1.\text{A}19)$$

where $-dw/w$ indicates the rate at which the valuation of the additional consumption of the hypothetical individual always receiving the per capita consumption declines. Since weights w are a function of per capita consumption (c), multiplying and dividing dw/w by the rate of growth of per capita consumption (dc/c) yields $dw/w = (c/w)(dw/dc)(dc/c)$. This expression allows for the discount rate to be presented as the product of the elasticity of w, $\mu = (c/w)(dw/dc)$ – referred to in the literature as the elasticity of the marginal utility of per capita consumption – and the rate of growth of per capita consumption $\dot{c} = (dc/c)$. Thus, (1.A19) may be written as

$$1 + d = (1 - \mu \dot{c})(1 + n)$$

from where expression (1.22) is obtained.

2. Foreign Exchange

2.1 THE CLASSIFICATION OF GOODS

The shadow price of a good depends on (the money value of) the effects that a demand or supply change for that good has on people's welfare, and these effects depend on how markets adjust to those demand or supply changes. Thus goods may be classified according to how an additional demand is met. One group includes those goods whose additional demand is met fully by withdrawals from other uses; here these goods will be said to be *in fixed supply* and will be analyzed in Chapters 3 and 4, and Appendix 6.1. When the additional demand is met fully by additional production, the good is said to be *produced* at the margin, or simply produced; this type of good will be considered in Chapter 6. The final group is that of the so-called *traded* goods, whose additional demand would be met by additional imports (*imported at the margin*), or reductions in exports (*exported at the margin*). Schematically, the classification may be presented as in Table 2.1.

Note that the classification criteria are not based on the origin (destination) of the input (output) actually used (sold) by the project, but on the direct effects resulting from the additional demand (supply) on domestic production (consumption), foreign trade, and alternative uses. Thus, if a project buys an input from a domestic producer, and other users import an equivalent amount as a result, the input would be imported at the margin.

Table 2.1   Classification of goods according to how demand changes are met

Changes in	Imports or exports	Production	Consumption
Imports or exports	Traded	Partially traded	Partially traded
Production	Partially traded	Produced	Partially produced
Consumption	Partially traded	Partially produced	Fixed supply

There may be goods with mixed characteristics, as indicated by the off-diagonal cells in Table 2.1. For example, the additional demand may be met partially by increasing production and partially by withdrawals from other uses, both induced by a price increase. This would generally be called a nontraded good, and it would be partially produced at the margin. Also, an additional demand may be partially met by increasing production and/or withdrawing from other uses, and partially by increasing imports or reducing exports. These goods are normally called partially traded.[1]

Sometimes goods are also classified as traded and nontraded at the margin according to whether a supply or demand change affects foreign trade directly. The disadvantage of this classification is that defining a good as nontraded does not specify how the domestic market adjusts to supply or demand changes. It should be noted that the classification of goods as traded or nontraded is different from that classifying goods according to what would happen *if* foreign trade incentives and disincentives (tariffs, export taxes, quotas, etc.) were different. Goods that would be nontraded (traded) in that hypothetical situation are said to be nontradable (tradable) in the actual situation with respect to the hypothetical. It is common in the literature to call nontradable (tradable) those goods that would be nontraded (traded) in a free trade situation. Note that this classification assumes knowledge of which goods would be traded and which would not under a set of relative prices that differs from the prevailing one. Finally, it should be borne in mind that some authors do not use these terms rigorously, and frequently refer to tradable goods when they actually mean traded. As a result, sometimes the true meaning has to be inferred from the context.

Shadow price ratios (*sprs*) for produced goods will be presented in detail in Chapter 6, but it should be intuitively clear that their efficiency prices would depend on the efficiency cost of producing the additional quantity. That additional production would require using foreign exchange, labor, and land, thus shadow price ratios for these primary inputs would also be needed. For that reason, before discussing methods to calculate *spr* for marginally produced goods, this chapter will be devoted to the estimation of *spr* for foreign exchange, and Chapters 3 and 4 to the *sprs* of labor and land. The analysis of the *spr* of foreign exchange will be preceded by a brief introductory presentation on the pricing of marginally traded goods.[2]

---

1. Londero (1996b) discusses partially traded goods in detail.

2. Gittinger (1982) and Londero (1987) treat the pricing of traded goods in more detail. Also see Chapter 7.

2.2   PRICING MARGINALLY TRADED GOODS

The case of a marginally imported good is presented in Figure 2.1.(a). For demand D_0, total consumption q_0 is met by domestic production q_d plus imports $q_0 - q_d$ at a domestic price determined by the cost, insurance and freight (hereafter CIF) one, the exchange rate, the tariff, and the domestic distribution costs. Additional demand $q_w - q_0$ does not affect the domestic price and would be fully met by additional imports, since small changes in domestic demand would not affect the international price. The additional quantity would be supplied at the users' price p^u,[3] made up of the CIF price, tariffs t^m, domestic indirect taxes t, and domestic distribution costs *dis*

$$p^u = p^{cif} + t^m + t + dis \qquad (2.1)$$

Since the tariff is a transfer, the cost at efficiency prices of meeting the additional demand will be equal to the cost of providing the foreign exchange plus that of domestic distribution:[4]

$$p^e = p^{cif} \, sprfe + dis \, spr_{dis}$$

where *sprfe* and spr_{dis} are, respectively, the shadow price ratios of foreign

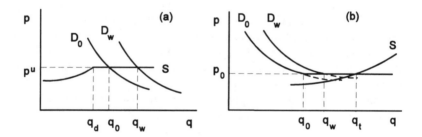

Figure 2.1 Marginally traded goods

---

3. A users' or purchasers' price is that paid by the buyer (final or intermediate), and therefore includes distribution margins. The producers' price is that received by the producer, and therefore excludes distribution margins but includes indirect taxes (net of subsidies) of the transaction between the producer and the distributor. Finally, a basic price is the producers' price minus the indirect taxes (net of subsidies) of the transaction. See Bulmer-Thomas (1982, Ch. 6).

4. There could be efficiency effects attributable to the project originating in its fiscal impact and the instruments used to re-establish the fiscal equilibrium disturbed by the project (Drèze and Stern, 1987; Ahmad and Stern, 1989; Squire, 1989). See Chapter 5.

exchange and distribution costs. This expression shows what the project analyst requires in order to price imported goods: one *spr* for foreign exchange and another for distribution margins.

The case of a marginally exported good is similar. Figure 2.1(b) represents the case of an input with a domestic consumption of q_0 at factory-gate price p_0. This price is equal to the 'free on board' (hereafter FOB) price, plus export subsidies, minus other export costs such as transportation from the factory to the port, port handling and storage, or commercialization margins of trading companies. The additional demand $q_w - q_0$ does not affect the domestic price, which depends on the price in the international market where the domestic producer is a 'price taker'. As a result, the cost to the domestic buyer of using an additional unit of input q may be broken down into the forgone foreign exchange (FOB price), the subsidies no longer received (s^x), the saving of other export costs (dis^x), indirect taxes (t) and distribution costs associated with its domestic use (dis^d):

$$p^u = p^{fob} + s^x - dis^x + t + dis^d$$

$$p^u = p^{fob} + s^x + t - \Delta dis \qquad (2.2)$$

As in the case of the imported input, once the domestic price has been expressed in this manner, the efficiency price may be calculated using shadow price ratios for the foreign exchange and for the distribution costs, which would normally be produced at the margin. That is,

$$p^e = p^{fob} \, sprfe + \Delta dis \, spr_{dis}$$

In summary, pricing traded goods requires a *sprfe*, as well as *spr*s for nontraded services (e.g. transport, commerce). The next section is devoted to deriving the traditional operational formula for the *sprfe*.

2.3   THE SHADOW PRICE RATIO OF FOREIGN EXCHANGE

The efficiency price of foreign exchange, like any other efficiency price, is defined as the sum of the compensating variations attributable to a unit change in the demand or supply of foreign exchange, and its shadow price ratio would be the ratio of that shadow price to the market price: the prevailing exchange rate. Intuitively, if a US$100 additional supply of foreign exchange makes $1500 worth of additional domestic consumption possible, then the efficiency price of foreign exchange would be $15. The process that results in this increase in consumption may be outlined as follows. The additional supply would reduce the equilibrium exchange rate, which in turn would lead to reductions in the domestic prices of imported goods. These price reductions would result in the additional domestic consumption of imported goods, and in 'resource savings' due to the reductions in the domestic production of marginally imported goods. The lower exchange rate would also reduce the domestic prices of exported goods, leading to an increase in their domestic consumption and 'resource savings' associated with reductions in their production.

The preceding description refers to the concept of an equilibrium exchange rate. Thus, a brief explanation of what is meant by 'equilibrium' and how it may differ from the prevailing market exchange rate is required. A cost benefit analysis is a comparative-static analysis aimed at assessing whether a project (or other actions) represents a 'total welfare improvement'. To that effect, two equilibrium situations, one with and one without the project, are compared for each period over the life of the project. It is conceivable that for the initial period, the comparison could be initiated under the prevailing short-run situation, followed by adjustment hypotheses for the subsequent years. Such an approach, however, would not only be extremely difficult to implement, but would also make the result dependent on the initial year, which is normally unknown.[5] Alternatively, with as against without the project comparisons could be made under long-run equilibrium conditions and project flows priced accordingly. Shadow prices would be independent of the date for starting project execution and, if necessary, separate consideration could be made of temporary situations that may currently affect prices, such as short-run unemployment or international prices significantly different from their long-run values. This is the approach implicitly followed in practice, since constant market prices are normally used for the preparation of financial flows, and constant *sprs* are applied to those market prices.

Henceforth, references to the equilibrium exchange rate are to the long-run-equilibrium exchange rate. That is, the exchange rate that keeps both domestic and foreign accounts in equilibrium for *given* values of other fundamental variables, such as protection levels, international prices, available technology, and so on, on which the equilibrium position depends.[6] The equilibrium real exchange rate may be expressed as

---

5. Such an approach may be followed when simulation models allow for year-to-year comparisons of with and without the project situations, as may be the case in the simulation of electricity generation systems (see Londero, 1987, Ch. 10). However, results depend on assumed project starting dates, and simulations may need to be redone when these dates change.

6. For further discussion along these lines see Harberger (1986) and Edwards (1988). Clark et al. (1994) provide a review of alternative indicators.

$$erer = eer\ P^w_* / P^d_*$$

where *eer* is the nominal equilibrium exchange rate, P^w_* is a price index for traded goods corresponding to equilibrium prices and quantities, and P^d_* is a price index for nontraded goods corresponding to equilibrium prices and quantities, all for given values of the other fundamental variables. These considerations are implied in the following chapters.[7]

In order to identify the effects of an additional supply of foreign exchange, consider an investment project that increases exports not subject to any foreign trade tax. Thus, in Figure 2.2, S_0 is the supply of foreign exchange in the situation without the project when only good *x* is exported, and S_1 is that supply in the situation with the project. *D* is the demand for foreign exchange resulting from the demand for the only marginally imported good *m*, which is also produced domestically. Initially it will be assumed that the domestic transport and trade margins are nil, an assumption that will be eliminated in section 2.4. As a result, the equilibrium domestic prices of such goods in the situation without the project would be

$$p^m_0 = p^{cif,m}_0\ eer_0\ (1 + t^m)$$

$$p^x_0 = p^{fob,x}_0\ eer_0\ (1 - t^x)$$

(2.3)

where $p^{cif,m}_0$ and $p^{fob,x}_0$ are CIF and FOB prices expressed in foreign exchange, eer_0 is the equilibrium exchange rate, and t^m and t^x are the (*ad valorem*) trade tax rates. These taxes are initially assumed to be the only sources of discrepancy between border and domestic prices. In practice there may be other trade interventions, like quotas, import deposits, subsidized export financing, and so on. In those cases, estimates for the *ad valorem* equivalent to the effects of those interventions would have to be incorporated in t^m and t^x. Export sales are normally exempt from domestic indirect taxes, but imports are normally subject to them; these indirect taxes are temporarily ignored. These subjects will be considered in section 2.4.

Adjustment to the additional supply of foreign exchange will be made by means of a reduction in the (long-term) equilibrium exchange rate to eer_1. Thus, the domestic prices of *m* and *x* would be reduced to:

$$p^m_1 = p^{cif,m}_0\ eer_1\ (1 + t^m)$$

$$p^x_1 = p^{fob,x}_0\ eer_1\ (1 - t^x)$$

(2.4)

---

7. This formula assumes a flexible exchange rate. If the exchange rate were fixed, the correct formula would be $erer = er\ P^w_* / P^{de}_*$, where P^{de}_* would be the equilibrium prices for the nontraded goods. See Londero (1997).

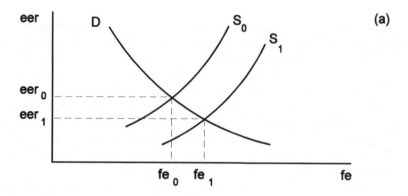

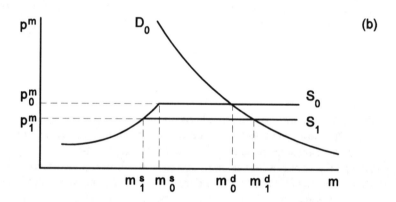

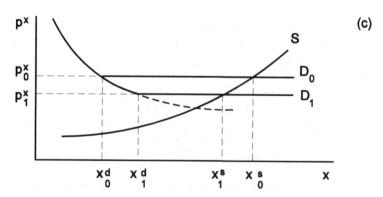

Figure 2.2 An increase in the supply of foreign exchange

where international prices $p_0^{cif,m}$ and $p_0^{fob,x}$ are assumed not to be affected by small variations in the domestic demand of a country.

Estimating the shadow price of foreign exchange requires estimating the CV of those affected. Starting with the consumers, the compensating variations of the reduction in the prices of the traded goods can be approximated by the increase in consumers' surplus (Δcs) – Figures 2.2(b) and (c) – a linear approximation to which yields[8]

$$\Delta cs^m = (p_0^m - p_1^m)\, m_0^d + \tfrac{1}{2}\,(p_0^m + p_1^m)(m_1^d - m_0^d) - p_1^m\,(m_1^d - m_0^d)$$

$$\Delta cs^x = (p_0^x - p_1^x)\, x_0^d + \tfrac{1}{2}\,(p_0^x + p_1^x)(x_1^d - x_0^d) - p_1^x\,(x_1^d - x_0^d)$$

(2.5)

That is, the reduction in the domestic value of the quantity that they would have consumed in the absence of the reduction in the exchange rate, plus their willingness to pay for the additional consumption, minus what they actually pay for this consumption.

It will now be useful to analyze the income changes of those affected that are associated with Δcs (Table 2.2), and to that effect each term of expression (2.5) will be treated separately. The first term is the change in the market value of the quantities consumed in the situation without the project. Substituting expressions (2.3) and (2.4) in that first term yields the following:

$$(p_0^m - p_1^m)\, m_0^d = p_0^{cif,m}\,(1 + t^m)(eer_0 - eer_1)\, m_0^d$$

$$(p_0^x - p_1^x)\, x_0^d = p_0^{fob,x}\,(1 - t^x)(eer_0 - eer_1)\, x_0^d$$

In turn, each of the above expressions can be broken down into three parts, each part representing the losses to those who, in the situation without the project, receive the expenses forgone by the consumers in the situation with the project. The first is the reduction in government revenue (Government column in Table 2.2) by way of receipts from the trade taxes corresponding to sales in the situation without the project because of the reduction in the *eer*:

$$p_0^{cif,m}\,(eer_0 - eer_1)(m_0^d - m_0^s)\, t^m$$

$$p_0^{fob,x}\,(eer_0 - eer_1)(m_0^d - m_0^s)\, t^x$$

The second part is the reduction in factor incomes ('Other factor owners' column in Table 2.2) due to the reduction in the domestic prices, which affects

---

Table 2.2   Income changes attributable to an additional supply of exports

Source	Project	Consumers
Change in the market value of the quantity of m consumed without the project	—	$p_0^{cif,m}\Delta eer(1+t^m)m_0^d$
Change in the market value of the quantity of x consumed without the project	—	$p_0^{fob,x}\Delta eer(1-t^x)x_0^d$
Consumers' willingness to pay for Δm^d	—	$\frac{1}{2}(p_0^m+p_1^m)\Delta m^d$
Consumers' willingness to pay for Δx^d	—	$\frac{1}{2}(p_0^x+p_1^x)\Delta x^d$
Paid by the consumers for Δm^d	$p_0^{cif,m}eer_1\Delta m^d$	$-p_0^{cif,m}eer_1(1+t^m)\Delta m^d$
Paid by the consumers for Δx^d	$p_0^{fob,x}eer_1\Delta x^d$	$-p_0^{fob,x}eer_1(1-t^x)\Delta x^d$
Willingness to receive for Δm^s	—	—
Willingness to receive for Δx^s	—	—
Received for Δm^s	$p_0^{cif,m}eer_1\Delta m^s$	—
Received for Δx^s	$p_0^{fob,x}eer_1\Delta x^s$	—
Total	$p_0^{cif,m}eer_1(\Delta m^d+\Delta m^s)+$ $p_0^{fob,x}eer_1(\Delta x^d+\Delta x^s)$	[a]
Changes in real incomes	Project's net revenue	Change in consumers' surplus

Note: [a] Total omitted due to complexity .

Source: Figure 2.2 as explained in the text.

the producers of import substitutes by

$$p_0^{cif,m}(eer_0-eer_1)(1+t^m)m_0^s$$

the importers of the marginally traded goods by

$$p_0^{cif,m}(eer_0-eer_1)(m_0^d-m_0^s)$$

Other factor owners	Government	Total
$-p_0^{cif,m}\Delta eer(1+t^m)m_0^s-p_0^{cif,m}\Delta eer(m_0^d-m_0^s)$	$-p_0^{cif,m}\Delta eer(m_0^d-m_0^s)t^m$	—
$-p_0^{fob,x}\Delta eer(1-t^x)x_0^d-p_0^{fob,x}\Delta eer(x_0^s-x_0^d)$	$-p_0^{fob,x}\Delta eer(x_0^s-x_0^d)t^x$	—
—	—	$\tfrac{1}{2}(p_0^m+p_1^m)\Delta m^d$
—	—	$\tfrac{1}{2}(p_0^x+p_1^x)\Delta x^d$
—	$p_0^{cif,m}eer_1 t^m\Delta m^d$	—
—	$-p_0^{fob,x}eer_1 t^x\Delta x^d$	—
$\tfrac{1}{2}(p_0^m+p_1^m)\Delta m^s$	—	$\tfrac{1}{2}(p_0^m+p_1^m)\Delta m^s$
$\tfrac{1}{2}(p_0^x+p_1^x)\Delta x^s$	—	$\tfrac{1}{2}(p_0^x+p_1^x)\Delta x^s$
$-p_0^{cif,m}eer_1(1+t^m)\Delta m^s$	$p_0^{cif,m}eer_1 t^m\Delta m^s$	—
$-p_0^{fob,x}eer_1(1-t^x)\Delta x^s$	$-p_0^{fob,x}eer_1 t^x\Delta x^s$	—
[a]	[a]	$\tfrac{1}{2}(p_0^m+p_1^m)(\Delta m^d+\Delta m^s)+$ $\tfrac{1}{2}(p_0^x+p_1^x)(\Delta x^d+\Delta x^s)$
Changes in factor incomes	Change in government revenue	Value at efficiency prices

and the producers of the exported good in their sales to both domestic and export markets by

$$p_0^{fob,x}(eer_0-eer_1)(1-t^x)x_0^d+p_0^{fob,x}(eer_0-eer_1)(x_0^s-x_0^d)$$

The second terms of expression (2.5) are the willingness to pay for the additional quantities of goods m and x, which express the values of the maximum quantities of other goods that the consumers would be prepared to forgo rather than do without the additional quantities of m and x. In this sense these are not an actual income flows but measures of the income equivalent to such quantities.

Finally, the third terms are the amounts paid by the consumers for the additional consumption, and may be broken down by replacing domestic prices by expression (2.4):

$$p_1^m (m_1^d - m_0^d) = -p_0^{cif,m} \, eer_1 \, (1 + t^m)(m_1^d - m_0^d)$$

$$p_1^x (x_1^d - x_0^d) = -p_0^{fob,x} \, eer_1 \, (1 - t^x)(x_1^d - x_0^d)$$

Thus, what the consumers pay for the additional quantities is equal to part of what the project receives from the sale of foreign exchange generated by exports

$$p_0^{cif,m} \, eer_1 \, (m_1^d - m_0^d)$$

$$p_0^{fob,x} \, eer_1 \, (x_1^d - x_0^d)$$

plus the corresponding change in receipts from trade taxes by the government

$$p_0^{cif,m} \, eer_1 \, t^m \, (m_1^d - m_0^d)$$

$$p_0^{fob,x} \, eer_1 \, t^x \, (x_1^d - x_0^d)$$

With regard to the effects on the producers of the traded goods, under competitive conditions the supply function would reflect the minimum amount they are willing to accept for the changes in production

$$\tfrac{1}{2} \, (p_0^m + p_1^m)(m_1^s - m_0^s)$$

$$\tfrac{1}{2} \, (p_0^x + p_1^x)(x_1^s - x_0^s)$$

To the extent that market prices of the inputs for producing m and x are equal to their efficiency prices, there would be no further effects to record. Resources released by the reductions in domestic production are assumed to be absorbed elsewhere in the economy at similar prices, which in turn equal their efficiency prices. If that were not a reasonable assumption to make, the differences between market and efficiency prices of the additional supply of inputs generated by the additional supply of foreign exchange would have to be estimated and incorporated into the *sprfe*.[9]

---

9. In these cases, the *sprfe* could be calculated by using input–output techniques. See Londero (1994).

Buyers actually paid, and factor owners no longer receive,

$$p_0^{cif,m} \, eer_1 \, (1 + t^m)(m_1^s - m_0^s)$$

$$p_0^{fob,x} \, eer_1(1 - t^x)(x_1^s - x_0^s)$$

for the reductions in production. Each of these amounts equals the net change in project revenue

$$p_0^{cif,m} \, eer_1 \, (m_1^s - m_0^s)$$

$$p_0^{fob,x} \, eer_1 \, (x_1^s - x_0^s)$$

plus the change in government revenue

$$p_0^{cif,m} \, eer_1 \, t^m \, (m_1^s - m_0^s)$$

$$p_0^{fob,x} \, eer_1 \, t^x \, (x_1^s - x_0^s)$$

Finally, note that due to the long-run equilibrium nature of the argument, there is an assumption that the additional supply of foreign exchange is fully used to increase imports $(\Delta m = \Delta m^d + \Delta m^s)$ and reduce exports $(\Delta x = \Delta x^d + \Delta x^s)$; that is

$$eer_1 \, (S_1 - S_0) = eer_1 \, [p_0^{cif,m} \, (\Delta m^d + \Delta m^s) + p_0^{fob,x} \, (\Delta x^d + \Delta x^s)]$$

$$eer_1 \, (S_1 - S_0) = eer_1 \, (p_0^{cif,m} \, \Delta m + p_0^{fob,x} \, \Delta x) \qquad (2.6)$$

From the perspective of the potential compensation criterion, Table 2.2 should be examined column by column. The first one records the project's revenue from the sale of exports. The second shows the CV of the consumers benefitting from the effect of the greater supply of foreign exchange on consumer goods. (Strictly speaking, this column should be subdivided into one column for each consumer.[10]) In other words, the total in the first column is the reduction in the income of the consumers that would leave them at the same level of welfare they enjoyed before the increase in the supply of foreign exchange (fall in the price of consumer goods). As the additional supply of foreign exchange causes a reduction in the *eer*, incomes of other factor owners are reduced by the extent shown in the third column. The fourth column records the changes in tax revenue brought about by the project. Since the government would not alter its foreign trade tax policy as a result of marginal

---

10. The reader will recall that to add CVs, judgments are required concerning the welfare 'value' of income changes for each consumer affected.

changes in revenue, these changes would result (most likely) in an increase in expenditure, a reduction in the deficit, or (least likely), a reduction in other taxes, which in turn would affect peoples' economic welfare. Although the sign of the net effect on the government is not defined, it will be assumed to be positive.[11]

For the project to be a potential Pareto improvement, the gainers (the consumers, the project and the government) should receive enough additional income to be able to compensate the losers (factor owners) and leave a remainder that exceeds project costs (not shown in Table 2.2). The overall balance of the table is the willingness to pay for the consumption made possible by the increase in the supply of foreign exchange plus the efficiency value of the resources released in the production of traded goods. This sum is the additional income attributable to the increase in the supply of foreign exchange that would remain after (potentially) compensating the respective losers, a sum that would become available to compensate those who are net losers as a result of the project costs.

The same result can be achieved by applying equal weights to the marginal income changes of all affected, allowing for the columns in Table 2.2 to be added up horizontally. Thus, for example, in the first row, the gain by consumers is equal to the loss of the remaining exporters and the government, as a result of which the respective *net effect on total welfare* is nil. The net result of the horizontal sum of the columns is the willingness to pay for the consumption made possible by the increase in the supply of foreign exchange plus the efficiency value of the resources released due to the reductions in the production of traded goods.

What has been explained so far allows for a simple formula to be presented for the shadow (efficiency) price of foreign exchange when the exchange rate adjusts the supply and demand of foreign exchange. In this simple example, the sum of the compensating variations of the additional supply of foreign exchange will be:

$$\tfrac{1}{2}(p_0^m + p_1^m)\, \Delta m + \tfrac{1}{2}(p_0^x + p_1^x)\, \Delta x$$

By substituting (2.3) in the above equation it becomes

$$\tfrac{1}{2}(eer_0 + eer_1)[p_0^{cif,m}\,(1 + t^m)\, \Delta m + p_0^{fob,x}\,(1 + t^x)\, \Delta x] \qquad (2.7)$$

The additional supply of foreign exchange generated by a project would normally have a minimum influence on the exchange rate. Thus, for all

---

11. This is consistent with the approximation $eer_0 = eer_1$, which will be incorporated in the analysis later (see expressions (2.8) and (2.9)).

practical purposes $\frac{1}{2} (eer_0 + eer_1) = eer$, and expression (2.7) may be written as

$$eer \, [p_0^{cif,m} (1 + t^m) \, \Delta m + p_0^{fob,x} (1 + t^x) \, \Delta x] \qquad (2.8)$$

In such a case, the direct income changes attributable to the additional supply of foreign exchange would be those recorded in Table 2.3. The resulting efficiency value of the additional supply of foreign exchange would be the consumers' willingness to pay for the additional consumption of traded goods, plus the producers' willingness to receive for the resources released. The shadow price of foreign exchange will be the change in economic welfare attributable to the marginal increase in the supply of foreign exchange per unit of that additional amount of foreign exchange. Thus, from (2.6) and (2.7) the *spfe* would be

$$spfe = \frac{eer \, [p_0^{cif,m} (1 + t^m) \, \Delta m + p_0^{fob,x} (1 + t^x) \, \Delta x]}{p_0^{cif,m} \, \Delta m + p_0^{fob,x} \, \Delta x} \qquad (2.9)$$

The *spfe* is normally expressed as a ratio to its market price: the official or prevailing exchange rate (*oer*); that is, that exchange rate at which the project transactions are valued. This ratio will be called the shadow price ratio of foreign exchange (*sprfe*)

$$sprfe = \frac{eer}{oer} \, \frac{[p_0^{cif,m} (1 + t^m) \, \Delta m + p_0^{fob,x} (1 + t^x) \, \Delta x)}{(p_0^{cif,m} \, \Delta m + p_0^{fob,x} \, \Delta x)} \qquad (2.10]$$

Note that the *sprfe* corrects the prevailing exchange rate as a measure of the efficiency price first for the difference with the equilibrium exchange rate, and then for the differences between market and efficiency values of the additional consumption and additional production of traded goods. Only when project flows are valued at long-run equilibrium prices can the correction *eer/oer* be omitted. Also note that the ratio *eer/oer* is one plus the real depreciation required for reaching the external equilibrium. Therefore, it indicates the increase in the exchange rate that is required *relative to the prices of nontraded goods* for reaching equilibrium.

Generalizing expression (2.10) for many imported consumer goods m_i and exported goods x_j would result in

$$sprfe = \frac{eer \, [\Sigma_i \, p_i^{cif,m} \, \Delta m_i \, (1 + t_i^m) + \Sigma_j \, p_j^{fob,x} \, \Delta x_j \, (1 - t_j^x)]}{oer \, (\Sigma_i \, p_i^{cif,m} \, \Delta m_i + \Sigma_j \, p_j^{fob,x} \, \Delta x_j)} \qquad (2.11)$$

Table 2.3   Income changes attributable to an additional supply of exports when effects on the exchange rate are negligible

Source	Project	Consumers
Willingness to pay for Δm^d	—	$p^m \Delta m^d$
Willingness to pay for Δx^d	—	$p^x \Delta x^d$
Paid for Δm^d	$p_0^{cif,m} eer_1 \Delta m^d$	$-p_0^{cif,m} eer_1 (1+t^m)\Delta m^d$
Paid for Δx^d	$p_0^{fob,x} eer_1 \Delta x^d$	$-p_0^{fob,x} eer_1 (1-t^x)\Delta x^d$
Willingness to receive for Δm^s	—	—
Willingness to receive for Δx^s	—	—
Received for Δm^s	$p_0^{cif,m} eer_1 \Delta m^s$	—
Received for Δx^s	$p_0^{fob,x} eer_1 \Delta x^s$	—
Total	$p_0^{cif,m} eer_1 (\Delta m^d+\Delta m^s)$ $+ p_0^{fob,x} eer_1 (\Delta x^d+\Delta x^s)$	—
Changes in real incomes	Project's net revenue	Change in consumers' surplus

Source: Table 2.2.

or in a simpler notation

$$sprfe = eer/oer \left[\Sigma_i \, \varphi_i \, (1 + t_i^m) + \Sigma_j \, \varphi_j \, (1 - t_j^x) \right] \qquad (2.12)$$

in which

$$\varphi_i = \frac{p_i^{cif,m} \, \Delta m_i}{\Sigma_i p_i^{cif,m} \, \Delta m_i + \Sigma_j p_j^{fob,x} \, \Delta x_j} \qquad \varphi_j = \frac{p_j^{fob,x} \, \Delta x_j}{\Sigma_i p_i^{cif,m} \, \Delta m_i + \Sigma_j p_j^{fob,x} \, \Delta x_j}$$

are the shares of each good i (j) in the additional supply of foreign exchange brought about by the project. It should be pointed out that the weights φ_i and φ_j refer to the value of the additional imports and exports *attributable* to the change in the exchange rate brought about by the increase in the supply of foreign exchange. That is, in the case of imports

$$\Delta m_i = \frac{\partial m_i}{\partial eer} \frac{\partial eer}{\partial fe} \, dfe \qquad (2.13)$$

Other factor owners	Government	Total
—	—	$p^m \Delta m^d$
—	—	$p^x \Delta x^d$
—	$p_0^{cif,m} eer_1 t^m \Delta m^d$	—
—	$-p_0^{fob,x} eer_1 t^x \Delta x^d$	—
$p^m \Delta m^s$	—	$p^m \Delta m^s$
$p^x \Delta x^s$	—	$p^x \Delta x^s$
$-p_0^{cif,m} eer_1(1+t^m)\Delta m^s$	$p_0^{cif,m} eer_1 t^m \Delta m^s$	—
$-p_0^{fob,x} eer_1(1-t^x)\Delta x^s$	$-p_0^{fob,x} eer_1 t^x \Delta x^s$	—
—	$p_0^{cif,m} eer_1 t^m(\Delta m^d + \Delta m^s)$ $-p_0^{fob,x} eer_1 t^{x}(\Delta x^d + \Delta x^s)$	$p^m(\Delta m^d + \Delta m^s) +$ $p^x(\Delta x^d + \Delta x^s)$
Changes in factor incomes	Changes in government revenue	Value at efficiency prices

Consequently, these marginal changes *should not* be estimated by simply comparing the lists of imports between two periods, since the Δm_i and Δx_j thus observed incorporate the effects of changes in other determinants of import and export levels, and not just those attributable to a change in the supply or demand of foreign exchange.

It should also be noted that import and export changes as presented in (2.13) are not truly equal to those measured under the *ceteris paribus* demand and supply curves used in the partial equilibrium derivation presented in this chapter. Partial equilibrium Δm_i and Δx_j assume that all other things remain equal, while there are cross-price and income effects resulting from the change in the *eer*. Therefore, partial equilibrium measures of Δm_i and Δx_j should be considered approximations. Appendix 2.1 to this chapter presents a general equilibrium derivation of the equivalent expression to (2.10).

Expression (2.12) corresponds to the traditional formula for the *sprfe* as presented in, *inter alia*, Harberger (1973, 1977), but it differs in that it takes into account the difference between the equilibrium and the prevailing exchange rates. This formula is often shown in terms of the price elasticities of imports and exports, a formulation that is easily derived from (2.12) and (2.13). Substituting by $M_i = p_i^{cif,m} m_i$ and $X_j = p_j^{fob,x} x_j$, multiplying the numerator and denominator by the *eer*, and multiplying and dividing all terms by M_i (or

X_j in the case of φ_j), the weight may be expressed as

$$\varphi_i = \frac{M_i\,(eer/M_i)(\partial M_i/\partial eer)}{\Sigma_i\,M_i\,(eer/M_i)(\partial M_i/\partial eer) + \Sigma_j\,X_j\,(eer/X_j)(\partial X_j/\partial eer)} \qquad (2.14)$$

Substituting in the above expression by price elasticities

$$\eta_i = (eer/M_i)(\partial M_i/\partial eer)$$

$$\varepsilon_j = (eer/X_j)(\partial X_j/\partial eer)$$

and then replacing (2.14) in (2.12) results in

$$sprfe = \frac{eer}{oer}\;\frac{[\Sigma_i\,M_i\,\eta_i\,(1 + t_i^m) + \Sigma_j\,X_j\,\varepsilon_j\,(1 - t_j^x)]}{\Sigma_i\,M_i\,\eta_i + \Sigma_j\,X_j\,\varepsilon_j} \qquad (2.15)$$

It should be noted that elasticities correspond to the equilibrium values of imports, exports and the exchange rate (see Appendix 2.1).

A Simplified Formula

Using expression (2.12) or (2.15) for calculating the *sprfe* requires that the price elasticities of exports and imports be known – information which in practice is not available. As a result, the *sprfe* is often calculated on the assumption that the weights φ are equal to the average share of each product in total imports and exports, or, equivalently, that all import and export elasticities are equal ($\eta_i = \varepsilon_j$, for all i, j). In these cases, the formula becomes

$$sprfe = \frac{eer}{oer}\;\frac{M + T^m + X - T^x}{M + X} \qquad (2.16)$$

in which $M = \Sigma_i\,M_i$, $T^m = \Sigma_i\,M_i\,t_i^m$, $X = \Sigma_j\,X_j$, and $T^x = \Sigma_j\,X_j\,t_j^x$. It should be noted that when average shares are used, only exports and imports of goods and services that are elastic to the exchange rate should be included. Chapter 8 provides a quantitative estimation for the case of Colombia.[12]

Finally, an expression very similar to (2.16) has been presented in various texts as the formula for calculating the 'standard conversion factor', which would be used to convert values expressed in the consumption numeraire to

---

12. Also see Parot (1992).

the foreign exchange numeraire.[13] These expressions do not include the corrections for the *eer*, and it is not clear how differences between the *eer* and the *oer* are taken into account.

2.4   MORE REALISTIC ASSUMPTIONS

Non-tax Interventions

So far the analysis has been limited to trade taxes as the only transfers explaining the difference between border and domestic prices. In practice, several non-tax interventions affect the domestic prices of traded goods, and consequently the CVs and the *spfe*. The creativity showed in designing non-tax interventions in foreign trade is significant, asking for equivalent ingenuity on behalf of economists to estimate the corresponding *ad valorem* equivalents. In this section, only a brief look at these interventions will be taken with the objective of showing the general approach in trying to estimate these *ad valorem* equivalents.[14]

On the export side, one of the most common non-tax interventions is subsidized export credit. When exporters receive this incentive, the equilibrium domestic price of the exported good becomes

$$p^x = p^{fob}\, eer\, (1 - t^x + fs^x)$$

where the *ad valorem* equivalent to the financial subsidy fs^x would be estimated by the difference between the present value of the loan at the market interest rate[15] and its present value at the subsidized interest rate, expressed as a proportion of the FOB value.

Similarly, in the case of import deposits the equilibrium domestic price of the imported good would become

$$p^m = p^{cif}\, eer\, (1 + t^m + fc^m)$$

---

13. Squire and van der Tak (1975, Ch. IX), Bruce (1976), Gittinger (1982, Ch. 7), and Squire, et al. (1979, Appendix C). See section 2.5.

14. Grennes (1984) and Vousden (1990) discuss trade restrictions and the equivalent tariff under different scenarios. Krishna et al. (1994, 1995) illustrate the case of export quotas and test for the assumption of competitive markets. Chapter 7 provides an example of simple estimates for import deposits, quantitative restrictions, and export financing.

15. The implicit assumption is that there is a financial market that represents the opportunity cost for the importer; otherwise, an appropriate opportunity cost would have to be identified.

where the *ad valorem* equivalent to the financial cost fc^m may be estimated by the difference between the present value of investing the deposit at the market interest rate and the present value of holding the import deposit, all expressed as a proportion of the CIF value. Chapter 8 discusses the estimation of the *ad valorem* equivalents of financial incentives and import deposits for Colombia, and provides the quantitative results.

There may also be quantitative restrictions, exemplified here by import quotas. These quotas may be temporary to compensate for a short-term disequilibrium, or may be of a more permanent nature, comparable to import taxes. The distinction is important because it is desirable that the numerator of an *spr* refers to the long-run shadow price and the denominator to the prevailing price. This stems from the fact that it is neither possible to calculate the series of *sprs* that follow the adjustment trajectory of short-run shadow prices to long-run equilibrium ones, nor is it possible to know when the project would be started. If the quantitative restrictions are of a short-run nature, the corresponding effects should be included in the *eer*. Its ratio to the *oer* would be higher if there were temporary quantitative restrictions. If those restrictions are considered a permanent part of the commercial policy, instead, then the *ad valorem* equivalents would have to be estimated and included in the numerator of the *sprfe*.

Another consideration in the case of quantitative restrictions is that the same good may have two market prices. One would be the price for those who import the good directly, and the other for those who purchase it in the market, since the market price would include the quasi rent generated by the quota.

Consider first the case of temporary quantitative restrictions. If the project imports the good directly, project flows record purchases at the *oer*. Therefore, the project economist can ignore the quantitative restrictions, since the *sprfe* should include the corresponding effects through the *eer/oer*. Domestic purchases of goods subject to temporary quotas, instead, should be valued at market prices that include the quasi rent of the quota in the distribution margins. The case of nontraded goods that use inputs subject to quotas is similar. The market prices of the inputs – or, if some producers import their inputs directly, their gross operating surpluses – would include the resulting quasi rent. In these cases the *sprfe* would continue to be the same, but taking into account the effects of temporary quotas would require special *sprs* for these gross operating surpluses. These corrections would result in lower *sprs* for the distribution margins and these nontraded goods, but this approach may not be practicable, and therefore the efficiency prices of imported goods subject to quotas would tend to be overvalued.[16]

---

16. A full understanding of these considerations requires knowledge on the calculation of *sprs* for nontraded goods. See Chapter 6.

When quantitative restrictions are permanent (as permanent as tariffs), it is the *eer* resulting from the existence of these restrictions that should be used, and the *ad valorem* equivalent of the quasi rents derived from those restrictions should be incorporated into the numerator of the *sprfe*. As a result, the *eer* would be lower than that without the quotas, but the numerator of (2.10), (2.15), or (2.16) would incorporate the *ad valorem* equivalent of the quantitative restrictions. As in the case of temporary quotas, this *sprfe* would allow for the proper pricing of goods imported directly by the project, but would overestimate the value of the foreign exchange incorporated in nontraded goods or in traded goods purchased at wholesale.

In the case that the *ad valorem* equivalents of quotas need to be estimated, there are two main questions: (1) would the quota be changed in response to the additional availability of foreign exchange and how?; and (2) how is the quota allocated and, consequently, who appropriates the rents generated by it? The first part of the first question determines whether the goods subject to the import quota enter into the formula for the *spfe*, since a quota that is not affected by changes in the demand or supply of foreign exchange would not affect prices or quantities consumed.[17] How the quota is affected determines the weights that goods subject to import quotas have in the formula for the *spfe*. The second question determines the approach to measuring the *ad valorem* equivalent of the quota and the distributional effects associated with it. For example, if the import quota is auctioned by the government imposing it, the per unit equivalent to the auction price may be used as an approximation to the difference between border and domestic prices. If, on the other hand, the quota is allocated on an *ad hoc* basis, estimating its *ad valorem* equivalent would be considerably more difficult, since it would require estimation of the composition of the market prices of these traded goods from market data, instead of the more simple approach of starting from trade data and adding *ad valorem* estimates of trade interventions.

Intermediate Goods

Thus far, the assumption that only consumer goods were being imported, simplified the presentation considerably, since CVs could be measured directly. When there are imported intermediate goods, the theoretical approach remains that of measuring the CVs of those affected, but this measurement requires following the input–output chain – a task that in practice becomes impossible. As a result, valuation is indirect through expected connections between demand for the intermediate good and consumers' willingness to pay for the consumer goods that could be produced with these intermediate goods.

---

17. Other than for the effect of the change in the *eer*, normally ignored in calculating the *spfe*.

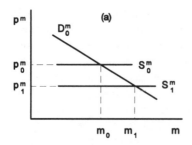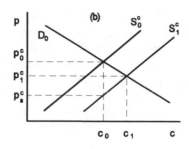

Figure 2.3 A reduction in the domestic price of an imported input

An increase in the supply of foreign exchange and its associated reduction in the *eer* would reduce the price of imported intermediate good m in Figure 2.3(a). That, in turn, would increase the supply of consumption good c, assumed here to be the only use of m (Figure 2.3(b)). Producers of c would not be affected (Table 2.4), since under competition they simply continue to receive a total revenue equal to total cost. The initial reduction in the cost of imports for production c_0

$$\Delta p^m m_0 = (\Delta p^c + \Delta p_s^c) c_0 = p_1^{cif,m} m_0 \Delta eer (1 + t^m)$$

would be balanced by the reduction in the price of the output and the increase in costs due to increases in input prices. The additional cost of producing $\Delta c = c_1 - c_0$, composed of the additional imports plus the other inputs required, equals the value of the corresponding sales:

$$p_1^c \Delta c = (p_1^c \Delta c - p_1^m \Delta m) + p_1^m \Delta m$$

Factor owners would be affected by the change in their rents (producers' surpluses), which originate from two sources. First, from the production of c, where they would be affected by

$$\Delta r = (p_1^c - p_s^c) c_0 + p_1^c (c_1 - c_0) - p_1^m \Delta m - \frac{1}{2} (p_0^c + p_1^c)(c_0 - c_1) \quad (2.17)$$

$$\Delta r = \Delta p_s^c c_0 + (p_1^c \Delta c - p_1^m \Delta m) - \frac{1}{2} (p_1^c + p_s^c) \Delta c$$

income received for providing the additional resources for increasing the production of c, minus their willingness to receive for providing these additional resources, which is assumed to equal the prices they receive (i.e. market prices equal efficiency prices). Then, they would also be affected by the reduction in the domestic value of foreign exchange $-p_1^{cif,m} m_0 \Delta eer$, which primarily affects the domestic producers of traded goods. The additional supply of foreign exchange reduces the equilibrium exchange rate and thus tends to increase the rents of factors used in the production of nontraded goods relative to the rents of factors used in the production of traded goods.

As a result of the reduction in the *eer*, consumers of *c* gain their CVs of the price reduction, measured by the change in their consumers' surpluses,

$$\Delta cs^c = (p_0^c - p_1^c)\, c_0 + \tfrac{1}{2}\, (p_0^c + p_1^c)(c_0 - c_1) - p_1^c\, (c_1 - c_0) \qquad (2.18)$$

$$\Delta cs^c = \Delta p^c\, c_0 + \tfrac{1}{2}\, (p_0^c + p_1^c)\, \Delta c - p_1^c\, \Delta c$$

That is, the reduction in the value of the quantity consumed in the absence of the price reduction, plus the consumers' willingness to pay for the additional consumption, minus what they actually pay for the additional quantity.

The government gains the tariff revenue associated with the additional imports that are purchased with part of the foreign exchange generated by the project, but loses the effect of the reduction in the *eer* on tariff revenue.

Finally, the efficiency value of this part of the foreign exchange generated by the project; that is, the part used to increase imports of *m* is obtained by adding the CVs of all affected, and it is a familiar result: willingness to pay for the additional consumption minus the efficiency value of the additional resources required to attain that production increase. Furthermore, if it is assumed that Δeer is insignificantly small, it becomes the domestic value of the imported input.

Domestic Taxes and Distribution Margins

Derivations have been conducted thus far under the simplifying assumption that there are no domestic taxes or distribution margins (commerce, transportation, handling and storage, etc.). This assumption made it possible to write expressions (2.3) and (2.4) for the market prices of traded goods as

$$p^m = p^{cif}\, eer\, (1 + t^m)$$

$$p^x = p^{fob}\, eer\, (1 - t^x)$$

In practice, market prices paid by the user normally include unit distribution margins *dis*. In the case of imports, the assumption is that both the imported and the domestically produced good are identical and command the same users' price in the domestic market.[18] Then, the users' price of the marginally

---

18. Londero (1996b) considers the case when the imported and the domestically produced goods are different, but close substitutes.

Table 2.4   Income changes attributable to a reduction in the domestic price of imported inputs

Source	Project	Government
Market value of the quantity of m imported without the project	—	$-t^m p_1^{cif.m} m_0 \Delta eer$
Other inputs for producing c_0	—	—
Change in the market value of c_0	—	—
Paid for Δm	$eer_1 p_1^{cif.m} \Delta m$	$t^m eer_1 p_1^{cif.m} \Delta m$
Other inputs for producing Δc	—	—
Consumers' willingness to pay for Δc	—	—
Paid by the consumers for Δc	—	—
Willingness to receive for other inputs to produce Δc	—	—
Total	$p_1^{cif.m} eer_1 \Delta m$	$t^m eer_1 p_1^{cif.m} \Delta m - t^m p_1^{cif.m} m_0 \Delta eer$
Changes in real incomes	Project's revenue	Change in tax revenue

Source: Figure 2.3, as explained in the text.

imported good, the domestic distribution margins for the domestically produced one, dis^d, and indirect taxes t – assumed equal for both the imported and the domestically produced good – determine the basic price, p^b, which domestic producers would take into account for determining output levels. The domestic price paid by the consumer for the imported good, or users' price, would thus be:

$$p^m = p^{cif} eer (1 + t^m)(1 + t) + dis^m = p^b (1 + t) + dis^s \qquad (2.19)$$

since indirect taxes are normally charged on the domestic value of the import at the customs gate. Expression (2.19) indicates that, at the users' price level, the domestic price of the imported good would be equal to the domestic price of the domestically produced one, which equals the domestic basic price, plus the indirect tax at rate t, plus the distribution margin for the domestically produced good.

An increase in the supply of foreign exchange would reduce the eer and, consequently, the domestic prices of imported goods. These domestic price

Factor owners	Producers of c	Consumers of c	Total
$-p_1^{cif,m}m_0\Delta eer$	$(\Delta p^c + \Delta p_s^c)c_0$	—	—
$\Delta p_s^c c_0$	$-\Delta p_s^c c_0$	—	—
—	$-\Delta p^c c_0$	$\Delta p^c c_0$	—
—	$-p_1^m \Delta m$	—	—
$p_1^c \Delta c - p_1^m \Delta m$	$-(p_1^c \Delta c - p_1^m \Delta m)$	—	—
—	—	$\frac{1}{2}(p_1^c + p_0^c)\Delta c$	$\frac{1}{2}(p_1^c + p_0^c)\Delta c$
—	$p_1^c \Delta c$	$-p_1^c \Delta c$	—
$-\frac{1}{2}(p_1^c + p_s^c)\Delta c + p_1^m \Delta m$	—	—	$-\frac{1}{2}(p_1^c + p_s^c)\Delta c + p_1^m \Delta m$
$\Delta p_s^c c_0 + \frac{1}{2}\Delta p_s^c \Delta c - p_1^{cif,m}m_0\Delta eer$	—	$\Delta p^c c_0 + \frac{1}{2}\Delta p^c \Delta c$	$p_1^m \Delta m + \frac{1}{2}(p_0^c - p_s^c)\Delta c$
Change in rents	Change in producers' income	Change in consumers' surplus	Value at efficiency prices

reductions would in turn result in additional domestic consumption Δm^d and resource savings due to a reduction in domestic production Δm^s. Under the simplifying assumption that producers' prices equal marginal production costs at efficiency prices of the imported good, the efficiency value of the additional consumption generated by the additional foreign exchange via the market of the imported good would be

$$\Delta m^d (p^m - dis^{m'}) + \Delta m^s (p^m - dis^{s'}) \qquad (2.20)$$

where the primes indicate values at efficiency prices. The first term is the willingness to pay for the additional consumption, minus the efficiency value of the additional distribution costs attributable to the additional imports required to effect that consumption. The second term is the users' price minus the efficiency value of the distribution margin of the domestic production, minus the indirect tax. By substituting (2.19) in (2.20) the efficiency value would be

$$\Delta m^d \ [p^{cif} \ eer \ (1 + t^m)(1 + t) + dis^m - dis^{m\prime}] +$$

$$\Delta m^s \ [p^b \ (1 + t) + dis^s - dis^{s\prime}] \qquad (2.21)$$

The process followed in order to arrive at expression (2.21) allows for three assumptions implicit in the traditional formula for the *sprfe* to be made explicit: producers' prices equal long-run marginal production costs at efficiency prices, producer prices of the imported and the domestically produced goods are equal, and distribution costs at market and at efficiency prices are equal, that is,

$$p^{cif} \ eer \ (1 + t^m)(1 + t) = p^b \ (1 + t)$$

$$dis^m = dis^{m\prime}$$

$$dis^s = dis^{s\prime}$$

Then, if these assumptions hold, the valuation frequently used in practice is obtained, that is

$$p^{cif} \ eer \ (1 + t^m)(1 + t)(\Delta m^d + \Delta m^s) \qquad (2.22)$$

In the case of exports, the equality between the export price and the domestic market price is no longer to be expected at the basic level, since many exporting firms may pay the export distribution costs themselves. Thus, assuming that exporting firms pay export distribution costs and that exports are exempt from domestic indirect taxes, the two marginal revenues equated in the maximization process would be

$$p^{fob} \ eer \ (1 - t^x) - dis^x = (p^{xd} - dis^d) / (1 + t) \qquad (2.23)$$

where p^{xd} is the users' price of the exported good in the domestic market, and dis^d is the corresponding distribution margin. An increase in the supply of foreign exchange would reduce the *eer* and the ensuing domestic price reductions would result in additional domestic consumption of the exported good Δx^d,

$$\Delta x^d \ \{[p^{fob} \ eer \ (1 - t^x) - dis^x](1 + t) + dis^d + dis^{x\prime} - dis^{d\prime}\} \qquad (2.24)$$

For the sake of simplicity, it will be assumed that $dis^x \times t = 0$ and expression (2.24) will be approximated by

$$\Delta x^d \ [p^{fob} \ eer \ (1 - t^x)(1 + t) - (dis^x - dis^{x\prime}) + (dis^d - dis^{d\prime})] \qquad (2.25)$$

As a result, the value of the additional consumption would be the amount paid by the consumer, minus the efficiency value of the *net* additional distribution costs.

The additional supply of foreign exchange would also result in resource savings due to the reduction in domestic production Δx^s. Under the assumption that producers' prices to the domestic market equal the long-run marginal cost at efficiency prices,[19] the efficiency value of the resource savings would be

$$\Delta x^s \left(p^{xd} - dis^d + dis^{d\prime}\right) = \Delta x^s \left[p^{fob} \, eer \, (1 - t^x) - (dis^x - dis^{x\prime})\right] \quad (2.26)$$

The additional consumption would save export distribution costs and require additional domestic distribution services, while the reduction in production would only release resources under the same heading.

In summary, when exports are exempt from indirect taxes, as they usually are in practice, the value of the additional consumption attributable to the increase in the supply of foreign exchange will be the sum of (2.25) and (2.26)

$$\Delta x^d \left[p^{fob} \, eer \, (1 - t^x)(1 + t) - (dis^x - dis^{x\prime}) + (dis^d - dis^{d\prime})\right] +$$

$$\Delta x^s \left[p^{fob} \, eer \, (1 - t^x) - (dis^x - dis^{x\prime})\right] \quad (2.27)$$

Note that the assumptions used are similar to the case of imports, namely that producers' prices equal long-run marginal production costs at efficiency prices, and that basic prices of the imported and the domestically produced goods are equal. If the value at market prices of the distribution margins is, for practical purposes, equal to their value at efficiency prices, the effects $(dis - dis')$ will be nil and the *sprfe* can be calculated as

$$sprfe = eer/oer \left[\Sigma_i \, \varphi_i \, (1 + t_i^m)(1 + t_i) +\right.$$

$$\left. \Sigma_j \, \varphi_j^d \, (1 - t_j^x)(1 + t_j) + \Sigma_j \, \varphi_j^s \, (1 - t_j^x)\right] \quad (2.28)$$

Since marginal coefficients are difficult to estimate, expression (2.28) is simplified to

$$sprfe = \frac{eer}{oer} \, \frac{M + T^m + T^{md} + X - T^x + T^{xd}}{M + X} \quad (2.29)$$

where $T^{md} = \Sigma_i \, M_i \, (1 + t_i^m) \, t_i$ is the collection of indirect taxes out of imports,

---

19. Otherwise, see Londero (1994). The assumption that the weighted average of the export and domestic prices equals the long-run marginal cost at efficiency prices complicates the algebra, adding little to the substance.

and $T^{xd} = \alpha^{xd} \Sigma_j X_j (1 - t_j^x) t_j$ is an estimate of the indirect taxes paid by the share α^{xd} of domestic sales attributable to a change in exports induced by a change in the *eer*. Equation (2.29) corresponds to (2.16) when imports and domestic sales of marginally exported goods pay domestic indirect taxes. In practice, however, the indirect taxes on the changes in the domestic consumption of exports are often ignored, perhaps because α^{xd} is difficult to estimate.

Partial Summary

The calculation of the *sprfe* in accordance with expressions (2.11) or (2.15), or the operational versions (2.16) and (2.29), presupposes that the following main conditions are met:

(a)   in the long run, adjustment to an excess demand for foreign exchange takes place through changes in the real exchange rate;

(b)   if other incentives or disincentives to import or export exist, they are taken into account through an equivalent *ad valorem* tax or subsidy;

(c)   the domestic prices of intermediate goods adequately reflect their efficiency prices;

(d)   the market values of the distribution services are equal to their values at efficiency prices.

In these circumstances, an additional unit of foreign exchange converted into the national currency at the prevailing exchange rate may be expressed in units of consumption by multiplying it by a *sprfe* calculated in accordance with what is shown in this section.

2.5   DOMESTIC AND FOREIGN EXCHANGE NUMERAIRES

The publication of a manual for the appraisal of industrial projects by the Organization for Economic Co-operation and Development (Little and Mirrlees, 1969), and two subsequent books that enjoyed wide distribution (Little and Mirrlees, 1974; Squire and van der Tak, 1975), led some economists to believe that it was simpler to use foreign exchange expressed in the domestic currency at the prevailing exchange rate as the numeraire.[20] So presented, it would just be a difference in the unit of account used to express costs and benefits, and switching from one numeraire to the other should pose

---

20. For other comparisons of the two numeraires see, *inter alia*, Joshi (1972), Dasgupta (1972), Little and Mirrlees (1974, Ch. 18), Curry and Weiss (1994, Ch. 5-6) and ADB (1997).

no significant problem. If in order to express an amount of foreign exchange (converted into the domestic currency at the *oer*) into efficiency prices it is multiplied by the *sprfe*, any cost or benefit expressed in the consumption numeraire may be expressed in the 'foreign exchange numeraire' by dividing it by the *sprfe*, while imports or exports would simply be valued at the prevailing exchange rate. The use of one or the other numeraire would just be a matter of preference.

Consider a government project that substitutes imports for a total of

$$oer \, \Delta m_s \, (1 + t_s^m) = 150$$

using imported inputs for a total of

$$oer \, \Delta m_i \, (1 + t_i^m) = -26$$

where $t_s^m = 0.5$ and $t_i^m = 0.3$. The efficiency value of the foreign exchange savings for a *sprfe* of 1.2 would be

$$oer \, (\Delta m_s + \Delta m_i) = (100 - 20) \times 1.2 = 96$$

Expressing this efficiency value in the foreign exchange numeraire would start by asking what would be the increase (reduction) in the supply (demand) of foreign exchange Δfe valued at the prevailing exchange rate that would have provided a consumption increase of 96; that is, $96 = \Delta fe \times sprfe$, from where $\Delta fe = 96 / 1.2 = 80$.

Expressing an efficiency value in another numeraire only means using a different unit of account, as in the way that distances may be measured in miles or kilometers. Therefore, the use of a different numeraire does not change the conclusions of a cost–benefit analysis. If B_t is the net benefit in the consumption numeraire of a project in year t, d is the discount rate, PV is present value, and r is the internal rate of return, it follows that

$$PV(B_t, d) > 0 \rightarrow (1/sprfe) \, PV(B_t, d) > 0$$

$$PV(B_t, r) = 0 \rightarrow (1/sprfe) \, PV(B_t, r) = 0$$

That is, neither the sign of the net present values (nor the ranking according to the cost–benefit ratios), nor the magnitude of the internal rate of return would be affected by a true change in numeraire.

When estimating a distributional impact as required by the approach proposed by Little and Mirrlees, care should be exercised in properly registering all the flows attributable to the project. Table 2.5 presents the case

Table 2.5   Distributive effects in two numeraires

	Project	Government	Total
Foreign exchange	100	20	120
Import taxes	50	-50	—
Efficiency value in:			
Consumption numeraire	150	-30	120
Foreign exchange numeraire	150/1.2	-30/1.2	100

of a project that substitutes imports of good s, under the assumption that both the imported and the domestically produced goods pay the same distribution margins. Then, the project output at market prices would be equal to the value of the substituted import, which is recorded split into foreign exchange (100) and import taxes (50). The example in the top half of Table 2.5 corresponds to the consumption numeraire. Under the assumption that trade taxes make up the entire difference between the *oer* and the *spfe*, the additional foreign exchange available in the market would result in extra trade-tax revenue for the government in (*sprfe* - 1) per unit value. Consequently, the project earns sales revenue, and the government is affected by the difference between the trade-tax revenue lost due to the reductions in the imports of s and the additional trade-tax revenue resulting from the alternative use of the foreign exchange released by the import substitution.

As explained above, expressing these effects in the foreign exchange numeraire simply requires dividing the income changes by the *sprfe*, which is recorded in the bottom line of Table 2.5. There it should be noted that the effects on government revenue are recorded, but in a different numeraire.[21] With that in mind, it is difficult to imagine why anybody would conduct a cost–benefit analysis in the foreign exchange numeraire when an estimate of the distributional effects is required.

It should be noted that the numeraire proposed by Little and Mirrlees (1974) is not simply foreign exchange, but 'present uncommitted social income measured in terms of convertible foreign exchange of constant purchasing power' (p. 151). The reader interested in the practical applications need not worry about the definition. When the rubber meets the road, these authors assume that uncommitted social income and uncommitted public income are equally valuable, and that uncommitted public income equals the

---

21. Cf. Little and Mirrlees (1974, p. 149), where the effects of the alternative use of the foreign exchange were omitted, and flows were not expressed in the numeraire.

'social value of public investment', implying that public consumption and public investment are equally valuable at the margin. These assumptions are more clearly stated by Squire and van der Tak (1975, pp. 135, 140). The reasons for selecting such a cumbersome numeraire seem to be less known. Little explained (Schwartz and Berney, 1977, pp. 142–5) that they aimed at 'producing an interest rate that the World Bank would believe', and that rate would be in the order of a 10% cut-off rate.

The assumptions required to make Little and Mirrlees' approach operational in the form it was proposed – that is, optimal allocation at the margin by the government – would be hard to find in developing countries. Eliminating these assumptions would lead to a treatment very similar to that of UNIDO (1972), which considers the use of separate shadow prices of investment for the government and for the private sector. Also, it is hard to imagine a case where a cost–benefit analysis involving the important issues incorporated by Little and Mirrlees into their analysis – allowing for shadow prices of investment different from unity and for different distributional weights for different income levels – would be made easier by using the numeraire they proposed. On the contrary, these important distributional issues are better handled and understood when using the domestic numeraire, estimating the distributional effects, and only then applying shadow prices of investment and distributional weights (UNIDO, 1972; Londero, 1987). Moreover, the mere process of estimating the distributional effects may itself create some significant external benefits (Londero, 1996a).

APPENDIX 2.1 A SIMPLE GENERAL EQUILIBRIUM DERIVATION[22]

The simple small open economy produces three consumption goods: a nontraded good (n), an imported good (m), and an exported good (x), with domestic prices p_n, p_m and p_x. Imports are subject to an *ad valorem* tariff t_m and export to a tax t_x. To simplify the notation, the price of the nontraded good is used as numeraire, thus

$$p_n = 1$$

$$p_m = p_m^w e (1 + t_m) \tag{2.A1}$$

$$p_x = p_x^w e (1 - t_x)$$

where p_j^w is the world price and e is the exchange rate. Net taxes are distributed by the government through lump-sum payments. Total consumption of each good C_j would equal total production (Q_j), plus imports (M_j), minus exports (E_j). Thus,

$$C_n = Q_n$$

$$C_m = Q_m + M_m \tag{2.A2}$$

$$C_x = Q_x - E_x$$

and balance of payments equilibrium would be

$$p_m^w M_m = p_x^w E_x + F \tag{2.A3}$$

where F is exogenous capital inflows. Total welfare is represented by the same welfare function used in Appendix 1.1

$$W = W[(1/N) \; \Sigma_i \; U^i(C_n^i; \; C_m^i; \; C_x^i] \tag{2.A4}$$

The change in welfare that is attributable to an additional unit of foreign

---

22. This derivation is based on Bacha and Taylor (1971) and Dornbusch (1974). There is a strain of general equilibrium literature deriving similar formulae from more detailed models (*inter alia*, Dinwiddy and Teal, 1986, 1990, 1996; Maneschi, 1990a, 1990b). These approaches separate the effects measured along compensated excess demand functions from those resulting from the reallocation of factors in the production of nontraded goods and those originating in the fiscal adjustment required due to the *net* effects attributable to the project.

exchange may be represented by

$$N \frac{\partial W}{\partial F} = \Sigma_i \frac{\partial W}{\partial U^i} \Sigma_j \frac{\partial U^i}{\partial C^i_j} \frac{\partial C^i_j}{\partial e} \frac{\partial e}{\partial F} \tag{2.A5}$$

That is, the additional supply of foreign exchange is expected to alter the exchange rate (i.e. the relative prices between trade and non traded goods) leading to changes in the consumption of the three goods.

According to utility maximization conditions,

$$\partial U^i / \partial C^i_j = \lambda^i p_j \tag{2.A6}$$

where λ^i is the Lagrange multiplier for consumer i, equal to his or her marginal utility of income. Substituting (2.A2) and (2.A6) in (2.A5) results in

$$N \frac{\partial W}{\partial F} = \Sigma_i \frac{\partial W}{\partial U^i} \lambda^i \Sigma_j p_j \frac{\partial C^i_j}{\partial e} \frac{\partial e}{\partial F} \tag{2.A7}$$

Taking the marginal utility of income for individual 1 as numeraire, and using the definition of distributional weight u^i from Chapter 1, equation (2.A7) may be presented as follows

$$\frac{N}{\lambda^1} \frac{\partial W}{\partial F} = \Sigma_i u^i \Sigma_j p_j \frac{\partial C^i_j}{\partial e} \frac{\partial e}{\partial F} = \Sigma_j p^j \Sigma_i u^i \frac{\partial C^i_j}{\partial e} \frac{\partial e}{\partial F} \tag{2.A8}$$

The shadow price of foreign exchange is a weighted average of all prices, where the weights are the consumption changes attributable to the change in its supply multiplied by the corresponding distributional weights.[23] Therefore, its value would depend on the distribution of the consumption changes among individuals. It should be noted that (2.A8) includes all consumption effects attributable to the change in the exchange rate attributable to the change in the supply of foreign exchange, and not just those measured *along* the (compensated) demand curve as presented in this chapter. The effects comprised in the partial derivatives also include the changes in government revenue assumed to be returned as lump-sum payments. Some of these government revenue changes are normally the only distributional effects taken into account when estimating the distributional impact of an investment

---

23. Note the similarity with the general expression (1.A16) for a shadow price.

project, since price changes attributable to the additional supply of foreign exchange are assumed to be negligibly small $(de \rightarrow 0)$.[24]

Expression (2.A8) may be simplified by defining a distributional adjustment parameter μ^e such that

$$\Sigma_i u^i \frac{\partial C_j^i}{\partial e} = \mu^e \Sigma_i \frac{\partial C_j^i}{\partial e} = \mu^e \frac{\partial C_j}{\partial e} \tag{2.A9}$$

and therefore

$$\mu^e = \frac{\Sigma_i u^i \dfrac{\partial C_j^i}{\partial e}}{\Sigma_i \dfrac{\partial C_j^i}{\partial e}} = \Sigma_i u^i \frac{\dfrac{\partial C_j^i}{\partial e}}{\dfrac{\partial C_j}{\partial e}} \tag{2.A10}$$

Substituting (2.A9) in (2.A10) results in

$$\frac{N}{\lambda^1} \frac{\partial W}{\partial F} = \mu^e \Sigma_j p_j \frac{\partial C_j}{\partial e} \frac{\partial e}{\partial F} \tag{2.A11}$$

Since this is an open economy, changes in consumption are due to changes in production and trade, which are obtained by differentiating (2.A2)

$$\frac{\partial C_m}{\partial e} = \frac{\partial Q_m}{\partial e} + \frac{\partial M_m}{\partial e}$$

$$\frac{\partial C_x}{\partial e} = \frac{\partial Q_x}{\partial e} - \frac{\partial E_x}{\partial e} \tag{2.A12}$$

Optimality in production requires that marginal rates of transformation dQ_i / dQ_j equal relative prices p_i / p_j; therefore, in equilibrium,

---

24. See the analysis of section 2.2, Tables 2.1 and 2.2.

$$\Sigma_j \, p_j \, \frac{\partial Q_j}{\partial e} = 0 \qquad\qquad (2.A13)$$

Substituting (2.A12) and (2.A13) in (2.A11) yields

$$\frac{N}{\lambda^1} \frac{\partial W}{\partial F} = \mu^e \, (p_m \frac{\partial M_j}{\partial e} - p_x \frac{\partial E_j}{\partial e}) \, \frac{\partial e}{\partial F} \qquad\qquad (2.A14)$$

If changes in utility for all consumers have the same weight in the welfare function and the marginal utilities of income are the same for all consumers, then $\mu^e = 1$. In such a case, substituting (2.A1) in (2.A12) would provide

$$\frac{N}{\lambda^1} \frac{\partial W}{\partial F} = e \, [p_m^w \, (1 + t_m) \frac{\partial M_j}{\partial e} - p_x^w \, (1 - t_x) \frac{\partial E_j}{\partial e}] \, \frac{\partial e}{\partial F} \qquad\qquad (2.A15)$$

As noted by Tower and Pursell (1987), in (2.A15) partial derivatives of imports and exports with respect to the exchange rate are not compensated own-price elasticities, but general equilibrium derivatives with respect to the exchange rate. Two additional assumptions are required in order to obtain the traditional formula for the efficiency price of foreign exchange (Dornbusch, 1974): zero cross-price elasticities between traded goods and zero marginal propensities to spend on traded goods. In this case, the resulting formula will be equivalent to equation (2.10) using own-price derivatives when the *oer* equals the *eer*.

3. Labor

3.1 THE SHADOW PRICE OF LABOR

In neoclassical microeconomics, the supply of labor and the demand for consumption goods are treated similarly. Working for a salary is conceived of as being performed at the cost of alternative uses of that time (so-called leisure), and the welfare derived from the consumption of commodities made possible by wage income competes with the welfare derived from those alternative uses. Moreover, it is assumed that the additional income required to induce an additional hour of work of a certain type increases with the number of hours worked; that is, an extra hour of salaried work of a certain type could only be obtained at the expense of a salary increase (the individual's supply of labor is an increasing function of the salary). Note that the argument is formulated for hours of work of a certain type, since the individual may be willing to work a different time period for the same salary in different occupations.[1]

The market supply of labor would be the horizontal aggregation of the individual supply functions. Thus, an increase in the demand for labor, $L_1 - L_s$ in Figure 3.1(a), would result in an increase in the prevailing wage. In the absence of 'involuntary unemployment', the additional demand for labor would be met by a reduction of employment in alternative occupations

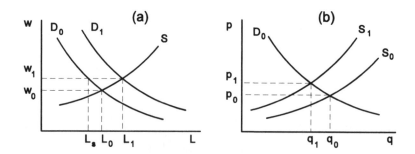

Figure 3.1 An additional demand for labor

1. Hourly valuations by the individual may differ for different occupations; for example, a riskier occupation may be associated with a higher supply price.

$(L_0 - L_s)$ and an increase in the number of hours of work, both induced by the wage increase. If occupations were such that the number of working hours could be adjusted freely, $\Delta w = w_1 - w_0$ would be the minimum salary increase required to induce the supply of additional hours $L_1 - L_0$. If the daily number of hours were fixed, Δw would be the salary increase that is necessary to induce the required additional number of working days.[2]

The efficiency cost of providing the additional hours of work required by a project may be analyzed following the same approach as in the case of foreign exchange; that is, by identifying those affected by the additional demand for labor, and measuring their CVs. The results of doing so are presented in Table 3.1. Starting with the project, it pays

$$w_1 (L_1 - L_s) = w_1 (L_1 - L_0) + w_1 (L_0 - L_s)$$

for its labor requirements. The workers gain the CV of the wage increase, approximately equal to the increase in their rent or producer's surplus[3]

$$\Delta w\, L_0 + w_1 (L_1 - L_0) - \tfrac{1}{2} (w_1 + w_0)(L_1 - L_0)$$

which equals the additional income for the same hours of work due to the wage increase, plus the amount received for the extra hours, minus the minimum sum they are willing to receive for these additional hours.[4]

Labor is Withdrawn from the Production of Consumption Goods

The salary increase also affects all other producers of goods and services. For the sake of simplicity, it will be initially assumed that only one consumption good q is produced, and that q is nontraded at the margin, represented in Figure 3.1(b). (The extension to the case of intermediate goods would be similar to that of foreign exchange and is left to the reader.) As a result of the wage increase, producers of the consumer good face a cost increase, which under competitive conditions would translate (almost) fully into a price increase $(p_1 - p_0)$; that is,

$$(p_1 - p_0)\, q_1 = (w_1 - w_0)\, L_s = (w_1 - w_0)\, L(q_1)$$

---

2. See Mishan (1981b).

3. Mishan (1981b) provides a simple demonstration that the increase in the producers' surplus is approximately equal to the CV of the additional hours of work.

4. Sometimes called the value of the 'disutility of effort'.

Shadow Prices for Project Appraisal

Table 3.1   Income changes attributable to an additional demand for labor

Source	Project	Workers
Market value of labor employed without the project	$-\Delta w (L_0 - L_s)$	$\Delta w L_0$
Other inputs for producing q_0	—	—
Market value of q_0	—	—
Willingness to receive for ΔL	—	$-\frac{1}{2}(w_1+w_0)(L_1-L_0)$
Received for ΔL	$-w_1(L_1-L_0)$	$w_1(L_1-L_0)$
Willingness to pay for Δq	—	—
Paid by the consumers for Δq	—	—
Value of the resources released	$-w_0(L_0-L_s)$	—
Total	$-w_1(L_1-L_s)$	$\Delta w L_0+\frac{1}{2}\Delta w(L_1-L_0)$
Changes in real incomes	Project's cost	Change in rents

Source: Figure 3.1 as explained in the text.

where $L(q_1) = L_s$ is the employment in the production of q when the output level is q_1. As a result, the consumers lose the CV of the price increase

$$(p_1 - p_0) q_1 + \frac{1}{2} (p_1 + p_0)(q_0 - q_1) - p_0 (q_0 - q_1)$$

represented here by the additional amount they pay for q_1, plus their willingness to pay for their reduction in the consumption of Δq, minus what they actually pay for that quantity.

The producers of q see their revenues increased in

$$(p_1 - p_0) q_1 = (w_1 - w_0) L_s = (w_1 - w_0) L(q_1)$$

equal to their additional costs for the new production level q_1. At the same time, the producers' revenues decline due to the sales reduction in

Factor owners	Producers of q	Consumers of q	Total
—	$-\Delta w\, L_s$	—	—
—	—	—	—
—	$\Delta p\, q_1$	$-\Delta p\, q_1$	—
—	—	—	$-\frac{1}{2}(w_1+w_0)(L_1-L_0)$
—	—	—	—
—	—	$-\frac{1}{2}(p_1+p_0)(q_0-q_1)$	$-\frac{1}{2}(p_1+p_0)(q_0-q_1)$
—	$-p_0(q_0-q_1)$	$p_0(q_0-q_1)$	—
—	$p_0(q_0-q_1)$	—	$p_0(q_0-q_1)-w_0(L_0-L_s)$
—	—	$-\Delta p\, q_1 - \frac{1}{2}\Delta p(q_0-q_1)$	$-\frac{1}{2}(w_1+w_0)(L_1-L_0)- \frac{1}{2}(p_1+p_0)(q_0-q_1)+ [p_0(q_0-q_1)-w_0(L_0-L_s)]$
—	Change in producers' income	Change in consumers' surplus	Value at efficiency prices

$$(p_1 - p_0)\, q_1 = (w_1 - w_0)\, L_s = (w_1 - w_0)\, L(q_1)$$

Under competitive conditions, this revenue reduction would be equal to the market value of the resources released when reducing production from q_0 to q_1, or the market value of the released resources. If the market prices of the released resources were equal to their efficiency prices, there would be no more transfers to register and the accounting of income changes would be complete.

The sum of the columns of Table 3.1 provides the compensating variations of those affected. Assigning equal weights to these money measures of welfare changes results in the efficiency cost of the labor hired by the project

$$\frac{1}{2}(w_1 + w_0)(L_1 - L_0) + \frac{1}{2}(p_1 + p_0)(q_0 - q_1) -$$

$$[p_0(q_0 - q_1) - w_0(L_0 - L_s)] \tag{3.1}$$

Table 3.2   Income changes attributable to an additional demand for labor when effects on the wage rate are negligible

Source	Project	Workers
Change in the market value of the quantity of labor supplied without the project	—	—
Willingness to receive for ΔL	—	$-w(L_1-L_0)$
Received for ΔL	$-w(L_1-L_0)$	$w(L_1-L_0)$
Change in the market value of the quantity of q consumed without the project	—	—
Consumers' willingness to pay for Δq	—	—
Paid by the consumers for Δq	—	—
Value of the resources released	$-w(L_0-L_s)$	—
Total	$-w(L_1-L_s)$	—
Changes in real incomes	Project's cost	Change in producers' surplus

Source: Table 3.1.

That efficiency cost may be described as the willingness to receive for the extra work,[5] plus the willingness to pay for the reduction in consumption required to release part of the labor hired by the project, minus the efficiency value of the other resources released as a result of reducing the production of consumption goods, under the assumption that the total market value of these resources equals their efficiency value.

In practice, wage and price changes attributable to the project are negligible; that is, $w_1 = w_0$ and $p_1 = p_0$.[6] In this case, income changes are

---

5. Lal (1973) questioned the inclusion of the willingness to receive for the additional work in the shadow price for unskilled labor in developing countries. Hamilton (1976, 1977) restated the traditional argument, which is the one followed here.

6. Care should be exercised with this assumption when distributional considerations are taken into account. See Londero (1987) and Wildasin (1988).

Consumers of q	Producers of q	Total
—	—	—
—	—	$-w(L_1-L_0)$
—	—	—
—	—	—
$-p(q_0-q_1)$	—	$-p(q_0-q_1)$
$p(q_0-q_1)$	$-p(q_0-q_1)$	—
—	$p(q_0-q_1)$	$p(q_0-q_1)-w(L_0-L_s)$
—	—	$-w(L_1-L_s)$
Change in consumers' surplus	Change in producers' income	Value at efficiency prices

considerably simpler, as shown in Table 3.2, and expression (3.1) simply becomes the market value of the additional demand for labor

$$w[(L_1-L_0)+(L_0-L_s)] = w(L_1-L_s) \tag{3.2}$$

In some cases it cannot be assumed that the efficiency value of the released resources equals the corresponding market value, because labor is withdrawn from the production of a good whose market price differs considerably from its efficiency price. In these cases, the market value of the released resources may be represented by

$$p(q_0-q_1) - w(L_0-L_s) = p(\Sigma_i a_{iq} + \Sigma_{h=1} f_{hq})(q_0-q_1)$$

where a_{iq} and f_{hq} are, respectively, the marginal value coefficients for the produced inputs i and for the nonproduced inputs and transfers h used in the production of q.[7] Then, the efficiency value of the additional demand for labor as presented in (3.1) becomes the willingness to receive for the extra work, plus the difference between the efficiency value of the forgone output and the efficiency value of the released inputs,[8] that is

$$w (L_1 - L_0) + [spr_q p - p (\Sigma_i spr_i a_{iq} - \Sigma_{h \neq l} spr_h f_{hq})] (q_0 - q_1) \qquad (3.3)$$

If the additional demand for labor could be fully met by unemployed workers, and the supply of labor was very elastic at the prevailing wage, the efficiency cost would simply be the worker's willingness to receive for the additional salaried work valued at the prevailing wage. On the other hand, if the supply of labor was completely inelastic, and thus the additional demand for labor could be met entirely by reducing employment in other occupations, the efficiency cost of labor would be the efficiency value of the sacrificed consumption required to release that labor, minus the efficiency value of the other resources released in that process.

The shadow price ratio for labor (at efficiency prices) is the ratio of its efficiency cost, represented by equation (3.3), to its market cost, represented by (3.2). In order to obtain a more concise formula, it is convenient to replace the additional production with a more precise definition

$$q_0 - q_1 = (\Delta q / \Delta L) (L_0 - L_s)$$

that is, the reduction in production per unit of withdrawn labor, multiplied by the amount of labor withdrawn. The wage may also be represented in a similar fashion as

$$w = p (1 - \Sigma_i a_{iq} - \Sigma_{h \neq l} f_{hq}) (\Delta q / \Delta L) \qquad (3.4)$$

that is, the price, minus the per unit value of all inputs and transfers (including the gross operating surplus) other than labor, all multiplied by the change in production resulting from employing one additional unit of labor along with all other required inputs according to the relevant coefficients. Thus, the ratio of the efficiency value (3.3) to the market value (3.4), or shadow price ratio, becomes

$$sprw = \frac{(L_1 - L_0)}{(L_1 - L_s)} + \frac{[spr_q - \Sigma_i spr_i a_{iq} - \Sigma_{h \neq l} spr_h f_{hq})] p (\Delta q / \Delta L) (L_0 - L_s)}{(1 - \Sigma_i a_{iq} - \Sigma_{h \neq l} f_{hq}) p (\Delta q / \Delta L) (L_1 - L_s)}$$

---

7. Full understanding of this expression may require material that is presented in Chapter 6.

8. Note that the next formula includes the case of q being an intermediate good, but does not discuss the calculation of spr_q.

which simplifies to

$$sprw = \frac{(L_1 - L_0)}{(L_1 - L_s)} + \frac{[spr_q - \Sigma_i \, spr_i \, a_{iq} - \Sigma_{h \neq l} \, spr_h f_{hq})]}{(1 - \Sigma_i \, a_{iq} - \Sigma_{h \neq l} f_{hq})} \frac{(L_0 - L_s)}{(L_1 - L_s)} \quad (3.5)$$

That is, a weighted average of one (first term) and the ratio of the efficiency to the market value of the other resources released (second term), where the weights are, respectively, the shares in total additional demand of the additional labor supplied and the labor withdrawn from other occupations. Since coefficients f_{hq} would include transfers such as trade taxes or normative excess profits (see section 6.1), equation (3.5) is quite general.

If there were external effects associated with the production of q, they should be incorporated in (3.5). For example, in the case of a negative externality with an efficiency value of $-e_q$ per unit of output, that value would simply be subtracted in the numerator from the efficiency value of the output

$$sprw = \frac{(L_1 - L_0)}{(L_1 - L_s)} + \frac{(spr_q - \Sigma_i \, spr_i \, a_{iq} - \Sigma_{h \neq l} \, spr_h f_{hq} - e_q)}{(1 - \Sigma_i \, a_{iq} - \Sigma_{h \neq l} f_{hq})} \frac{(L_0 - L_s)}{(L_1 - L_s)} \quad (3.6)$$

The general model presented thus far may be applied to different situations, some of which will be explored in the remainder of this chapter. To simplify the presentation, it will be assumed that wage changes attributable to the change in the demand for labor are negligible (Table 3.2), and thus are ignored. The reader is reminded, however, that small changes in the wage are multiplied by large employment quantities, and thus may carry important distributional implications (Londero, 1987; Wildasin, 1988).

A Digression: Popular Formulae

Under simplifying assumptions, mainly full substitution in production, perfect competition and profit maximization, the effects in the market for q – that is, the consumers' valuation of the reductions in consumption, minus the value of the changes in the use of the other associated inputs – may be also presented by resorting to the expected equality between the wage and the value of the marginal product of labor in the production of q. In such a case, expression (3.5) becomes

$$sprw = \frac{(L_1 - L_0)}{(L_1 - L_s)} + spr_q \frac{(L_0 - L_s)}{(L_1 - L_s)}$$

where q is the good produced by that labor in the situation without the project. This simplified approach focuses the analysis on the possible difference between p and the corresponding shadow price. Thus, if the market price of q equals its efficiency price, the efficiency value of the additional labor would simply be $w(L_1 - L_s)$ and the *sprw* would be equal to one.

The preceding results are often presented in terms of supply and demand elasticities. Say that the additional demand for labor dL is met by reducing uses elsewhere dL^d, and increasing the labor supplied dL^s, both induced by the (negligible) wage increase. Therefore, the market value of the labor demanded by the project $w\,dL$ would be

$$w\,dL = w^d\,dL^d + w^s\,dL^s$$

This expression distinguishes between demand and supply prices because they entail different opportunity costs, despite the fact that they are equal when expressed at market prices. The shadow value of the additional demand for labor may thus be presented as

$$sprw\,w\,dL = sprw^d\,w^d\,dL^d + sprw^s\,w^s\,dL^s$$

Therefore, the shadow price of labor for the dL change would be

$$sprw = \frac{sprw^d\,dL^d + sprw^s\,dL^s}{dL} \qquad (3.7)$$

since $w = w^d = w^s$. Changes in the quantities of labor demanded and supplied may in turn be expressed with reference to demand and supply elasticities with respect to the wage; that is,

$$dL^d = \eta\,(dw/w)\,L^d$$

$$dL^s = \varepsilon\,(dw/w)\,L^s \qquad (3.8)$$

Substituting (3.8) in (3.7), remembering that in equilibrium the quantity demanded equals the quantity supplied ($L^d = L^s$), and simplifying, results in the following expression for the shadow price of labor:

$$sprw = \frac{sprw^d\,\eta + sprw^s\,\varepsilon}{\eta + \varepsilon} \qquad (3.9)$$

This expression is equivalent to (3.5), since the shadow price ratio for the increase in the quantity supplied is equal to the workers' consumption loss; that is, $sprw^s = 1$. If the elasticity of the supply of labor is infinite, the additional demand is fully met by additional workers, there are no costs incurred in the rest of the economy, and the resulting $sprw$ is equal to one. If the elasticity of the supply of labor is equal to zero, all the additional demand is met by withdrawing labor from the production of other goods, and the shadow price of labor equals the shadow value of the associated reductions in the production of these goods per unit of withdrawn labor ($sprw = sprw^d$).

These approaches are appealing from a presentational viewpoint, since they greatly simplify the notation. On the other hand, they are less useful for (1) understanding the step by step effects of the changes in the demand and supply of labor, (2) identifying the implicit assumptions at each step, and (3) tracing the entailed distributional effects. Therefore, they are less useful for confronting the complications at the applied level. For these reasons, this chapter will continue using the more detailed approach of equation (3.5).

3.2 DUAL LABOR MARKETS

Labor is Withdrawn from the Production of Traded Goods

So far the argument has been developed under the assumption that labor is withdrawn from the production of a nontraded consumption good, allowing for the CV of the price increase to be measured directly. Labor, however, may be withdrawn from the production of marginally traded goods (Figure 3.2). In that case, willingness to pay for the reduction in consumption would be replaced by the efficiency value of the reduction in exports, or the increase in imports that is attributable to the wage increase resulting from the additional demand for labor. If, for example, labor is withdrawn from the production of a marginally exported good x – in the absence of external effects – the

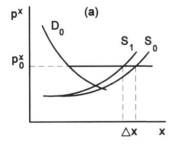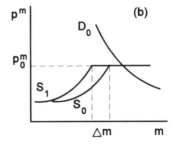

Figure 3.2 Labor is withdrawn from the production of traded goods

efficiency value of that labor would be the efficiency value of the reduction in the production of the exported good, net of the efficiency value of the other resources released in reducing its production:

$$[sprfe\ p^{fob} - spr_{dis}\ (\Delta dis/\Delta x) - p^x\ (\Sigma_i\ spr_i\ a_{ix} + \Sigma_{h \bullet l}\ spr_h f_{hx})]\ (\Delta x/\Delta L)$$

where *dis* is other distribution costs incurred between the production site and the point of export (transport, storage, port handling, etc.), p^x is the producer price of *x*, a_{ix} and f_{hx} are the value coefficients for the inputs used in the production of *x* calculated with respect to that producer price, and spr_i and spr_h are their respective shadow price ratios. Note that if *x* were subject to an export tax the cost of labor would be significantly higher, since the expression $\Sigma_{h \bullet l}\ spr_h f_{hx}$ would contain the export tax multiplied by an *spr* equal to zero.

The *sprw* in the case of an exported good would thus be

$$sprw = \frac{(L_1 - L_0)}{(L_1 - L_s)} +$$

$$\frac{sprfe - spr_{dis}\ dis_x - (p^x/p^{fob})(\Sigma_i\ spr_i\ a_{ix} + \Sigma_{h \bullet l}\ spr_h f_{hx})}{1 - dis_x - (p^x/p^{fob})(\Sigma_i\ a_{ix} - \Sigma_{h \bullet l} f_{hx})}\ \frac{(L_0 - L_s)}{(L_1 - L_s)} \qquad (3.10)$$

where dis_x is the value coefficient with respect to p^{fob}.

Similarly, if labor were withdrawn from the production of a marginally imported good, in the absence of external effects, the associated efficiency cost would be

$$[sprfe\ p^{cif} - spr_{dis}\ (\Delta dis/\Delta m) - p^m\ (\Sigma_i\ spr_i\ a_{im} + \Sigma_{h \bullet l}\ spr_h f_{hm})]\ (\Delta m/\Delta L)$$

where *dis* is the *net* distribution costs – that is, those saved from domestic production minus those incurred due to the additional imports. Assuming that the net additional distribution costs are nil, the corresponding *sprw* would be

$$sprw = \frac{(L_1 - L_0)}{(L_1 - L_s)} +$$

$$\frac{sprfe - (p^m/p^{cif})(\Sigma_i\ spr_i\ a_{im} + \Sigma_{h \bullet l}\ spr_h f_{hm})}{(1 - \Sigma_i\ a_{iq} - \Sigma_{h \bullet l} f_{hq})}\ \frac{(L_0 - L_s)}{(L_1 - L_s)} \qquad (3.11)$$

Equation (3.10) may be simplified by assuming that the wage equals the factory gate price value of the marginal product in the marginally exported activity; that is,

$$w = [p^{fob} (1 - t^x) - \partial dis/\partial x] (\partial x/\partial L) \, dL \qquad (3.12)$$

Thus, the efficiency cost of providing the amount of labor required by the project would be the willingness to receive for the additional supply, plus the efficiency value of this marginal product,

$$w (L_1 - L_0) + [sprfe \, p^{fob} - spr_{dis} (\partial dis/\partial x)] (\partial x/\partial L) (L_0 - L_s)$$

and the associated shadow price ratio would be

$$sprw = \frac{(L_1 - L_0)}{(L_1 - L_s)} + \frac{(sprfe - spr_{dis} \, dis_x)}{(1 - t^x - dis_x)} \frac{(L_0 - L_s)}{(L_1 - L_s)} \qquad (3.13)$$

where dis_x is the value coefficient calculated with respect to p^{fob}. The resulting *sprw* would be a weighted average of one and the shadow price ratio of the exported good. Note in expressions (3.10) and (3.13) that the efficiency cost of labor withdrawn from the production of an exported good would be higher, the higher the export tax.

The same approach may be applied to the case of an imported good. Assuming that the net additional distribution costs are nil, the efficiency cost of providing the amount of labor required by the project would be

$$w (L_1 - L_0) + sprfe \, p^{cif} (\partial m/\partial L) (L_0 - L_s)$$

and the associated shadow price ratio would be

$$sprw = \frac{(L_1 - L_0)}{(L_1 - L_s)} + \frac{sprfe}{(1 + t^m)} \frac{(L_0 - L_s)}{(L_1 - L_s)} \qquad (3.14)$$

a weighted average of one and the shadow price ratio of the imported good.

Dual Urban Labor Markets

Consider the case of a dual labor market, represented in Figure 3.3, in which there is a subset of productive activities where workers are protected by labor legislation and represented by unions. This subset is sometimes referred to as the formal sector, where the labor market results in higher than free-market wages and higher firing costs. This segment of the market coexists with

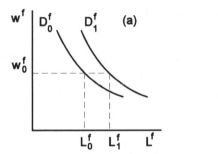 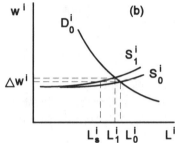

Figure 3.3 Dual labor market

another, often referred to as the informal sector, in which unions are less powerful or nonexistent, and labor legislation does not apply or is not enforced. These conditions normally result in lower wages and firing costs, and frequently disguised unemployment in the sense that employment may be augmented by increasing the average hours of work per person without necessarily raising wages significantly. An increase in the demand for labor generated by the project ($D_1^f - D_0^f$) would not affect the wage in the formal sector and would be met by workers previously employed in the informal sector ($D_1^f - D_0^f = S_0^s - S_1^s$). Since the informal sector is primarily a producer of nontraded goods and services, the *sprw* would be calculated according to an expression similar to (3.11) and resulting in

$$ sprw = \frac{w^i}{w_0^f} \left[\frac{(L_0 - L_1)}{(L_0 - L_s)} + spr_q \frac{(L_1 - L_s)}{(L_0 - L_s)} \right] \qquad (3.15) $$

In practice, q would be a basket of goods with efficiency prices above and below market prices. If the average of the corresponding *spr*s is equal to one, the shadow price ratio of labor is equal to the ratio of the informal to the formal sector wage. Note that in equation (3.15) it is implicitly assumed that both occupations are equally valued by the workers, and therefore the wage difference is not attributable to the nature of the occupation but to that of the market. If, for example, the formal sector occupation carried a higher personal risk to the worker than the informal one, the ratio of the informal to the formal wage would underestimate the *sprw*. A similar situation would arise if the formal sector occupation implied higher costs to the worker, such as transportation or clothing.

Rural–Urban Migration

The preceding case highlights the importance of market adjustment to the additional demand in the estimation of the *sprw*. Since it is the supply in the informal market that is affected in the end, the value associated with its reduction determines the efficiency cost. From such a perspective, it is also possible to go back one additional step in the adjustment process and consider the possibility that the reduction in the supply of labor to the informal sector may induce migration from the rural areas. A classical approach to the subject is that of Sen (1966, 1972). It consists of identifying those affected by the formal sector hiring and separating the associated realized welfare effects into changes in incomes and changes in effort expended (Table 3.3).[9]

The project hires a worker from the urban informal sector to perform L hours of salaried work at the hourly formal sector wage w^f. The newly hired worker gains the difference between the wages in both sectors, loses his valuation of the formal sector work $d^f L$, and gains that of his informal sector occupation $d^i L$. The informal employer has no problem replacing the worker at the prevailing wage, thus experiencing no income changes.

The creation of a permanent additional job in the urban formal sector is met by withdrawing one worker from the urban informal sector, and only one rural worker migrates to the urban areas as a result. In the rural area, traditional and capitalistic institutions coexist; therefore, labor allocation in these areas may only partially take place according to market rules. The rural worker is employed in family agriculture, where all members contribute their work and share in the resulting income y^m. In order to simplify the presentation, it is assumed that migration does not affect employment of the pre-existing informal sector workers. Thus the rural migrant occupies the job made available by the formal sector hiring, gains the difference between the informal wage and his or her share in the rural family income, and is affected by the difference between his or her subjective valuation of the new job $d^{im} L$ and his valuation of the hours worked in the family plot $(d^{rm} L^{rm})$.[10]

The rural family no longer has to share their income with the migrating

---

9. The analysis of migration flows may be conducted by contrasting expected and realized welfare. Cost–benefit analysis, instead, is a comparative-static exercise. Therefore, it should be conducted in terms of realized, rather than expected, welfare. See Sen (1972).

10. The preceding outline omits taking other migration costs and benefits into account, such as adjustment to a different culture or better opportunities for the family (strictly monetary migration costs may be small when spread over the life of the migrant). As long as rural–urban net migration is positive, however, it may be suspected that the realized benefits of migration exceed the costs. If that were the case, a net benefit would have been omitted and the shadow price of labor would have been overestimated.

Table 3.3 Single migration when market and efficiency prices of the forgone output are equal

	Income changes	Effort changes	Total
Project	$-w^f L$	—	$-w^f L$
Informal sector worker	$(w^f - w^i)L$	$(d^i - d^f)L$	$[(w^f - w^i) + (d^i - d^f)]L$
Migrant worker	$w^i L - y^{rm}$	$-d^{im}L + d^{rm}L^{rm}$	$(w^i - d^{im})L - y^{rm} + d^{rm}L^{rm}$
Rural family	$y^{rm} - w^r L^r$	$-d^{rf}L^{rf}$	$y^{rm} - w^r L^r - d^{rf}L^{rf}$
Rural workers	$w^r(L^r - L^o)$	$-d^r(L^r - L^o)$	$(w^r - d^r)(L^r - L^o)$
Other farms	$(w^r - v^r)L^o$	—	$(w^r - v^r)L^o$
Total	$-v^r L^o$	$-d^f L + (d^i - d^{im})L + d^{rm}L^{rm} - d^{rf}L^{rf} - d^r(L^r - L^o)$	$-d^f L + (d^i - d^{im})L + (d^r - v^r)L^o + d^{rm}L^{rm} - d^{rf}L^{rf} - d^r L^r$

member, but stands to lose the migrant's marginal product. To compensate for that potential loss, the family increase their work (L^{rf}) and hire wage labor (L^r) at the prevailing rural wage w^r. For the sake of simplicity, it is assumed that the extra work by the family plus the hired labor exactly compensate for the migrant's marginal product. Thus, the rural family gains the income share of the migrant at the cost of extra effort and wage expenses.

The remainder of the adjustment takes place in the rural labor market. Rural (probably landless) workers supply the additional demand by the family farm L^r by increasing the supply of hours ($L^r - L^o$) and diverting hours from other farms L^o. As a result, they gain the wage income for the additional hours, and lose their valuation of those hours. Finally, the farms no longer pay wages for the L^o hours, and lose the value of the corresponding marginal product $v^r L^o$. For the sake of simplicity, it is assumed that there is no seasonality in employment (or alternatively that unit values represent yearly averages), and that the market value of the marginal product equals its efficiency value. In practice, these two assumptions are far from being realistic, but relaxing them now would complicate the notation without contributing to the substance of the argument. They will be relaxed later on once the main argument has been made.

The sum of all income changes provides the efficiency value of L hours of additional work in the formal sector. Expressed as an economic cost (i.e. changing the sign) this would be

$$EC(L) = d^f L - (d^i - d^{im}) L + (v^r - d^r) L^o +$$

$$(d^{if} L^f + d^r L^r - d^{rm} L^{rm}) \tag{3.16}$$

That is, the minimum sum that the informal sector worker is willing to accept in order to do the formal sector job, minus any difference between the subjective valuations of the informal sector job, plus any difference between the marginal product in rural agriculture and the workers' valuation of performing that job, plus any difference between the migrant's valuation of his or her work in the family plot and the valuation of the same number of total hours by the family and the hired worker. In practice, it is often, but not always explicitly, assumed that:

1. subjective valuations of the informal sector job by the informal sector worker and by the migrant are equal $(d^i - d^{im} = 0)$;[11]
2. labor markets for rural commercial agriculture are competitive and free of interventions, thus making the wage equal to the (market and efficiency) value of the marginal product and to the individual valuation of such work (i.e. $v^r - d^r = 0$); and
3. there is no difference between the subjective valuation of the work by the migrant and that required to compensate for his or her departure (i.e. $d^{if} L^f + d^r L^r - d^{rm} L^{rm} = 0$).

As a result of these assumptions, the efficiency cost of the additional employment created in the formal sector would be the minimum sum needed to attract a worker to that job $d^f L$, normally estimated by the informal sector wage for an equivalent occupation. Therefore, the shadow price ratio of labor would simply be the ratio of the informal to the formal sector wage. In particular, it should be noted that it is assumption 2) that makes the resulting efficiency price independent from the existence of forgone agricultural output in commercial agriculture.

Expression (3.16) allows for the effects of different assumptions to be explored. For example, if all agriculture were fully capitalistic, the efficiency cost of labor would simply be $(d^f + v^r - d^r) L$. In this case there would only be an argument for an efficiency cost higher than d^f if the efficiency price of the agricultural output exceeded its market value, or if the market value of the marginal product exceeded the wage.

If the supply of family labor were infinitely elastic and the family was able to fully compensate for the migrating member, a correction to an efficiency cost of $d^f L$ would be required only if the value of the family's extra effort was different from that of the migrant. It can also be shown that if there was

---

11. Since migrants do accept employment at the informal sector wage, $d^i - d^{im} \geq 0$.

forgone output in family agriculture due to a partial replacement of the migrant's hours of work, the efficiency cost of labor would increase by the *difference* between the value of that forgone output and the net result of extra effort valuations by the migrants and the providers of labor to family agriculture (i.e. $d^f L^f + d^r L^r - d^{rm} L^{rm}$, where $L^f + L^r < L^{rm}$).

It is more common for the market value of the forgone output to differ from its efficiency value. In this case, the efficiency cost of labor has to reflect the difference, and the following example is aimed at capturing such an effect (Table 3.4). Assume now that there is seasonality in rural employment and that during peak periods rural workers are employed in export agriculture at wage w^{rx} and an associated compensating variation of d^{rx} per unit of work done. Thus, when one family member migrates to the urban area, the rural family no longer has to share their income with the migrating member and loses the income that the member contributed in money ($w^{rx} L^{rx}$) and in kind ($v^{rm} L^{rm}$) through his or her work in family agriculture. The rural family tries to compensate by increasing their family work, and thus gains the value of the marginal product of their own additional work $v^f L^f$ at a cost $d^f L^f$. To simplify the presentation, it is assumed that the rural family does not hire extra workers. Assuming that during these peak periods there is full employment in the rural sector and labor supply is totally inelastic, the migration would reduce farms' export revenue by the value of the marginal product $v^x L^{rx}$ and save those farms the corresponding wage amount $w^x L^{rx}$. It is also assumed that exports are subject to an *ad valorem* tax t^x and the shadow price ratio of foreign exchange differs from one; therefore the market value of the marginal product differs from its efficiency value. Since exports would be affected, the government would lose the associated export tax revenue $v^x L^{rx} (p^{fob}/p^p) t^x$, plus the taxes it would have earned from the disposition of that foreign exchange $v^x L^{rx} (p^{fob}/p^p)(sprfe - 1)$.

$$v^x L^{rx} (p^{fob}/p^p) t^x + v^x L^{rx} (p^{fob}/p^p)(sprfe - 1)$$

where p^p is the farm-gate price at which the marginal product v^x is valued and the remaining symbols are those from (3.12).

The efficiency cost of hiring a worker in the formal sector may now be calculated by adding the two column totals and applying the same simplifying assumptions. First, due to underemployment during the off-peak season the rural family fully compensates for the marginal product of the migrant ($v^f L^f - v^{rm} L^{rm} = 0$), and the associated efforts are equally valued ($d^{rm} L^{rm} - d^f L^f = 0$). Second, during peak periods the rural wage clears a competitive market, that is $d^{rx} = v^{rx} = w^x$. Finally, the private valuation by the informal worker of employment in the informal sector is equal to that of the migrant $d^i = d^{im}$. As a result of these assumptions, the cost of hiring a worker in the formal sector would be

Table 3.4 Single migration and differences between market and efficiency price of the forgone output

	Income changes	Effort changes	Total
Project	$-w^i L$	—	$-w^i L$
Informal sector worker	$(w^f - w^i) L$	$(d^i - d^f)L$	$[(w^f - w^i) + (d^i - d^f)]L$
Migrant worker	$w^i L - y^{rm}$	$-d^{im}L + d^{rm}L^{rm} + d^{rx}L^{rx}$	$(w^i - d^{im})L - y^{rm} + d^{rm}L^{rm} + d^{rx}L^{rx}$
Rural family	$-w^x L^{rx} + y^{rm} - v^{rm}L^{rm} + v^{rf}L^{rf}$	$-d^{rf}L^{rf}$	$-w^x L^{rx} + y^{rm} - v^{rm}L^{rm} + v^{rf}L^{rf} - d^{rf}L^{rf}$
Export agriculture	$w^x L^{rx} - v^{rx}L^{rx}$	—	$w^x L^{rx} - v^{rx} L^{rx}$
Government	$-[v^{rx}L^{rx}(p^{fob}/p^p)](t^x + sprfe - 1)$	—	$-[v^{rx}L^{rx}(p^{fob}/p^p)](t^x + sprfe - 1)$
Total	$-v^{rx}L^{rx} - v^{rm}L^{rm} + v^{rf}L^{rf} - [v^{rx}L^{rx}(p^{fob}/p^p)](t^x + sprfe - 1)$	$-d^i L + (d^i - d^{im})L + d^{rm}L^{rm} - d^{rf}L^{rf} - d^{rx}L^{rx}$	$(d^{rx}L^{rx} - v^{rx}L^{rx}) - d^i L + (d^i - d^{im})L + (v^{rf}L^{rf} - v^{rm}L^{rm}) + (d^{rm}L^{rm} - d^{rf}L^{rf}) - [v^{rx}L^{rx}(p^{fob}/p^p)](t^x + sprfe - 1)$

$$EC(L) = d^i L + [w^x L^{rx}(p^{fob}/p^p)](t^x + sprfe - 1) \qquad (3.17)$$

the valuation of the formal sector job plus the effects of the difference between the market and the efficiency price of the exported good. Replacing the producer price p^p by

$$p^p = p^{fob}(1 - t_x - dis_x),$$

assuming that the informal sector wage represents the minimum sum the worker is willing to receive in order to work in the formal sector (that is, $d^f = w^i$), and dividing by $w^f L$, the shadow price ratio of labor becomes

$$sprw = \frac{w^i L}{w^f L} + \frac{w^x L^{rx}}{w^f L} \frac{(t_x + sprfe - 1)}{1 - t_x - dis_x} \qquad (3.18)$$

that is, the ratio of the informal to the formal wage corrected by the effects of withdrawing labor from export agriculture, where the farm-gate price of the output differs from its efficiency price due to export taxes and the effects of the shadow price ratio of foreign exchange.

Multiple Migration

It has been suggested that more than one worker may migrate per additional worker hired in the formal sector, and that such additional migration may increase the welfare cost attributable to employing an additional worker in the urban formal sector.[12] In order to explore this proposition, the effects of multiple migration are now incorporated into the preceding simplified models, starting from the example presented in Table 3.3 and then moving on to the case where the efficiency and market price of the forgone output differ. If there is multiple migration, the first two rows of Table 3.3 would be unaffected because the project would continue to employ a single worker withdrawn directly from the informal sector. The analysis will thus focus on the adjustment in the rural markets.

The additional employment in the formal sector induces the migration of more than one rural worker (Table 3.5). Thus, the migrants' total income would increase by the wage of the only additional urban job available in the informal sector, but would be reduced by their participation in the family income $\Sigma_j y_j^m$, where $j = 1, \ldots N$ are the migrant workers. The migrants also incur the cost associated with their valuation of working in the informal sector $d^{im} L$, but gain their valuation of working in the family plots $\Sigma_j d_j^{rm} L_j^{rm}$.[13] The rural families no longer share their incomes with the migrants, and no longer receive their contributions to family production. On the production side, the rural family is assumed to fully compensate the production of the migrants, thus no production effects are shown in the corresponding row of Table 3.5.[14] Such compensation is done by increasing their own work L_j^f per migrant j and hiring salaried labor L_j' during peak periods. This compensation implies for the rural family an additional effort valued as $\Sigma_j d_j^{rf} L_j^f$ and a total monetary cost

---

12. See Todaro (1969, 1976), Harris and Todaro (1970), Harberger (1971), and comments by Sen (1972, 1975) and Mazumdar (1976).

13. If more than one informal sector job would be available for the migrants, they would receive additional income but also incur in extra effort. Similarly, if the hours of informal sector work were less than those previously performed by the worker who transferred to the formal sector, they would receive less income and incur in less effort. Similar effects would affect the informal sector workers, who would lose the income that the migrants gain, and gain the valuation of the work the migrants perform.

14. Full compensation on the production side is a simplifying assumption; see below.

Table 3.5 Multiple migration when market and efficiency prices of the forgone output are equal

	Income changes	Effort changes	Total
Project	$-w^i L$	—	$-w^i L$
Informal sector worker	$(w^f - w^i)L$	$(d^i - d^f)L$	$[(w^f - w^i) + (d^i - d^f)]L$
Migrant workers	$w^i L - \Sigma_j y_j^{rm}$	$-d^{im}L + \Sigma_j d_j^{rm} L_j^{rm}$	$(w^i - d^{im})L - \Sigma_j y_j^{rm} + \Sigma_j d_j^{rm} L_j^{rm}$
Rural families	$\Sigma_j y_j^{rm} - w^r \Sigma_j L_j^r$	$-\Sigma_j d_j^{rf} L_j^{rf}$	$\Sigma_j y_j^{rm} - w^r \Sigma_j L_j^r - \Sigma_j d_j^{rf} L_j^{rf}$
Rural workers	$w^r(\Sigma_j L_j^r - \Sigma_j L_j^o)$	$-d^r(\Sigma_j L_j^r - \Sigma_j L_j^o)$	$(w^r - d^r)(\Sigma_j L_j^r - \Sigma_j L_j^o)$
Other farms	$(w^r - v^r)\Sigma_j L_j^o$	—	$(w^r - v^r)\Sigma_j L_j^o$
Total	$-v^r \Sigma_j L_j^o$	$-d^f L + (d^i - d^{im})L + \Sigma_j d_j^{rm} L_j^{rm} - \Sigma_j d_j^{rf} L_j^{rf} - d^r(\Sigma_j L_j^r - \Sigma_j L_j^o)$	$-d^f L + (d^i - d^{im})L - (v^r - d^r)\Sigma_j L_j^o + \Sigma_j d_j^{rm} L_j^{rm} - \Sigma_j d_j^{rf} L_j^{rf} - d^r \Sigma_j L_j^r$

of $w^r \Sigma_j L_j^r$. Rural workers withdraw from alternative occupations (assumed to pay the same wage and represent the same value of effort) L_j^o hours to compensate for migrant j and partly work additional $L_j^r - L_j^o$ hours, receiving the additional wages paid by the family and incurring the additional cost of working more hours. Finally, other farms are affected by the departure of workers to the family plots.

The efficiency cost of labor would then be

$$EC(L) = d^f L - (d^i - d^{im}) L + (v^r - d^r) \Sigma_j L_j^o +$$

$$(\Sigma_j d_j^{rf} L_j^{rf} + d^r \Sigma_j L_j^r - \Sigma_j d_j^{rm} L_j^{rm}) \tag{3.19}$$

That is, the worker's valuation of performing the formal sector job, minus any difference between the subjective valuations of the informal sector job, plus any differences between: (1) the rural wage and the efficiency value of labor's marginal product in rural commercial agriculture; and (2) the rural family and the rural worker's valuation of the extra work net of the migrants' valuation of the (assumed) same number of hours.

Following the same reasoning, it may be shown that if the rural family does not compensate for the rural migrants, the efficiency cost of the formal sector job would be

$$EC(L) = d^f L - (d^i - d^{im}) L + \Sigma_j (v_j^m - d_j^m) L_j^{rm} \qquad (3.20)$$

where v_j^m is the hourly value of the marginal product of the rural migrant when working in family agriculture.

Note from equations (3.19) and (3.20) that only under a value judgement assigning a zero value to changes in the hours of work would the efficiency cost of labor be equal to the sum of the values of the marginal products of all migrants, and/or those of the workers that replace them. Such a value judgement would contradict fundamental principles of traditional applied welfare economics. In particular, it would contradict the principle that each individual determines whether he or she has been affected and the amount that compensates for the corresponding effects (see Chapter 1).[15]

Some traditional assumptions allow for considerable simplification of equations (3.19) and (3.20). If rural labor markets are cleared by the competitive wage and the market price of the forgone output equals its efficiency price, it would be expected that $v^r - d^r = 0$. Also, the private valuation of the informal sector job is assumed to be the same for the informal worker as for the migrant $d^i - d^{im} = 0$. Finally, the valuation by migrant workers of their effort at the family farms is assumed to be equal to that necessary to compensate for their departure $\Sigma_j (d_j^f L_j^f + d^r L_j^r - d_j^{rm} L_j^{rm}) = 0$. As a result, the efficiency cost of labor would be the minimum sum that the worker is willing to receive for accepting the additional job created.

The final example would be that of multiple migration when labor is withdrawn from a sector where the market price for the output differs from the corresponding efficiency price. To that effect, the example of Table 3.4 will be used as reformulated in Table 3.6. The reasoning behind each cell will not be repeated, since it is similar to that in Table 3.4. The sole difference is that account has been taken of the effects of multiple workers migrating from rural to urban areas. Reordering the sum of the Total column, the efficiency cost of labor would be

$$EC(L) = d^f L + \Sigma_j [v^{rx} L_j^{rx}(p^{fob}/p^p)](t^x + sprfe - 1) - (d^i - d^{im}) L +$$

$$\Sigma_j L_j^{rx} (d_j^{rx} - v^{rx}) + \Sigma_j (v^{rm} L_j^{rm} - v^f L_j^f) - \Sigma_j (d_j^{rm} L_j^{rm} - d_j^f L_j^f) \qquad (3.21)$$

That is, the willingness to receive for the additional job created, plus the difference between the market and the efficiency values of the forgone marginal product, minus any difference between the private valuations of the

---

15. Arguments for ignoring workers' private valuation of extra effort expended were presented by Lal (1973) and examined by Hamilton (1976, 1977).

Table 3.6 *Multiple migration when market and efficiency prices of the forgone output differ*

	Income changes	Effort changes	Total
Project	$-w^fL$	—	$-w^fL$
Informal sector worker	$(w^f-w^i)L$	$(d^i-d^f)L$	$[(w^f-w^i)+(d^i-d^f)]L$
Migrant workers	w^iL- $\Sigma_j(y_j^{rm}-w^xL_j^{rx})$	$-d^{im}L+\Sigma_j d_j^{rm}L_j^{rm}+$ $\Sigma_j d_j^{rx}L_j^{rx}$	$(w^i-d^{im})L-$ $\Sigma_j(y_j^{rm}-w^xL_j^{rx})+$ $\Sigma_j d_j^{rm}L_j^{rm}+\Sigma_j d_j^{rx}L_j^{rx}$
Rural families	$\Sigma_j(y_j^{rm}-v^mL_j^{rm}+$ $v^fL_j^f)$	$-\Sigma_j d_j^f L_j^f$	$\Sigma_j(y_j^{rm}-v^mL_j^{rm}+$ $v^fL_j^f)-\Sigma_j d_j^f L_j^f$
Export agriculture	$\Sigma_j(w^xL_j^{rx}-v^xL_j^{rx})$	—	$\Sigma_j(w^xL_j^{rx}-v^xL_j^{rx})$
Government	$-\Sigma_j[v^xL_j^{rx}(p^{fob}/p^p)]$ $(t^x+sprfe-1)$	—	$-\Sigma_j[v^xL_j^{rx}(p^{fob}/p^p)]$ $(t^x+sprfe-1)$
Total	$-\Sigma_j(v^xL_j^{rx}+$ $v^mL_j^{rm}-v^fL_j^f)-$ $\Sigma_j[v^xL_j^{rx}(p^{fob}/p^p)]$ $(t^x+sprfe-1)$	$-d^fL+(d^i-d^{im})L+$ $\Sigma_j d_j^{rm}L_j^{rm}+$ $\Sigma_j d_j^{rx}L_j^{rx}-\Sigma_j d_j^f L_j^f$	$-d^fL+(d^i-d^{im})L-$ $\Sigma_j L_j^{rx}(d_j^{rx}-v^x)-$ $\Sigma_j(v^mL_j^{rm}-v^fL_j^f)+$ $\Sigma_j(d_j^{rm}L_j^{rm}-d_j^f L_j^f)-$ $\Sigma_j[v^xL_j^{rx}(p^{fob}/p^p)]$ $(t^x+sprfe-1)$

informal sector job, plus the sum over the number of migrants of any differences between: (1) the valuation of effort in the export job and the market value of the marginal product, (2) the hourly productivity of the migrant, and/or (3) the private valuation of the corresponding effort. Under the normal simplifying assumptions, the efficiency cost of labor would become

$$EC(L) = d^f L + \Sigma_j [v^x L_j^{rx}(p^{fob}/p^p)](t^x + sprfe - 1) \qquad (3.22)$$

and the corresponding shadow price ratio would be

$$sprw = \frac{w^i L}{w^f L} + \frac{\Sigma_j w^x L_j^{rx}}{w^f L}\,\frac{(t_x + sprfe - 1)}{1 - t_x - dis_x} \qquad (3.23)$$

In this example, multiple migration increases the efficiency cost of employing one additional unit of labor, and thus its shadow price ratio. Note that if the export tax did not exist, and the *sprfe* were equal to one, the shadow price ratio would be the ratio of the informal to the formal wage. The additional cost due to the multiple migration results from affecting the production of a good whose market price is below its efficiency price, and thus creating a cost per unit of migrating worker.

The examples in this section have shown that the effects of multiple migration on the shadow price of labor depend on the specifics of the markets involved. Attributing more costs than those associated with the single migration case requires careful evaluation of those markets and clear identification of the sources of the additional costs.

3.3   OTHER SPECIAL CASES

Avoided Emigration

In some countries, the lack of employment opportunities leads to significant emigration. In such cases, the creation of additional employment may affect emigration and thus the economic cost of labor. Consider the case in which the additional demand for labor is covered by a worker who, in the absence of the project, would have emigrated (Table 3.7). If employed by the project, the worker would receive the domestic wage w^{dom}, which will have to be no smaller than his willingness to receive d^{dom} when the alternative of emigration does not exist. To simplify the presentation, it is assumed that any possible change in the equilibrium wage is negligible. Since emigration may imply some gain for the worker, d^{dom} needs to be completed with that possible gain $w^{for} - d^{for}$ resulting from the difference between the foreign wage and the respective willingness to receive. The compensating variation of taking the domestic job will then be

$$d^m = d^{dom} + (w^{for} - d^{for})$$

which will be the minimum sum the worker is prepared to accept. His or her net gain will thus be $w^{dom} - d^m$.

Since in the absence of the project the worker would have emigrated, there is no domestic loss of production due to the hiring. There could be, however, a production loss and other effects in the planned country of destination of the potential migrant, but traditional value judgements in cost–benefit analysis only take into account the effects on the economic welfare of the 'residents' (see section 1.2). The worker is assumed to remit a proportion a of his or her wage to the family when he or she emigrates. Assuming that the entire difference between *sprfe* and the prevailing exchange rate is due to taxes,

Table 3.7   Income changes attributable to employing a worker who would have emigrated

	Project	Worker	Government	Total
With the project				
Wage	$-w^{dom}$	w^{dom}	—	—
Willingness to receive	—	$-d^{dom}$	—	$-d^{dom}$
Without the project				
Wage	—	$-(1-\alpha)w^{for}-\alpha w^{for}$	$-\alpha w^{for}(sprfe-1)$	$-(1-\alpha)w^{for}-\alpha w^{for}sprfe$
Willingness to receive	—	d^{for}	—	d^{for}
Total	$-w^{dom}$	$w^{dom}-d^{m}$	$-\alpha w^{for}(sprfe-1)$	$-d^{m}-\alpha w^{for}(sprfe-1)$

the government loses the corresponding foreign exchange premium.

The sum of the totals of each column of Table 3.7 indicates the minimum income to be created by employing this worker that is required to make the compensation possible, or the efficiency cost of hiring the worker. This sum will be equal to his or her willingness to receive for not migrating d^{m}, plus the premium on the foreign exchange which he or she would have remitted if he or she had emigrated:

$$EC(L) = d^{m} + \alpha\, w^{for}\, (sprfe - 1) \qquad (3.24)$$

Assuming that the salary offered by the project w is equal to the willingness to receive for not migrating d^{m}, the shadow price ratio for emigrating labor would be

$$sprw = 1 + \frac{\alpha\, w^{for}\, (sprfe - 1)}{w} \qquad (3.25)$$

one plus the share of the foreign exchange premium on remittances in the wage paid by the project.

Foreign Labor

If temporary labor were to be hired abroad, special considerations should be taken into account. The most important consideration is that a temporary foreign worker is a nonresident for the cost–benefit analysis. Therefore, the changes in his or her income as well as the effects on the foreign production of goods in the without project situation, are excluded from the computation of the economic cost. Conversely, what does matter are the costs that employing the temporary foreign worker imposes on residents. It follows that it is important to distinguish between savings and consumption, because the former have a special impact in the form of remittances to the country of origin,[16] and consumption expenditures imply resource costs to the economy.

The effects of hiring a temporary foreign worker are summarized in Table 3.8. The project pays the wage, which is broken down into three parts: the domestic expenditure $w(1 - t^d)(1 - s)$, where s is the savings rate and t^d is the applicable direct tax rate, savings (remittances) $w(1 - t^d)s$, and the direct taxes paid $w\,t^d$. Remittances are priced with the *sprfe* as in the preceding examples, since they imply an outflow of foreign exchange. The income tax is attributable to the project, since without the project this worker would not have been employed in the country that hires him or her, and is shown as a transfer from the project to the government. The government also receives the taxes that explain the difference between the *sprfe* and the prevailing exchange rate. The efficiency cost of employing the temporary worker is given by the value of the foreign exchange remitted plus the value at efficiency prices of the domestic expenditure on goods and services. If the market prices of the basket of consumption goods are considered acceptable approximations of their efficiency prices, the corresponding efficiency cost of labor would be

Table 3.8   *Income changes attributable to hiring temporary foreign labor*

	Project	Government	Total
Consumption	$-w(1-t^d)(1-s)$	—	$-w(1-t^d)(1-s)$
Savings (remittances)	$-w(1-t^d)s$	$-[w(1-t^d)s]$ $(sprfe-1)$	$-w(1-t^d)s\,sprfe$
Direct taxes	$-wt^d$	$w\,t^d$	—
Total	$-w$	wt^d- $w(1-t^d)s(sprfe-1)$	$-w(1-t^d)-$ $w(1-t^d)s(sprfe-1)$

---

16. In what follows, no distinction is made between immediate remittances, temporary savings in the domestic market, and future remittances, thus making savings equal to remittances.

$$EC(L) = w\,(1 - t^d) + w\,(1 - t^d)\,s\,(sprfe - 1) \tag{3.26}$$

the efficiency value of the domestic consumption plus the efficiency value of the remittance. Thus, the shadow price ratio would be

$$sprw = (1 - t^d) + (1 - t^d)\,s\,(sprfe - 1) \tag{3.27}$$

It should be noted that the preceding analysis assumes that the foreign worker is temporary; that is, that he or she remains a nonresident during the analysis period. However, this may not be the case, and 'foreign labor' may have to be valued as such only for the initial periods, and then as a weighted average of foreign and domestic labor with weights declining over time in order to reflect the number of workers that become residents as time goes by.[17] This weighting scheme would be a special case of the value judgement determining who is included in the 'total' welfare function (see section 1.2).

Contributions to a Compulsory Social Security System

A compulsory social security system introduces a difference between the cost to the employer of hiring a unit of labor and the monetary income received by the worker. The cost to the employer will be equal to the monetary income received by the worker plus the contributions of the employer and the worker to the social security system. Consider the case of a worker employed in the informal sector at wage w^i who is hired in the formal sector at a cost to the employer equal to w^f and subject to a total social security contribution at the rate of t_{ss}. In such a case, represented in Table 3.9, the worker receives a net income equal to the cost to the employer, minus the social security contribution, plus his or her compensating variation of participating in it CV_{ss}; the worker also loses his or her informal sector wage, but gains the compensating variation of working there d^i.

As a result (column sums in Table 3.9), the project pays the cost to the employer; the worker gains the net income, plus his or her valuation of the social security benefits, minus the informal sector wage, plus the corresponding willingness to receive; and the social security receives the compulsory payment and pays the benefits. If it is assumed that in the informal sector the wage equals the willingness to receive, the total of all income changes, or efficiency cost of labor, would be

$$EC(L) = d^i + (c_{ss} - CV_{ss}) \tag{3.28}$$

17. Note that the definition of 'resident' for cost–benefit analysis is a value judgement that need not coincide with the legal definition.

Table 3.9 Income changes attributable to employing under a compulsory social security system (worker receiving benefits)

	Project	Worker	Social security	Total
Wage	$-w$	$w(1 - t_{ss}) + CV_{ss} - w^j$	$w\,t_{ss} - c_{ss}$	$CV_{ss} - c_{ss} - w^j$
Willingness to receive	—	$-d^j + d^i$	—	$-d^j + d^i$
Total	$-w$	$w(1 - t_{ss}) + CV_{ss} - w^j - d^j + d^i$	$w\,t_{ss} - c_{ss}$	$-d^j + CV_{ss} - c_{ss} - w^j + d^i$

the willingness to receive, plus the cost of providing social security, minus the compensating variation of that benefit. In practice, there could be good estimates for d^j and c_{ss}, but it would be difficult to estimate CV_{ss}.

If the worker was already covered by social security, his or her transfer to another occupation at the same wage would not affect the social security or his or her associated costs or benefits.[18] In such a case the efficiency cost of hiring the worker would just be d^j.

If, on the other hand, the social security contribution was paid, but the workers did not receive any benefit (Table 3.10), under the assumption of an informal wage equal to the corresponding willingness to receive, the efficiency cost of hiring the worker would also be just the willingness to receive for the new occupation. There would also be a transfer from the employer and the

Table 3.10 Income changes attributable to employing under a compulsory social security system (worker not receiving benefits)

	Project	Worker	Social security	Total
Wage	$-w$	$w(1 - t_{ss}) - w^j$	$w\,t_{ss}$	$-w^j$
Willingness to receive	—	$-d^j + d^i$	—	$-d^j + d^i$
Total	$-w$	$w(1 - t_{ss}) - w^j - d^j + d^i$	$w\,t_{ss}$	$-d^j - w^j + d^i$

18. Assuming that the change of job does not affect the cost of providing the service. This cost may be affected if, for example, the worker transfers to a riskier occupation.

worker to the social security for the amount paid as compulsory contribution.[19]

Workers Receiving Unemployment Compensation

The final case to be considered is that of workers receiving unemployment compensation. Since this compensation may vary over time, it should be kept in mind that the with- and without-project situations should be compared on a yearly basis for the period of expected employment. Consider the case of a worker who without the project would be receiving unemployment compensation in the amount of co_t, where t indicates the time period (Table 3.11). When hired by the project, the worker would earn the prevailing wage net of contributions to the compensation scheme t_c, would stop receiving the compensation, and would incur the cost of his valuation of employment d.

Care should be exercised, however, in the estimation of d, since it is the compensating variation of accepting employment when the worker is receiving unemployment compensation. Therefore, d is the minimum sum necessary to pay the now employed worker in order for him or her to enjoy the same welfare level he would have enjoyed without project; that is, receiving unemployment compensation and not working. Thus, if the minimum wage the worker would accept is $100 and the unemployment compensation was $60, that minimum sum would be $40. It follows that as long as that minimum sum is positive – that is, the worker is not willing to pay in order to work[20]– the wage would exceed the efficiency cost.

The compensation scheme would receive the contribution of the now employed worker, would cease to transfer the unemployment compensation to

Table 3.11 Income changes attributable to employing a worker receiving unemployment compensation

	Project	Worker	Compensation scheme	Total
Wage	$-w$	$w(1-t_c)-co_t$	$wt_c+co_t+\Delta c$	—
Willingness to receive	—	$-d$	—	$-d$
Total	$-w$	$w(1-t_c)-co_t-d$	$wt_c+co_t+\Delta c$	$-d+\Delta c$

---

19. The incidence of that payment would depend on market characteristics.

20. See Sen (1975) and Mishan (1988, Ch. 11, Section 5).

the worker, and may also experience cost reductions Δc due to less paperwork, no need for verification of status, and possible reduction in the provision of social services. In the end, the efficiency cost of labor withdrawn from the pool of unemployment compensation beneficiaries would be

$$spw = -d + \Delta c \qquad (3.29)$$

In words, it would be the willingness to receive for accepting the employment, minus the cost savings by the compensation scheme.

3.4   THE UNIDO AND THE LITTLE–MIRRLEES SHADOW PRICES FOR LABOR

The formulae for the shadow price of labor proposed by UNIDO (1972) and by Little and Mirrlees (1974) may be easily derived from the simple case of the dual labor markets presented at the beginning of section 3.2. One of the most important characteristics of these two approaches is their recognition that the marginal rate of return may exceed the rate of discount, and as a result an additional unit of savings (investment) would be more valuable that an additional unit of consumption; in UNIDO's nomenclature, a unit of investment is valued at P^{inv} units of consumption.

When additional units of income have different consumption values depending on whether they are saved or consumed, knowing *who* receives the income changes becomes necessary. The income changes brought about by the hiring of a unit of labor may be presented as in Table 3.12. Assuming that there are no differences in the subjective valuations of the two occupations ($d^f = d^i$), that the informal sector wage equals the corresponding efficiency value, and that workers have a marginal propensity to consume equal to one, the efficiency price of labor measured in consumption units would be

$$spw = -s \, w^f \, P^{inv} - (1 - s) \, w^f + w^f - w^i$$

the consumption value of the forgone savings ($s \, w^f \, P^{inv}$) resulting from paying the wage, where s is the marginal propensity to save of the project owners, the corresponding consumption loss [$(1 - s) \, w^f$], and the additional consumption by the workers ($w^f - w^i$). The above expression simplifies to

$$spw = -s \, w^f \, (P^{inv} - 1) - w^i \qquad (3.30)$$

which is UNIDO's (1972) expression (15.8) for the shadow price of labor.

Little and Mirrlees (1974) chose to use public investment as the numeraire expressed in foreign exchange, and assumed that public investment and public

Table 3.12   The simple dual labor market

	Project	Workers	Total
Wage paid	$-w^f$	$w^f - w^i$	$-w^i$
Value of extra work	—	$-d^f + d^i$	$-d^f + d^i$
Total	$-w^f$	$w^f - w^i - d^f + d^i$	$-w^i - d^f + d^i$

consumption were equally valuable at the margin. Under these assumptions, the shadow price of labor for a public sector project could be presented as

$$spw^{LM} = -[w^f - (1/P^{inv})(w^f - w^i)]/sprfe \tag{3.31}$$

where P^{inv} represents the consumption value of public investment. In words, the shadow price of labor is the cost of the (uncommitted) public funds used to finance the wages, minus the value of the additional consumption expressed in units of investment, all expressed in foreign exchange at the official exchange rate.[21]

These formulae are only provided to establish the link between traditional efficiency analysis and the UNIDO and Little–Mirrlees proposals. The economist interested in applying these approaches may, however, want to refrain from using simple formulae, since the specific assumptions required to arrive at them may not be applicable to the case in hand. The correct application of these methods requires starting by estimating the distributional impact of the project, and only then applying appropriate marginal savings rates and shadow prices of investment (see UNIDO, 1972, 1980; and Londero, 1987).

21. This expression is that of Little and Mirrlees (1969, Section 13.3; 1974, Section 14.11) under the assumptions that workers do not save and the cost of providing the consumption basket in the worker's sector of origin is the same as in the new occupation (Little and Mirrlees, 1974, p. 272). Also see Little and Mirrlees (1974, Ch. 18).

4. Land

4.1 INTRODUCTION

As with any other shadow price, that of land is better understood if obtained by identifying those affected by an additional demand (supply), and measuring and aggregating their compensating variations. In the case of land, this seemingly simple approach presents some practical complications. First, the market price of used land is largely determined by the present value of the associated rent. Estimating that rent requires estimating the difference between revenue and costs, since rent is a residual. Therefore, when removing land from alternative uses it is be necessary to estimate those effects and compute their present values. In practice, however, simplified approaches are used to estimate this component of the *spr* for land.

Second, there could be significant external effects associated with the use of land. Those effects that impact other markets would have to be estimated, since the market value of land captures only those appropriated by the landowner. There would also be external effects that are not captured by markets. These effects should also be taken into account, since the objective is, to repeat, to identify everyone affected and measure their welfare changes. The measurement of the welfare changes associated with these external effects has been discussed at length in a prolific, highly specialized literature on the measurement of environmental costs and benefits. That literature includes the proposal of using surveys to ask those affected for their money-measure of the effects and it analyzes the statistical methods for deriving willingness to pay estimates. As a result, estimates are based on people's judgements regarding their responses to hypothetical situations, rather than on actual transactions. This characteristic is an important source of controversy. For these reasons, these methods will only be mentioned in this chapter.

4.2 NO EXTERNAL EFFECTS

Consider a simple case in which the availability of land (all of the same quality) is fixed – that is, all land is in use – and there are no external effects. The project's increase in the demand for land (Figure 4.1(a)) would increase its price, which in turn would induce an increase in the price of the goods that

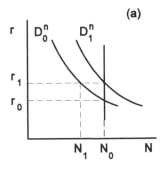 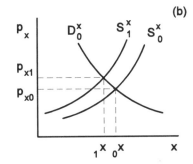

Figure 4.1 An increase in the demand for land

use land as an input (good x in Figure 4.1(b)), and thus reduce their production. Therefore, the land used by the project would be diverted from the production of other goods. The compensating variations of those affected by the increase in the price of land are presented in Table 4.1 under the assumption that market prices for outputs and inputs are equal to their efficiency prices. Withdrawing (a stock of) land from its current uses would result in a *flow* of effects over time. Therefore, the money values of those effects are to be recorded in the form of present values. In particular, the price of a certain piece of land ΔN is assumed to be equal to the private present value of the expected net income (rent) derived from its ownership. If the price were higher, the owner would benefit from selling the land and investing the money at the discount rate. If the price were lower, the owner would not sell it, since investing the proceeds would provide him or her with a smaller income flow.

In the absence of abnormal profits from any other source, and assuming that land is the only input in fixed supply and rent is the only benefit derived from land ownership,[1] the price of land would be the present value of the difference between the value of production at users' prices and supply costs (excluding land, including capital costs and distribution margins), that is

$$p_n = PV[(\Delta x_t/\Delta N)(p_{xt} - \Sigma_{i \neq N} q_{ixt} p_{it})] \qquad (4.1)$$

where $\Delta x_t = x_{0t} - x_{1t}$ is the yearly loss in production attributable to reducing the availability of land in ΔN, p_{xt} is the users' price of x at time t, q_{ixt} is the use of input i (including capital goods) required per unit of output x delivered to the market in year t, the second expression in parentheses is the rent content of one unit of output, and the expression in square brackets is the annual rent

---

1. In particular, assuming that land does not provide other benefits like 'prestige', or insurance against variability in the return of other assets (Gittinger, 1982, p. 257).

Table 4.1   Income changes attributable to an additional demand for land

Source	Project	Landowners
Market value of land with the project	—	$\Delta p_n N_1 = PV(\Delta r)N_1$
Other inputs for producing x_0	—	—
Market value of x_1	—	—
Willingness to receive for ΔN	—	—
Received for ΔN	$-p_{n1}\Delta N =$ $PV(r_1\Delta N)$	$p_{n1}\Delta N - p_{n0}\Delta N =$ $PV(\Delta r)\Delta N$
Willingness to pay for Δx	—	—
Paid by the consumers for Δx	—	—
Value of the other resources released	—	—
Total	$-p_{n1}\Delta N$	$\Delta p_n N_0 = PV(\Delta r)N_0$
Changes in real incomes	Project's cost	Change in landowners' surplus

Source: Figure 4.1, as explained in the text.

attributable to an additional unit of land.

In Table 4.1, the project purchases the land at its market price in the situation with the project p_{n1}. Landowners gain an extra rent due to the additional demand for land – rent that is paid by the project, $(r_1 - r_0)\Delta N$, and by the producers of x. Producers are assumed to earn no abnormal profits, thus price equals marginal cost, and small differences between the prices of the other inputs in the situations with and without the project are ignored for the sake of simplicity. Consumers lose the compensating variation of the price increase induced by the increase in rent attributable to the additional demand of land by the project.

The resulting efficiency cost of land, which is the sum of the 'Total' column of Table 4.1, is the difference between the present value of the willingness to pay for the reduction in the consumption of x and the present value of the other resources used in the production of x and released when reducing production in Δx_1. If for the sake of simplicity it is assumed that the only source of the increase in the cost of producing x is the increase in the

Producers of x	Consumers of x	Total
$-\Delta p_n N_1 = -PV(\Delta r)N_1$	—	—
—	—	—
$PV[\Delta p_x x_1]$	$PV[-\Delta p_x x_1]$	—
—	—	—
$p_{n0}\Delta N = PV(r_0\Delta N)$	—	—
—	$PV[-\tfrac{1}{2}(p_{x1}+p_{x0})\Delta x]$	$PV[-\tfrac{1}{2}(p_{x1}+p_{x0})\Delta x]$
$-PV[p_{x0}\Delta x]$	$PV[p_{x0}\Delta x]$	—
$PV[p_{x0}\Delta x - r_0\Delta N] =$ $PV[\Sigma_{i\neq N}\, q_{ix}\, p_i]$	—	$PV[\Sigma_{i\neq N}\, q_{ix}\, p_i]$
—	$PV[-\Delta p_x x_1 - \tfrac{1}{2}\Delta p_x \Delta x]$	$PV[-\tfrac{1}{2}(p_{x1}+p_{x0})\Delta x +$ $\Sigma_{i\neq N}\, q_{ix}\, p_i]$
Change in producers' surplus	Change in consumers' surplus	Value at efficiency prices

price of land (assumed in Table 4.1), the CV of the consumers would be (approximately) equal to the increase in rent, and thus

$$\tfrac{1}{2}(p_{n1} + p_{n0})\,\Delta N \approx PV[\Delta x_t\, \tfrac{1}{2}(p_{x1t} + p_{x0t}) - \Sigma_{i\neq N}\, q_{ixt}\, p_{it}] \qquad (4.2)$$

That is, the willingness to pay for the land diverted from the production of x would be (approximately) equal to the difference between the willingness to pay for the reduction in consumption and the value of the released resources other than land. If price changes are negligible, expression (4.2) may be simplified

$$p_n\,\Delta N = PV[\Delta x_t\, (p_{xt} - \Sigma_{i\neq N}\, q_{ixt}\, p_{it})] \qquad (4.3)$$

From (4.3) it follows that if, as it has been assumed thus far, market prices of outputs and inputs equal their efficiency prices, and price changes are negligible, the efficiency cost of land would be approximately equal to its market price. If market prices differ from efficiency prices, the shadow price ratio of land – that is, the ratio of its efficiency value to its market value – would be

$$spr_n = \frac{PV[\Delta x/\Delta N\,(spr_{xt}\,p_{xt} - \Sigma_{i \neq N}\,q_{ixt}\,spr_{it}\,p_{it})]}{PV[\Delta x/\Delta N\,(p_{xt} - \Sigma_{i \neq N}\,q_{ixt}\,p_{it})]} \tag{4.4}$$

The shadow price ratio of land would be a weighted average of *sprs* of the outputs, minus a weighted average of the *sprs* of the inputs other than land used in the production of those outputs, since in practice x is a basket of goods; that is,

$$spr_n = \frac{\Sigma_x\,PV[(\Delta x/\Delta N)(spr_{xt}\,p_{xt} - \Sigma_{i \neq N}\,q_{ixt}\,spr_{it}\,p_{it})]}{\Sigma_x\,PV[(\Delta x/\Delta N)(p_{xt} - \Sigma_{i \neq N}\,q_{ixt}\,p_{it})]} \tag{4.5}$$

The preceding expression is difficult to implement if taken literally, but it provides the applied economist with a sound basis for making estimates. In practice, information would only be available to estimate spr_n based on annual data. Therefore, the expression used would be

$$spr_n = \frac{\Sigma_x\,[(\Delta x/\Delta N)(spr_x\,p_x - \Sigma_{i \neq N}\,q_{ix}\,spr_i\,p_i)]}{\Sigma_x\,[(\Delta x/\Delta N)(p_x - \Sigma_{i \neq N}\,q_{ix}\,p_i)]} \tag{4.6}$$

Note that this expression may be estimated using input–output techniques, as explained in Appendix 6.1.

Expression (4.6) becomes much simpler under the familiar simplifying assumptions of full substitution in production, perfect competition and profit maximization. In this case,

$$spr_n = \frac{\Sigma_x\,[spr_x\,p_x\,\partial x/\partial N]}{\Sigma_x\,[p_x\,\partial x/\partial N]} \tag{4.7}$$

the present value of forgone output at shadow prices, divided by the present value of that same output at market prices.

4.3 USABLE LAND AS A PARTIALLY PRODUCED GOOD

So far it has been assumed that the amount of land is fixed. If there is a frontier, marginal land may be incorporated into the productive area. It would then be 'produced' at the margin in the sense that additional units may be made available at the cost of incorporating them into production (e.g. clearing, leveling). The price of the marginal land would be equal to these incorporation costs and such land would not receive rent. Therefore, at the margin, the additional demand for land would be satisfied not only by withdrawing it from alternative uses (dN_1), but also by incorporating marginal land (dN_s). The efficiency cost of land for the project would be a weighted average of the costs associated with these two sources.

Equations (4.6) and (4.7) are presented in terms of rent per unit of land. Therefore, these costs would have to be annualized in order to incorporate them into the formulae for spr_n. Assuming that these costs have an infinite life, the annuity would be obtained simply by multiplying them by the discount rate δ,[2] and the formula for the $sprs$ would be

$$spr_n = \frac{dN_1 \, \Sigma_x \, [(\Delta x/\Delta N)(spr_x \, p_x - \Sigma_{i \neq N} \, q_{ix} \, spr_i \, p_i)] + dN_s \, \delta \, \Sigma_i \, q_{in} \, p_i \, spr_i}{dN_1 \, \Sigma_x \, [(\Delta x/\Delta N)(p_x - \Sigma_{i \neq N} \, q_{ix} \, p_i)] + dN_s \, \delta \, p_{ns}} \quad (4.8)$$

$$spr_n = \frac{dN_1 \, \Sigma_x \, [spr_x \, p_x \, \partial x/\partial N] + dN_s \, \Sigma_i \, (\partial q_{in}/\partial N) \, p_i \, spr_i}{dN_1 \, \Sigma_x \, [p_x \, \partial x/\partial N] + dN_s \, \delta \, p_{ns}} \quad (4.9)$$

where dN_1 is the additional demand for land met by withdrawing it from alternative uses, dN_s is that met by incorporating new land ($dN = dN_1 + dN_s$), p_{ns} is the market price of land, $\Sigma_i \, q_{in} \, p_i$ is the cost of incorporating one unit of land, and $\Sigma_i \, (\partial q_{in}/\partial N) \, p_i$ is the marginal cost of incorporating land, both costs assumed to be equal to the market price of land. It should be noted that equations (4.8) and (4.9) allow for differences between the price of the marginal land and the marginal cost of providing it.

4.4   OTHER ISSUES

It has been assumed thus far that land is of a uniform quality. In practice, even land of the same physical quality may present differences in price per unit due to differences in distance to the market (locational rents). Because of the need to take locational rents into account, land rent should either be measured with respect to an output valued at users' prices – including distribution costs as part of the value of the released resources ($\Sigma_{i \neq N} \, q_{ix} \, p_i$) – or at producers' prices

---

2. Note that differences between the private and the social rate of discount would require use of different discount rates in the numerator and the denominator.

(farm gate) and excluding distribution costs from the resources released.[3] In practice, however, land values would capitalize rents attributable to both the location and the physical quality of the land, but that would not change the basic formulae presented so far.

Another important aspect to take into consideration is the existence of taxes. In the expressions presented thus far, rent includes indirect taxes on the output and direct taxes. The landowner, however, would calculate the present value of the net-of-tax rent. As a result, while it may be argued that the individual's rate of discount equals the *private* rate of profit, there would be a discrepancy between the total and the privately appropriated rent, and the price of land would always underestimate the present value of total rent. In order to show this with a simple example, say that the rent per unit of land r is obtained annually in perpetuity and subject to a direct tax rate t^d. Therefore, the market value of that land would be expected to be

$$p^n N = \frac{\Sigma_t \, r \, (1 - t^d)}{(1 + \delta)^t} = \frac{r \, (1 - t^d)}{\delta} \tag{4.10}$$

Thus, when there are direct taxes imposed on rent, even if total rent at market and efficiency prices are equal, the market price of land would underestimate its efficiency value and shadow price ratios would have to be amended accordingly. If direct taxes applied exclusively to land, land prices could be corrected by multiplying the denominator of equations (4.8) and (4.9) by $(1 - t^d)$ in order to reflect that the market price includes that part of the rent that is appropriated by the landowner. If direct taxes applied to all returns on equity, however, some inconsistencies in the application of traditional efficiency analysis would arise, since the investor would be expected to equalize the private rate of discount δ with the private rate of return, which would differ from the rate of return on total investment. Such inconsistencies and their implications for efficiency analysis will be discussed in section 6.3.

It has been suggested that the ownership of land may also be the source of a consumption flow to the extent that it provides some special 'prestige', or some insurance against the variability in the return of other assets (Gittinger, 1982, p. 257). In such a case, an extra consumption flow should be included in expression (4.1) that would make its price greater than the present value of its rent. If the project is going to own the land (rather than rent it), there is no reason to ignore these opportunity costs by using only the present value of the rent. Ignoring these (real or imaginary) benefits of land ownership as perceived by landowners would clash with traditional value judgements in

---

3. In this latter case it is implicitly assumed that distribution costs at market prices equals these costs at efficiency prices.

cost–benefit analysis in a manner similar to ignoring the value of extra effort in the case of labor. Thus, if there are direct taxes on rent and there is an additional unit value of B associated with land property, a value assumed to be the compensating variation of those 'other benefits', the market price of land would be

$$p^n = B + \frac{\Sigma_t \, r \, (1 - t^d)}{(1 + \delta)^t} = \frac{r \, (1 - t^d) + \delta B}{\delta} \qquad (4.11)$$

where $b = \delta B$. Therefore, the shadow price ratios corresponding to equations (4.8) and (4.9) would be

$$spr_n = \frac{dN_1 \, \{\Sigma_x \, [(\Delta x/\Delta N)(spr_x \, p_x - \Sigma_{i \neq N} \, q_{ix} \, spr_i \, p_i)] + \delta B_1\} + dN_s \, \delta \, (\Sigma_i \, q_{in} \, p_i \, spr_i + B_s)}{(1 - t^d) \, dN_1 \, \{\Sigma_x \, [(\Delta x/\Delta N)(p_x - \Sigma_{i \neq N} \, q_{ix} \, p_i)] + \delta B_1\} + dN_s \, \delta \, p_{ns}}$$
$$(4.12)$$

$$spr_n = \frac{dN_1 \, [\Sigma_x \, (spr_x \, p_x \, \partial x/\partial N) + \delta B_1] + dN_s \, \delta \, [\Sigma_i \, (\partial q_{ir}/\partial N) \, p_i \, spr_i + B_s]}{(1 - t^d) \, dN_1 \, \Sigma_x \, [p_x \, \partial x/\partial N] + dN_s \, \delta \, p_{ns}} \qquad (4.13)$$

where market price of marginal land p_{ns} includes benefits B_s, that is,

$$p_{ns} = \Sigma_i \, q_{in} \, p_i + B_s$$

$$p_{ns} = \Sigma_i \, p_i \, \partial q_{ir}/\partial N + B_s$$

where B_s would be the market price of unincorporated marginal land.

In practice, it is likely that the *spr* of land would be estimated based on the assumption of a fixed supply. Any new land incorporated as a result of the increase in its market price would tend to be small and geographically remote, and thus difficult to take into account. The extent to which land prices include more than the present value of expected rent is an empirical issue, but if they do, and that additional value relates to benefits perceived by landowners, traditional value judgements in cost–benefit analysis (section 1.2) would preclude their exclusion. The economist estimating shadow prices should only make sure that the difference between the market price of land and the present value of the rent is not due to other reasons.

4.5 EXTERNAL EFFECTS

There may be external effects attributable to the use of a specific piece of land that are registered by the market, but are not appropriated through the ownership of that specific land, and therefore are not captured by its market price. Consider the productive use of a wooded hillside overlooking an urban area. The benefits derived from the natural beauty of the wooded hillside are appropriated (to a large extent) through land ownership. However, they are not appropriated by the owner of the wooded land, but rather by the owners of the developed land at the foot of the hillside, and adjacent areas. The productive use of the hillside, therefore, would not only result in the forgoing of the expected rents of the landowner, but also in the forgoing of rents enjoyed by other landowners. The reduction in the value of these lands would, *ceteris paribus*, provide an estimate of the present value of the consumption loss attributable to the view of the undeveloped hillside.

It is certainly easier to explain the existence of these external effects and their market values, than it is to estimate them. There are two main reasons. First, such effects are not the result of repetitive (almost) identical transactions, and therefore historic market values of these effects cannot be used to estimate future ones. The fact that the market *will* reflect these effects is of little help to make the appraisal today. Moreover, there are so many factors affecting the price of land that attributing changes in its price to any of these factors is difficult. As a result, these effects are frequently estimated by resorting to the same techniques used to estimate the consumption value of effects that do not carry a market price. As mentioned at the beginning of this chapter, the use of these methods is not without controversy.[4]

Second, there may be general equilibrium effects that are important and difficult to bring into a simple estimate. For example, if there is a reduction in the flow of benefits to the owners of the properties on the foothills, the market value of the benefits enjoyed by other properties, and therefore their market prices, may increase, since there would be an overall reduction of land with these attributes.[5]

Finally, to complicate the problem even further, there may also be external effects that are not captured by the market. Such would be the case, for example, when the productive use of the wooded hillside took place along an interurban highway, affecting the enjoyment of passers by, rather than that of dwellers. In this situation, it is not even possible to conduct an ex-post estimate of effects based on market values because there is not a market for highways

---

4. For a presentation of these methods see Freeman (1993). The *Journal of Economic Perspectives* (Vol. 8, No. 4, 1994) provides an exchange of views on the subject.

5. Londero (2000) discusses a similar problem when analyzing the distributional effects of seemingly poverty targeted projects. For ex-post evaluations of benefit appropriation through land ownership see, *inter alia*, Haughwout (1997) and McDonald and Osuji (1995).

with different scenic attributes and different users' costs.[6] In these cases there may be no other alternative than resorting to 'willingness to pay surveys' in order to elicit the highway users' estimates of the welfare losses that would be imposed upon them by the development of the wooded hillside.

6. In the best of circumstances there may be two or three alternative routes that differ in many characteristics, making the attribution of effects to each individual characteristic practically impossible.

5. Fiscal Resources

5.1   THE PROBLEM

Resource allocation decisions affect not only the incomes of private individuals and firms, but government revenues and expenditures as well. The monetary values of these fiscal effects of resource allocation decisions, however, are not necessarily accurate measures of the costs or benefits attributable to such decisions. For example, the welfare loss to consumers of increasing taxes could differ from the additional amount of taxes paid. Those extra costs or benefits would depend on how the government adjusts to the fiscal effects. *Inter alia*, the government may change tax rates (including the inflation tax), efficiency in collection, expenditures, or transfers to future generations through borrowing.

The additional costs or benefits will also depend on the welfare effects of the different instruments. A government that designs its instruments in an optimal manner would make sure that, at the margin, all instruments suitable to compensate for a fiscal effect would have the same welfare cost per unit of fiscal resource, making the use of these instruments indifferent at the margin. For example, the government would be indifferent between raising indirect taxes and reducing current expenditures because, at the margin, both instruments would have the same welfare effect per unit. In this ideal world of optimal fiscal policy, there would be a unique welfare cost to the marginal change of any fiscal instrument.

In practice, however, fiscal policy is not optimal and different instruments normally have different marginal costs. The implication at the project level is that to attribute a shadow price ratio to the fiscal effects would require knowing the instrument that would be used to adjust for such effects. That is why the estimation of these shadow prices should take place at a central level.

This section provides only an introductory, primarily analytical treatment of the subject and with little reference to practice, since the estimation of the welfare cost of fiscal resources is not yet operational. The reader is encouraged to consult theoretical presentations by Atkinson and Stern (1974), Squire (1989), Ahmad and Stern (1989), and Sandmo (1997). Newbery and Stern (1987), and Ahmad and Stern (1991) provide a combination of theory and practice in the field of tax reform.

5.2   IMPLICATIONS OF SIMPLE MODELS

Using a simple model of public and private production with identical consumers and only consumption taxes, Atkinson and Stern (1974) showed that the necessary conditions for welfare maximization require the marginal rate of transformation of private goods into public goods (MRT) to be

$$\text{MRT} = \frac{\alpha}{\lambda^r} \, \Sigma_k \, \text{MRS}_k + \frac{\partial}{\partial e} [\Sigma_i \, t_i \, X_i] \qquad (5.1)$$

Where MRS_k is the marginal rate of substitution between the public good e and the private good k, α is the marginal utility of income, λ^r is the welfare marginal cost of raising revenue, t_i is the tax rate on private good i, and X_i is the net consumption of good i. In words, the marginal rate of transformation of private into public goods may have to be higher than the marginal rates of substitution in consumption if $\alpha > \lambda^r$, or if the additional production of the public good reduces tax revenue. Thus, *ceteris paribus*, if increasing the production of the public good increases tax collection (for example because of complementarity with highly taxed private goods) the rate of transformation may be lower; conversely, the MRT would have to be higher if private goods are substitutes in consumption of the public good, and therefore increasing the production of the public good reduces tax revenue. An important conclusion from the cost–benefit perspective is that this tax revenue effect of increasing the production of a public good depends on the characteristics of the public good itself, and is thus project specific. With regard to substitution effects, the rate of transformation of private into public goods would have to be higher the greater the marginal welfare cost of raising revenue λ^r with respect to the marginal utility of income α.

Atkinson and Stern showed that α/λ^r, known as the inverse of the 'marginal cost of funds' (MCF), may be expressed as

$$\alpha/\lambda^r = 1 + d - r \qquad (5.2)$$

The second term on the right-hand side, d, is called a 'distortionary effect' of taxation. It is shown to be ≤ 0 and interpreted as the 'excess burden (at the margin of tax revenue) associated with commodity as opposed to lump-sum taxation' (Atkinson and Stern, 1974, p. 123). The more 'distortionary' taxes are, the greater d would be in absolute value, the higher the MCF would be, and therefore the higher the MRT would have to be in order to justify an increase in public production.

The third term, r, is called the 'revenue effect', and is defined as the increase in revenue attributable to a unit increase in income. For normal goods, an increase in consumption taxes reduces real income and thus there is a negative 'income' effect on consumption-tax revenue. Similarly, if labor is taxed and leisure is also a normal good, additional taxation would reduce income and thus the 'consumption of leisure'. That is, it would increase work, and thus tax revenue. A similar effect would be obtained from the taxation of an inferior good. Therefore, the 'revenue effect' may be positive or negative depending on the goods being taxed.

Summing up the results of this highly simplified model, the (efficiency) optimal marginal rate of transformation of private goods into public goods may be different (higher or lower) than the sum of the marginal rates of substitution in consumption. It would be higher the lower the complementarity between public and taxed private goods, the higher the 'distortionary' effects of taxes, and the lower the importance of taxes on inferior goods or on normal factors.

The simple model just presented considers only consumption taxes. In practice, different taxes would have different impacts through different channels. Some taxes may affect not just the composition of consumption expenditures, but also saving and investment decisions, adding an intertemporal dimension to the problem (Ballard, Shoven and Whaley, 1985). Optimization using a more general model would require all tax instruments to have the same value at the margin. Those values would take into account not only expenditure switches in one period, but also the intertemporal effects resulting from induced changes in investment and savings behavior.

The simple model also ignores distributional considerations, which in practice are at the heart of tax and expenditure policy. Policy discussions concerning taxes and public expenditures are loaded with distributional considerations, and these often impact decisions. Whether practice would have to adjust to a normatively loaded theory, or the other way around, is an interesting discussion. What seems clear, however, is that it would not be defensible to use different welfare functions for tax and expenditure decisions.

The simple model considers only some of the costs associated with real tax systems. Slemrod and Yitzhaki (1996) propose to classify the overall costs of taxation into administrative costs of the tax authority, deadweight losses associated with the reallocation of consumers' expenditures due to taxes, compliance costs of the taxpayer, taxpayers' welfare costs attributable to the additional risks of evasion, and the avoidance costs of taxpayers. The simple model takes into account only the deadweight losses, and therefore omits many others.

On the other hand, the simple model is useful in highlighting important issues for applied cost–benefit analysis. The model implies that it would not be enough to have shadow prices for all resources involved in the transformation of private goods into public goods – shadow prices for the instruments that would be used to finance the net fiscal effects would normally be required as well. From the project analysis point of view, it would be important to distinguish those effects that are project specific, and therefore are either control variables for the project economist or need to be estimated as part of the analysis (e.g. project specific fiscal effects), from those that are related to the more general issues of tax and expenditure policy design (and administration).

An optimal fiscal policy would simplify the economic analysis of government allocation decisions considerably because there would be only one welfare cost to the fiscal resources (all instruments would have the same value per unit of fiscal revenue or expenditure). If that cost could be estimated, it could be used in cost–benefit analyses. In practice, however, governments do not conduct optimal fiscal policies. Different courses of action would have different effects on people's welfare and the combination of fiscal instruments selected would determine those costs and benefits. Then, in practice, the question is not just what cost is attributable to each instrument, but also which instruments would be used. The selection of fiscal instruments would generally be outside the control of the project analyst, and the information regarding which ones would be used and their associated costs would have to be provided to the analyst from the fiscal policy side.

The tax revenue effects of public production, instead, are project specific and ideally would have to be estimated on a project basis. From a theoretical perspective, those estimates would have to include direct and indirect fiscal effects through the purchase of inputs and the sale of outputs, as well as general equilibrium effects on substitutes and complements through price changes.

5.3   A SIMPLE PARTIAL EQUILIBRIUM EXAMPLE

The shadow price ratio of increasing/reducing public revenue using tax i may be expressed as[1]

$$sprpr_i = \frac{\lambda^r_i}{\alpha^k} = \frac{\Sigma_e u^e \Sigma_i p_i \, (\partial q^e_i / \partial t_i)}{(\partial R / \partial t_i) - (\partial C / \partial t_i)} \tag{5.3}$$

The intuitive meaning of this expression is that the shadow price ratio of raising funds is the welfare change attributable to an extra unit of revenue (λ^r_i), expressed in the numeraire; that is, in units of additional welfare derived from

---

1. For a demonstration see Appendix 5.1. In comparison with equations (5.1) and (5.2), where all consumers are assumed to be identical, α carries a subscript to indicate the individual chosen to define the numeraire (see Appendix 1.1). For an alternative presentation, see Ahmad and Stern (1991).

additional income to individual k (α^k). That ratio equals the weighted sum of the values of all consumption changes attributable to the change in tax t_i, where the weights u^e are the distributional weights presented in Chapter 1, expressed per unit of additional revenue (R) net of the additional monetary costs incurred to raise that extra revenue (C).

Expression (5.3) has been derived from a simple general equilibrium model (see Appendix 5.1), and consequently partial derivatives like $\partial q^e_i/\partial t_i$ represent the overall effects on the consumption of q by individual i attributable to changing the tax rate *after all adjustments to return to full equilibrium have taken place*. Therefore, these partial derivatives differ from traditional partial equilibrium measures based on *ceteris paribus* supply and demand curves. Nevertheless, a partial equilibrium example is provided next, since in practice it is likely that the applied economist will have to rely on partial equilibrium approximations.

Consider an increase in the consumption tax imposed on consumption good q, represented in Figure 5.1. To simplify the presentation, individuals are distinguished in their roles as consumers and factor suppliers. It is assumed that there are only two consumers, who also supply labor and land. The factor supply role of the landowner has been separated from that of consumer and supplier of labor. The producer, who could also be one of the consumers, is also distinguished from the landowner, although they could be the same individual.

The increase in the consumption tax raises the price paid by the consumer from p_0 to p_1, and as a result it reduces consumption from q_0 to q_1. Market prices may be conceived as

$$p_0 = p^b_0 (1 + t_0)$$

$$p_1 = p^b_1 (1 + t_0 + \Delta t)$$

where p^b_0 and p^b_1 are the basic prices, t_0 is the original tax rate, and Δt is the tax increase. Thus, defining increments in absolute values, the price increase may be conceived as

$$\Delta p = -\Delta p^b - \Delta p^b t_0 + p^b_1 \Delta t$$

the reduction in the basic price, plus the reduction in revenue attributable to the reduction in the basic price, plus the revenue increase due to increasing the tax rate.

As a result of the price increase, consumers lose the compensating variation of the price increase, equal to the additional expense for q_1 (see Table 5.1), plus the difference between their willingness to pay for $q_0 - q_1$ and what they actually pay for that quantity. Table 5.1 shows in brackets the decomposition

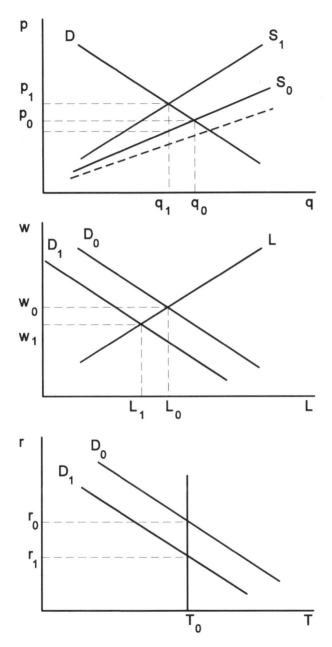

Figure 5.1 An increase in a consumption tax

Table 5.1   Effects of increasing a consumption tax

	Consumer 1	Consumer 2
Consumption good market		
Expenditure on q_1	$-\Delta p\, q_1^1$	$-\Delta p\, q_1^2$
[Tax revenue]	$[(\Delta t\, p^b - t_0\, \Delta p^b)\, q_1^1]$	$[(\Delta t\, p^b - t_0\, \Delta p^b)\, q_1^2]$
[Basic prices]	$[\Delta p^b\, q_1^1]$	$[\Delta p^b\, q_1^2]$
Willingness to pay for Δq	$-\tfrac{1}{2}(p_0 + p_1)\, \Delta q^1$	$-\tfrac{1}{2}(p_0 + p_1)\, \Delta q^1$
Paid for Δq	$p_0\, \Delta q^1$	$p_0\, \Delta q^2$
Labor market		
Received for L_1	$-\Delta w\, L_1^1$	$-\Delta w\, L_1^2$
Willingness to receive for ΔL	$\tfrac{1}{2}(w_0 + w_1)\, \Delta L^1$	$\tfrac{1}{2}(w_0 + w_1)\, \Delta L^2$
Received for ΔL	$-w_0\, \Delta L^1$	$-w_0\, \Delta L^2$
Land market	—	—
Total	$-\Delta p\, q_1^1 - \tfrac{1}{2}\Delta p\, \Delta q^1$ $-\Delta w\, L_1^1 - \tfrac{1}{2}\Delta w\, \Delta L^1$	$-\Delta p\, q_1^2 - \tfrac{1}{2}\Delta p\, \Delta q^2$ $-\Delta w\, L_1^2 - \tfrac{1}{2}\Delta w\, \Delta L^2$

Source: Figure 5.1 as explained in the text.

of the expenditure change into the tax revenue change and the basic price change. This decomposition facilitates showing the changes in revenue for the producer and the government in their respective columns.

As suppliers of labor, consumers lose the compensating variation of the reduction in wage income for L_1, minus the willingness to receive for the reduction in salaried work, plus the reduction in wage income due to reduction in hours worked.

The producer is basically unaffected by the consumption tax, since price equals marginal cost. The revenue change is exactly compensated for by the changes in factor incomes (wages and rents). The landowners, however, see their rents reduced.

The change in government revenue is the net result of three effects: (1) the tax increase; minus (2) the revenue reduction due to the reduction in the basic price; minus (3) the revenue reduction due to the quantity reduction

Producer	Landowner	Government	Total
—	—	—	—
—	—	$(\Delta t\, p^b - t_0\, \Delta p^b)\, q_1$	—
$-\Delta p^b\, q_1$	—	—	—
—	—	—	$-\frac{1}{2}(p_0 + p_1)\,\Delta q$
$-p_0^b\, \Delta q$	—	$-t^0\, p_0^b\, \Delta q$	—
$\Delta w\, L_1$	—	—	—
—	—	—	$\frac{1}{2}(w_0 + w_1)\,\Delta L$
$w_0\, \Delta L$	—	—	—
$\Delta r\, T_0$	$-\Delta r\, T_0$	—	—
—	$-\Delta r\, T_0$	$(\Delta t\, p^b - t_0\, \Delta p^b)\, q_1 - t^0\, p_0^b\, \Delta q$	$-\frac{1}{2}(p_0 + p_1)\,\Delta q + \frac{1}{2}(w_0 + w_1)\,\Delta L$

attributable to the price change.[2]

The efficiency value of the consumption tax increase is the willingness to pay for the reduction in consumption minus the willingness to receive for the reduction in salaried work. The efficiency loss in this example is high because the reduction in rents for the landowners is not compensated for by any gains. Note that a zero distributional weight for the landowner coupled with a unitary distributional weight for the remaining agents would significantly reduce the efficiency cost of the tax increase.

Finally, the partial equilibrium approximation to the shadow price ratio of public revenue raised with tax t_1 would be the weighted sum of the column

2. For the sake on simplicity, it is assumed that the marginal cost of raising revenue by increasing the consumption tax and the effects of the tax increase on the expenditure of other consumption goods (the second term of (5.A8)), are nil. That is $\partial C/\partial t_i = 0$ and $\Sigma_{i \neq j}\, t_i\, [\partial(q_i\, p_i)/\partial t_j] = 0$.

totals for all affected individuals in Table 5.1, divided by the additional revenue; that is

$$sprpr_i = - \frac{\Sigma_e u^e (-\Delta p\, q_1^e - \frac{1}{2}\Delta p\, \Delta q^e - \Delta w\, L_1^e - \frac{1}{2}\Delta w\, \Delta L^e) - u^l\, \Delta r\, T_0}{(\Delta t\, p^b - t_0\, \Delta p^b)\, q_1 - t^0\, p_0^b\, \Delta q} \quad (5.4)$$

The numerator is the weighted sum across all affected individuals – namely, consumers, providers of labor and landowners – of the CVs attributable to raising the consumption tax. Note that this is not the overall effect on those individuals, since the effects of spending the public sector revenue (e.g. the public project) have not been taken into account. Finally, the expression is preceded by a minus sign because in the project's accounts, the negative sign would be carried by the net fiscal effect that requires such a tax increase. Any costs to the public sector associated with the tax increase should be deducted from the denominator in order to obtain the net additional revenue, and any welfare effects of such costs would have to be added to the numerator (as in (5.3)).

The reader may want to use the same example to deduce the formula for a revenue increase that would be raised by increasing an income tax on wages and rents.

5.4   FISCAL POLICY AND NET FISCAL EFFECTS

Including the welfare costs of marginal fiscal changes attributable to the project requires measuring these fiscal effects. To illustrate some of the issues involved in this measurement, three instruments for adjusting to excess demands for funds will be discussed: public debt changes, expenditure changes, and tax changes. In order to simplify the presentation in a way consistent with practice, bond financing and reducing alternative investments would be considered as alternatives for investment outlays, and tax and expenditure changes as alternatives for smaller effects over longer periods of time.

Consider the simple case of a government investment decision requiring an initial outlay of $100 that provides a $10 annual revenue during 10 years:

Project A	Year 0	Year 1	. . .	Year 10
Government	– 100	10	. . .	10

If the size of the investment budget is independent from the project decision, that is, the investment budget is not a 'control variable' (Sen, 1972) for the analyst, incorporating one project in the budget would require displacing an equivalent amount of investment. Consider the example where the government contemplates financing the outlays in year 0 by reducing investments by $100, accomplished by not doing project B, the marginal investment, which would have resulted in the following financial flows for the government:

Project B	Year 0	Year 1	. . .	Year 10
Government	-100	7	. . .	7

The fiscal effects attributable to the project would simply be the difference between the effects of project A, minus those of the alternative course of action (project B). Therefore, there would be no fiscal effects attributable to the project in the first year, and there would be an additional revenue of $3 per year over 10 years. The present value of the net fiscal effect at a 10 percent rate of discount would be $15.23.

The government could also finance the initial outlay by issuing bonds. The bond issue would be attributable to the project if it were the marginal source of financing; that is, if its amount would be determined on a project basis. In such a case, the amount of the bond issue would be a control variable for the analyst, and therefore the financial flows associated with financing a $100 outlay with a bond placement would be attributable to project A. Otherwise, if the bond issue would take place regardless of the projects to be financed, for example, if it was used to reach a government investment target, project A would instead be displacing an alternative investment.

Say that the amount of the bond issue is attributable to the project. The government would raise $100 to finance the project at an interest rate equal to the rate of discount (10 percent), and repay the bond in equal principal payments over 10 years (i.e. $10 per year) plus interest. Thus, the government's outlays for principal and interest would be as follows:

Bond	Year 0	Year 1	. . .	Year 10
Government	100	-20	. . .	-11

The net fiscal effect of project A would be the difference between a revenue flow of $10 per year and the repayment flow of the bond. That difference amounts to a present value of -$31.86.

If the government conducted an optimal fiscal policy, the analysis of the project would present few problems to the analyst since all fiscal instruments would have the same welfare cost at the margin (including the reduction of current expenditures). In other words, there would be only one shadow price ratio for fiscal resources, since the tax structure and the allocation of current and capital expenditures would be optimal. The marginal rate of return of public investments would equal the rate of a discount and the rate of interest, since the government would presumably accept the revealed intertemporal preferences of the present generation as the rate of discount, and borrowing would be optimal; therefore, the present value of repaying the bonds would be equal to the amount raised to finance the project.[3] In these ideal circumstances it would be sufficient for the present value of net economic benefits (valuing the fiscal effects at the marginal cost of funds) to be positive for the project to be financed, since the investment budget would be determined according to the rate of discount and all financing instruments would have the same value.

If borrowing were suboptimal, the welfare cost of reducing government consumption in one unit would differ from that of reducing government investment, which in turn would differ from the cost of borrowing. If all other fiscal instruments had the same marginal welfare cost, the most important consequence would be the need to use shadow prices of investment funds (UNIDO, 1972; Londero, 1987) because of differences between the rate of discount and the marginal rate of return. In such a case, estimates of the distributional effects of the projects according to marginal propensities to save (UNIDO, 1972; Londero, 1987), required by the suboptimality of investment, would have to be complemented by estimates of how the fiscal effects would be financed using changes in government consumption, taxation and government investment, since the three would have different values at the margin. Estimates of the marginal cost of funds may have to take into account the effects on consumption and investment, and estimates of the shadow prices of investment funds (Londero, 1987) would have to account for fiscal effects and their welfare values.

With regard to the allocation of responsibilities, estimates of distributional effects would be conducted at the project level, while estimates of how fiscal effects would be financed, and of the shadow price ratios of public funds and investment funds would have to be provided to the project analyst.

Fiscal effects may have one shadow price ratio reflecting the marginal welfare values of changes in government consumption, taxation and investment as long as the financing of the fiscal effects is not project specific.

---

3. In this hypothetical case the marginal rate of return may be used as the rate of discount only because *it becomes equal to the rate of discount* as a result of the optimal borrowing. Otherwise, differences between marginal rates of return, marginal rates of interest and rates of discount require a distributional analysis and the use of shadow prices of investment. See Feldstein (1978), UNIDO (1972), Ray (1984), and Londero (1987). However, there may still be some intertemporal effects to register as long as the *private* rate of return differs from the rate of discount.

In this latter case, individual shadow price ratios for each fiscal instrument would be required.

In summary, a full account of project costs and benefits would normally require estimates of the net fiscal effects of projects, and of the compensating variations of the effects attributable to the associated future government expenditure and tax changes.

5.5 EMPIRICAL STUDIES

The operational application of the preceding discussion is still in its infancy, particularly in the case of developing countries. For developed countries, some empirical studies on the marginal cost of tax financing have been conducted using simulated experiments in which the government is *assumed* to follow certain courses of action. The marginal cost of the funds is then estimated using expressions derived from optimization exercises using highly simplified models, or costs are estimated using computable general equilibrium models under different assumptions about model parameters. Snow and Warren (1996) provide a general optimization model from which they deduce an expression for the marginal cost of funds. They then show that the best-known estimates for the US may be interpreted as special cases of the general model resulting from specific assumptions about government decisions and parameter values.

In the case of developing countries, case studies are also devoted to tax reform (Newbery and Stern, 1987; Ahmad and Stern, 1991), but pay little attention to the idea of estimating marginal welfare costs for a given tax and expenditure system to be used in cost–benefit analysis. A study aimed at improving cost–benefit analysis by introducing appropriate pricing of government funds would take the expected tax and expenditure system as given, since it would not be a 'control variable' for the project analyst, and would emphasize simplified, approximate measures of the marginal cost of alternative fiscal instruments. Those estimates would be confined to effects that are not project specific (like product-specific revenue effects), for which alternative simplified methods would also have to be devised. On the tax side, these studies should pay special attention to all costs involved in raising revenue, and take institutional constraints into account (Slemrod and Yitzhaki, 1996). Comparative applied studies using a common methodology would then allow the most important effects to be sorted out, and allow the formulation of country-specific approaches to estimate project specific revenue effects and the marginal cost of government financing of net fiscal effects. These studies should also shed some light on the implicit welfare functions guiding tax policy *in practice*, and contribute to unifying criteria on both the revenue and the expenditure sides of fiscal policy.

APPENDIX 5.1   A SIMPLE GENERAL EQUILIBRIUM DERIVATION

Given the welfare function used in Appendix 1.1, the problem of the government may be presented as that of maximizing welfare subject to a revenue constraint

$$R(t) - C(t) \leq R \tag{5.A1}$$

where t is a vector of tax rates, R is total revenue, and C is the monetary cost to the taxing authority of raising that revenue. Therefore, the optimizing government would maximize

$$\mathcal{L} = W[U^e(q_i^e)] - \lambda^r [R(t) - C(t)] \tag{5.A2}$$

Necessary conditions for that maximum are

$$\frac{\partial \mathcal{L}}{\partial t_i} = \frac{1}{N} \Sigma_e \frac{\partial W}{\partial U^e} \Sigma_i \frac{\partial U^e}{\partial q_i^e} \frac{\partial q_i^e}{\partial t_i} - \lambda^r [\frac{\partial R}{\partial t_i} - \frac{\partial C}{\partial t_i}] = 0 \tag{5.A3}$$

where λ^r is the marginal welfare of public revenue. Recalling that in equilibrium

$$\partial U^e_i / \partial q_i^e = \lambda^e p_i \tag{1.A3}$$

the consumer would make the marginal utility of q_i^e equal to the marginal cost of acquiring it, dividing both sides of (5.A3) by

$$(\partial W_t / \partial U^k_t) \lambda^k = W_k \lambda^k$$

using (1.A7), and rearranging, (5.A3) becomes

$$\frac{1}{N} \Sigma_e u^e \Sigma_i p_i \frac{\partial q_i^e}{\partial t_i} = \frac{\lambda^r}{W_k \lambda^k} - [\frac{\partial R}{\partial t_i} - \frac{\partial C}{\partial t_i}] \tag{5.A4}$$

Therefore, the marginal cost of public revenue expressed in the numeraire would be

$$\frac{\lambda^r}{W_k \lambda^k} = \frac{(1/N) \Sigma_e u^e \Sigma_i p_i (\partial q_i^e / \partial t_i)}{(\partial R / \partial t_i) - (\partial C / \partial t_i)} \tag{5.A5}$$

the per capita welfare change attributable to the changes in consumption caused by changing tax i per unit of net revenue. Note that in (5.A5) monetary costs of the tax authority are registered in the denominator, while the numerator registers all welfare costs of individuals including those derived from changes in factor supplies and the use of taxpayers' time for tax avoidance and tax evasion (Slemrod and Yitzhaki, 1996).

Expression (5.A5) implies that in an optimum situation the marginal cost of public revenue would be equal for all revenue instruments ($\lambda'_i = \lambda'_j = \lambda'$). In practice, however, different instruments may have different costs ($\lambda'_i \neq \lambda'_j$), and therefore there would be different marginal costs

$$\frac{\lambda'_i}{W_k \lambda^k} = \frac{(1/N) \, \Sigma_e \, u^e \, \Sigma_i \, p_i \, (\partial q^e_i / \partial t_i)}{(\partial R / \partial t_i) - (\partial C / \partial t_i)} \tag{5.A6}$$

associated with different taxes. Finally, and according to expressions (1.A12) to (1.A16), the effect of population size is the same for all shadow prices (and population change is captured in the discount rate). Thus, the shadow price of public funds (expression (5.3) in the text) would be

$$\frac{\lambda'_i}{W_k \lambda^k} = \frac{\Sigma_e \, u^e \, \Sigma_i \, p_i \, (\partial q^e_i / \partial t_i)}{(\partial R / \partial t_i) - (\partial C / \partial t_i)} \tag{5.A7}$$

Finally, $R = \Sigma_i \, p_i \, q_i \, t_i$, where $q_i = \Sigma_e \, q^e_i$. Therefore,

$$\partial R / \partial t_j = p_j \, q_j + \Sigma_{i \neq j} \, t_i \, [\partial(q_i \, p_i) / \partial t_j] \tag{5.A8}$$

Note that the numerator of expression (5.A7) is the weighted value of the consumption change, represented by the weighted sum of the compensating variations in (5.4), and that from the denominator the revenue increase may be expressed as $dR = (p_j \, q_j) \, dt_j + \Sigma_{i \neq j} \, t_i \, d(q_i \, p_i)$, which is the denominator of expression (5.4) when there are no additional monetary costs attributable to raising dR.

6. Produced Goods

The shadow prices for goods that are produced at the margin depend on the inputs required for their production and their respective shadow prices. This linkage structure between input coefficients, shadow prices of those inputs, and shadow prices of the outputs lends itself to the use of input–output techniques for estimating shadow prices of produced inputs. In fact many estimates have been conducted using these techniques. Earlier studies were prepared using existing input–output tables.[1] In these cases, the analysts were constrained by the aggregation level of the tables, which in many cases were inadequate for microeconomic analysis. In more recent studies, preference has been given to the preparation of an input–output table specifically for calculating shadow prices, allowing the analyst greater latitude in deciding aggregation and completeness with a view toward pricing requirements in cost–benefit analysis.[2]

This chapter starts with a presentation of the rationale for using input–output techniques to estimate *spr*s for marginally produced goods, providing a link between traditional demand and supply analysis and the preparation of an input–output table specifically for this use. The chapter illustrates the use of existing tables, as well as a more limited approach based on isolated cost structures, since the preparation of a specific input–output table would not always be possible.

6.1 THE RATIONALE FOR USING INPUT–OUTPUT TECHNIQUES

Input–output techniques are used to calculate the *spr* for those inputs whose additional demand is met by increasing production; that is, for those that are produced at the margin. The resulting *spr* may also be used to price consumption gains from saving resources, such as those resulting from vehicle operating cost savings in a road improvement project. The purpose of using

---

1. See Guerrero et al. (1977), Howard (1978), Schohl (1979), Tejada (1980), Weiss (1985). Powers (1981, Ch. 2) presents the methodology.

2. Scott, Macarthur and Newbery (1976), Hughes (1979a and 1979b), Londero (1981), Flament (1987), Mejía and Roda (1987), and Londero (1992).

input–output techniques is to capture backwards intersectoral effects. It consists of breaking down the users' cost of providing an extra unit in order to value the components at their respective *sprs*. Thus, it becomes necessary to know the long-run marginal cost at market prices of the good in question and the *spr* of the corresponding inputs. These *sprs* may be exogenous to the model, or be calculated from their own cost data and the *spr* of their inputs, and so on. In other words, the market value of the additional production is broken down in successive backwards steps along the output–inputs chain. In each backwards step, prices paid for the inputs may be broken down into the following four main categories:

1. The amount paid for inputs that are (assumed to be) diverted from alternative uses, since their supply is fixed with respect to small changes in demand (e.g. foreign exchange and skilled labor);[3]
2. The amount paid for unskilled labor, the supply of which is generally elastic with respect to small demand changes;
3. The value of transfers generated in the transactions (e.g. trade taxes or normative excess profits); and
4. Other inputs, the additional demand for which is met by additional production.

Thus, each step backwards along the intersectoral chain would result in a higher share of the market price expressed in nonproduced inputs (categories 1 and 2) and transfers (category 3), and a smaller share in produced inputs (category 4). The number of steps could be as high as required to make the residual in category 4 as small as desired; more formally, the residual tends to zero when the number of steps approaches infinity.

An example may help clarify the approach. The first row of Table 6.1 contains the composition of long-run marginal cost at market prices of providing $100 in additional value of production. This cost is broken down into $40 in additional production of inputs and $60 in nonproduced inputs and transfers. The $40 in marginally produced inputs may be further broken down into $10 in produced inputs and $30 in nonproduced inputs and transfers, and so on. After four rounds down the intersectoral chain, 95.5 percent of the original market value of $100 has been broken down into direct and indirect requirements of foreign exchange,[4] wages and taxes. Once the whole value at market prices has been decomposed, market values for foreign exchange, labor

---

3. Londero (1994) analyzes the case of an additional demand of foreign exchange leading to the additional production of exported or import-substituting goods.

4. In this chapter, foreign exchange is used to refer to foreign exchange expressed in the domestic currency at the prevailing exchange rate.

Table 6.1   *Break-down of a market price into its requirements of foreign exchange, nonproduced inputs, and transfers: iterative procedure*

	Produced inputs	Foreign exchange	Wages	Taxes	Market price
First round	40.0	35.0	20.0	5.0	100.0
Second round	10.0	22.0	7.0	1.0	40.0
Third round	2.0	5.0	3.0	—	10.0
Fourth round	0.5	0.7	0.6	0.2	2.0
Total after four rounds	0.5	62.7	30.6	6.2	100.0

and taxes may be expressed at efficiency prices, added up and expressed as a share of the market value.

Fortunately, the laborious iterative procedure of Table 6.1 may be avoided by using matrix algebra. To that effect, an input–output matrix with a sufficiently detailed classification of industries would be required, so as to be able to obtain *sprs* suitable for the pricing of project inputs and outputs. In order to present such a method, the relation between the marginal cost of good *j* and its market price may be stated as

$$\Sigma_i \Delta Q_{ij}\, p_i + \Sigma_h \Delta V_{hj}\, p_h \leq \geq \Delta Q_j\, p_j \qquad (6.1)$$

where:

$\Delta Q_{ij} =$ quantity of nontraded good or service *i* required to produce ΔQ_j additional units of good or service *j*

$\Delta V_{hj} =$ quantity of nonproduced input *h* ($h = 1, \ldots k$) required to produce ΔQ_j additional units of good or service *j*, or amount of transfers *h* ($h = k+1, \ldots m$) originating in the production of ΔQ_j (in which case $p_h = 1$).

Ideally, these marginal costs would be the present value of the additional costs attributable to increasing the production of *j* in ΔQ_j units; that is,

$$\Delta Q_{ij}\, p_i = PV(\Delta Q_{ijt}\, p_i)$$

$$\Delta Q_j\, p_j = PV(\Delta Q_{jt}\, p_j)$$

where *PV* indicates present value and *t* the period.[5] Thus, investment costs

---

5. Prices do not carry subscript *t*, since it is assumed that relative prices do not change over time.

would be included in $\Delta Q_{ij}\, p_i$ and in $\Delta V_{hj}\, p_h$. The costs of acquiring the produced inputs would be included in $\Delta Q_{ij}\, p_i$, while traded inputs would be broken down into foreign exchange (included in $\Delta V_{hj}\, p_h$), trade taxes and other produced inputs such as port handling, transport and commerce (included in the respective $\Delta Q_{ij}\, p_i$). Those present values would be calculated using the discount rate. Therefore, equation (6.1) may be written as an equality

$$\Sigma_i\,\Delta Q_{ij}\, p_i + \Sigma_h\,\Delta V_{hj}\, p_h + \Delta B_j = \Delta Q_j\, p_j \qquad (6.2)$$

where ΔB_j is the difference between the present market value of the additional production and the present value of long-run marginal costs at market prices. This difference will be called normative excess profits, and it will be positive (negative) when the internal rate of return *at market prices* is greater (smaller) than the discount rate.

Dividing both sides of (6.2) by ΔQ_j

$$\frac{\Sigma_i\,\Delta Q_{ij}}{\Delta Q_j}\, p_i + \frac{\Sigma_h\,\Delta V_{hj}}{\Delta Q_j}\, p_h + \frac{\Delta B_j}{\Delta Q_j} = p_j$$

The shadow price of j ($sp_j = spr_j\, p_j$) would be this long-run marginal cost valued at shadow prices; that is,

$$\frac{\Sigma_i\,\Delta Q_{ij}}{\Delta Q_j}\, p_i\, spr_i + \frac{\Sigma_h\,\Delta V_{hj}}{\Delta Q_j}\, p_h\, spr_h^v + \frac{\Delta B_j}{\Delta Q_j}\, spr_j^b = p_j\, spr_j$$

Thus, the shadow price ratio of j would be

$$\Sigma_i\,\frac{\Delta Q_{ij}\, p_i}{\Delta Q_j\, p_j}\, spr_i + \Sigma_h\,\frac{\Delta V_{hj}\, p_h}{\Delta Q_j\, p_j}\, spr_h^v + \frac{\Delta B_j}{\Delta Q_j\, p_j}\, spr_j^b = spr_j \qquad (6.3)$$

If coefficients for inputs, transfers and net benefits at market prices per unit value of additional production are independent of the magnitude of ΔQ_j, expression (6.3) may be presented as

$$\Sigma_i\, a_{ij}\, spr_i + \Sigma_h\, v_{hj}\, spr_h^v + b_j\, spr_j^b = spr_j \qquad (6.4)$$

where a_{ij}, v_{hj} are value coefficients of input or transfer per unit value of additional production, and b_j is normative excess profits per unit value of additional production. Expression (6.4) indicates that calculation of the *spr* of produced good or service j requires the *spr* of its produced inputs $i = 1, \ldots\, n$

as well as spr_h^v and spr_j^b. The *spr* of the produced inputs of good *j* would also have to be calculated from their respective equations (6.4). Thus, a complete system of equations (6.4) for all produced intermediate goods would be required. To that effect, and aiming at simplifying the notation, b_j and their corresponding *sprs* may be included under the common notation f_{hj} and spr_h^f, allowing the complete system of equations for the produced goods to be presented as

$$\Sigma_i\, a_{i1}\, spr_i + \Sigma_h f_{h1}\, spr_h = spr_1$$
$$\vdots$$
$$\Sigma_i\, a_{in}\, spr_i + \Sigma_h f_{hn}\, spr_h = spr_n$$

(6.5)

and in matrix form as

$$\mathbf{spr} = \mathbf{spr\ A} + \mathbf{spr^f\ F}$$ (6.6)

where
  spr = 1 × *n* vector containing spr_i (note that vector $[spr_i] = [spr_j]$)
  A = *n* × *n* matrix containing technical coefficients a_{ij}
  spr^f = 1 × *m* vector of *spr* for inputs and transfers assigned to $\mathbf{F} = [f_{hj}]$
Expression (6.6) allows vector **spr** to be presented as

$$\mathbf{spr} = \mathbf{spr^f\ F\ (I - A)^{-1}}$$ (6.7)

which may be interpreted as follows. From traditional input–output analysis it may be recalled that

$$[r_{ij}] = [\mathbf{I - A}]^{-1}$$

is the Leontief inverse, which provides total, direct and indirect, requirements of goods *i* required to produce an additional unit of *j*. By multiplying this matrix by **F**

$$\mathbf{F^*} = \mathbf{F\ [I - A]^{-1}}$$

the total produced input requirements are broken down into the corresponding total requirements of nonproduced inputs and transfers. Each element of the resulting matrix

$$f_{hj}^* = \Sigma_i f_{hj}\, r_{ij}$$

would be the sum of *h* requirements to produce the amount of *i* needed to increase j production in one unit value. Finally, $\mathbf{spr}^f \mathbf{F} [\mathbf{I} - \mathbf{A}]^{-1}$ gives those requirements at shadow prices, providing the long-run marginal costs at shadow prices as a proportion of the users' price (vector $\mathbf{spr}$). Therefore, each element of vector $\mathbf{spr}$ would be

$$spr_j = \Sigma_h \, spr_h^f f_{hj}^* \tag{6.8}$$

Calculations may be easily done on computers using spreadsheets (for small matrixes), by other commercial programs that perform matrix operations, or by programs specially designed for calculating *spr* (Londero and Soto, 1998; Lucking, 1993).

From a purely technical point of view, it would be desirable for input–output matrixes to be prepared on a commodity by commodity basis,[6] and valued at producers' prices.[7] The preparation of commodity by commodity matrixes, however, requires a large amount of resources, thus in practice they are frequently prepared on an industry by commodity basis. Similarly, valuing the matrix at producers' prices requires that detailed matrixes for distribution margins are available, and such is not normally the case; as a result, matrixes are frequently prepared at users' prices.

In summary, to estimate a set of *spr* it is necessary: (1) to prepare the matrix containing the cost structures of the *n* products involved; and (2) to estimate the *spr* for the *m* elements of matrix **F**. These *n* products will not cover the thousands of inputs involved in the input–output chain – less significant inputs may be aggregated into one or more composite inputs whose cost structures would be weighted averages of several cost structures for individual inputs.

6.2 A NUMERICAL EXAMPLE

Consider a simplified example where there are only three produced intermediate goods: machinery (1) and two current inputs (2) and (3). The cost structures for these goods are presented in Table 6.2. While all products utilize all others as inputs, elements on the principal diagonal of the **A** matrix (the a_{ii}) are nil, since own consumption has been deducted from total production. In order to produce, establishments also use foreign exchange (*fe*), labor (*w*), and pay import taxes (*t*). In sectors (1) and (2) there are no normative excess profits ($b_1 = b_2 = 0$), since market price equals long-run marginal cost, while in sector (3), a public utility, price is lower than long-run marginal cost

---

6. See Bulmer-Thomas (1982), and Londero (1990, 1999).

7. See Bulmer-Thomas (1982) and section 7.3 of this volume.

Table 6.2   Hypothetical input–output matrix

			Product	
Matrix	Input	(1)	(2)	(3)
	(1)	—	0.12	0.05
$[a_{ij}]$	(2)	0.27	—	0.14
	(3)	0.05	0.10	—
	fe	0.30	0.40	0.70
$[f_{hj}]$	*w*	0 35	0.35	0.20
	t	0.03	0.03	—
	b	—	—	-0.09
$\Sigma_i\, a_{ij} + \Sigma_h f_{hj}$	Total	1.00	1.00	1.00

$(b_3 < 0)$. Table 6.2 allows for system (6.7) to be presented as

$$[\text{spr}_1\ \ \text{spr}_2\ \ \text{spr}_3] = [\text{spr}_1^f\ \ \text{spr}_2^f\ \ \text{spr}_3^f\ \ \text{spr}_4^f] \begin{vmatrix} 0.3 & 0.4 & 0.7 \\ 0.35 & 0.35 & 0.2 \\ 0 & 0 & 0 \\ 0 & 0 & -0.09 \end{vmatrix} \begin{vmatrix} 1 & -0.12 & -0.05 \\ -0.27 & 1 & -0.14 \\ -0.05 & -0.10 & 1 \end{vmatrix}$$

$$\textbf{spr} \quad = \quad \textbf{spr}^f \qquad\qquad \textbf{F} \qquad\qquad (\textbf{I} - \textbf{A})^{-1}$$

To solve it, total requirements of foreign exchange, labor taxes and normative excess profits may be calculated first as $\textbf{F}^* = \textbf{F}\,(\textbf{I} - \textbf{A})^{-1}$, thus obtaining

$$\textbf{F}^* = \begin{vmatrix} 0.49 & 0.54 & 0.8 \\ 0.48 & 0.44 & 0.28 \\ 0.04 & 0.03 & 0.01 \\ -0.01 & -0.01 & -0.09 \end{vmatrix} = \begin{vmatrix} \textbf{fe}_j^* \\ \textbf{w}_j^* \\ \textbf{t}_j^* \\ \textbf{b}_j^* \end{vmatrix}$$

The reader may verify that for each sector (column) the sum of total requirements would be

$$\Sigma_h f_{hj}^* = fe_j^* + w_j^* + t_j^* + b_j^* = 1$$

Then, vector **spr** may be calculated according to expression (6.7). To that effect, consider that t and b are transfers with *spr* equal to zero, and assume that $sprfe = 1.1$ and $sprw = 0.4$. Thus

$$\mathbf{spr} = \mathbf{spr^f\ F^*} = [0.73\ \ 0.77\ \ 0.99]$$

For example, the *spr* for machinery produced by sector (1) results from

$$sprfe\ fe_1^* + sprw\ w_1^* + sprt\ t_1^* + sprb\ b_1^*$$

$$1.1 \times 0.49 + 0.4 \times 0.48 + 0 \times 0.04 + 0 \times (-0.01) = 0.73$$

In this case, the government receives tax revenue of 0.04 and grants a transfer of 0.01 to the purchaser of machinery through a price of input (3) lower than its long-run marginal cost. The final result shows that market price exceeds the efficiency cost by approximately 27 percent, due mainly to the difference between labor cost to the employer and the efficiency wage.

6.3 COST STRUCTURES FOR MARGINALLY PRODUCED GOODS

The availability of long-run marginal cost structures $[a_{ij}; f_{hj}]$ has been taken for granted so far. This section will start by briefly considering the data that it would be desirable to have in order to prepare those cost structures, and then discuss the data that are normally available.

It was mentioned at the beginning of this chapter that the columns of the input–output matrix should contain the difference between the present value of production costs attributable to supplying projection Q_{jt} of product j and the present value associated with projection $Q_{jt} + \Delta Q_{jt}$, that is,

$$[a_{ij}; f_{hj}] = [\frac{PV(\Delta Q_{ijt}\ p_i)}{PV(\Delta Q_{jt}\ p_j)}\ ;\ \frac{PV(\Delta F_{hjt}\ p_h)}{PV(\Delta Q_{jt}\ p_j)}]$$

where one of the F_{hjt} inputs (say F_{bjt}) captures the difference between the present value of sales and the present value of costs at market prices. Since costs in each year t include investment costs, F_{bjt} represents normative excess profits.

In practice, this approach can be used in few cases. One of them is electricity, where the existence of a planning process and the use of simulation models allow for a reasonable estimation of long-run marginal costs. In the majority of cases, however, a different method has to be used. A close substitute is to calculate the cost structures based on investment projects, which provide a good approximation to long-run marginal costs when the main effect of increasing demand is to bring forward such investment. The disadvantage in comparison with the preceding approach is that it fails to take into account the changes in the use of existing production capacity – changes that are taken into account by simulation models such as those used for planning electricity investments. The advantage in comparison with other procedures is that it permits a better estimation of investment costs and their composition.

Finally, the third alternative is to use cost structures prepared from current data originating in industrial censuses or surveys. These sources provide good data on current costs and sales, but are less reliable for estimating investment costs and their product composition.[8] That leads in practice to the use of the gross operating surplus as an approximation for the capital annuity, since in a *normal* year it may be expected that this surplus would be approximately equal to the capital annuity plus (minus) normative excess profits (i.e. those above the discount rate). For the good to be produced at the margin, the present value of sales (S_t) should be enough to cover capital costs (K_t), plus the present value of current costs including wages (C_t). If S_t is greater than C_t there would be normative excess profits (B); that is,

$$PV(S_t) = PV(K_t) + PV(C_t) + B \tag{6.9}$$

If present value coefficients for current costs are close to annual coefficients; that is, if

$$\frac{PV(C_t)}{PV(S_t)} \simeq \frac{C_t}{S_t}$$

then it follows that

$$\frac{PV(K_t) + B}{PV(S_t)} \simeq \frac{S_t - C_t}{S_t}$$

---

8. Some surveys request capital stock data. However, data provided correspond to the accounting valuation of the capital stock, which is affected by tax considerations and mismatches between inflation and asset revaluation procedures.

where $S_t - C_t$ is the gross operating surplus at market prices.[9]

The gross operating surplus may provide an approximation to the capital annuity, but does not help in breaking down that cost into at least traded and nontraded goods. Such a break-down may be estimated from secondary data (i.e. investment projects or surveys, see section 8.3) or performed according to the composition of broad aggregates. This latter method would blur the differences between industries and may lead to significant errors when there is special treatment, such as tariff exemptions, for some industries.

Another important aspect to take into consideration, already mentioned in discussing the shadow price of land, is that of taxes. Equation (6.9) is based on users' prices for the inputs and factory-gate prices for the outputs.[10] Thus, the gross operating surplus includes indirect taxes (net of subsidies) paid on the outputs, as well as direct taxes. Those taxes, however, are not taken into account by the private investor, who would calculate the present value of the after-tax profits. Thus, while it may be argued that the individuals' rate of discount, assuming it is unique, equals the *private* rate of profit, there would be a discrepancy between the total and the privately appropriated gross operating surplus. As a result, and in the absence of loan financing, the gross operating surplus would always exceed the capital annuity calculated at the private rate of discount. In other words, there would be normative excess profits in all industries made up from the amount of indirect taxes (net of subsidies) plus direct taxes.[11]

It may be argued that loan financing at a rate lower than the total rate of return may increase the rate of return on equity, closing the gap between the two rates of return. This line of argument, however, would also imply that there is a difference between the private rate of discount of some groups (those saving at the interest rate) and that of others (who invest only at higher rates), without adding anything with regard to the assumed equality between the rate of discount and the total rate of return.

Differences between the rate of discount and the marginal rate of return, for which there are other arguments, impose important changes in the way an efficiency analysis should be conducted. Briefly, a rate of return that exceeds the rate of discount implies that an extra unit of investment is more valuable

---

9. Lary (1968) compares estimates of the capital/labor ratios for US industries using both measures, and Balassa (1979) analyzes the orderings resulting from several alternative measures of capital intensity.

10. It could also be based on users' prices for the output if the same distribution costs charged to the outputs are also registered as costs to the industry, thus leaving the gross operating surplus at market prices unchanged.

11. Alternatively, it would have to be assumed that the social rate of discount exceeds the private one!

than an extra unit of consumption. Therefore, in order to express all costs and benefits in the same numeraire (consumption), units of investment (savings) attributable to the project should be valued using a shadow price ratio of investment funds.[12] Since marginal savings rates differ, frequently by income levels, such an approach requires estimating the distribution of costs and benefits generated by projects. These considerations are important, and the reader is encouraged to become familiar with them. However, they have been for the most part left out of this book, since they have received a detailed treatment in UNIDO (1972) and Londero (1987). Nevertheless, an effort has been made to present the derivation of formulae for shadow prices so as to facilitate the estimation of distributional effects.

6.4 PREPARING THE INPUT–OUTPUT TABLE

Traded Inputs

The building of an input–output matrix requires the preparation of the long-run marginal cost structures of supplying each of the m products involved. These cost structures are prepared according to how the additional demand is met. If the good is imported at the margin, the additional quantity would be supplied at a users' price p^u, made of the CIF price, tariffs t^m, indirect taxes t, and transport, commerce and other domestic distribution costs. Following the tradition of treating foreign exchange as a nonproduced input (i.e. ignoring the effects of additional demand for foreign exchange on the production of traded goods[13]), the cost structure of an imported good may be presented as in Table 6.3.

Foreign exchange normally accounts for a high percentage of total cost to the user. Therefore, the *spr* for an imported good may be estimated according to expression (6.3) if *spr*s for transport, commerce and other distribution costs are available from a shadow prices study. For that reason, input–output studies normally would not include the cost structures for imported goods in the input–output matrix. Exceptions may be made for traded inputs that are widely used, such as fuels or steel.

The case of an exported good is similar. The price paid for an additional unit may be broken down into the forgone foreign exchange due to reducing exports (FOB price), export subsidies no longer received (s^x), domestic export cost savings (transport, commerce, etc. $-dis^x$), indirect taxes charged on

---

12. See Marglin (1963a, 1963b), UNIDO (1972), and Londero (1987). The reader interested in the subject will greatly benefit from consulting Sen (1984, Part II).

13. Foreign exchange may be treated as a partially traded good. See Londero (1994).

Table 6.3   Schematic presentation of traded goods in the input–output matrix

Matrix	Input	Imported good	Exported good
	1	—	—
	.	.	.
	.	.	.
	.	.	.
$[A_{ij}]$	Transport	*tra*	*Δtra*
	Commerce	*com*	*Δcom*
	.	.	.
	.	.	.
	.	.	.
	n		
	1	—	—
	.	.	.
	.	.	.
	.	.	.
$[F_{hj}]$	Foreign exchange	p^{cif}	p^{fob}
	Trade taxes	t^m	s^x
	Indirect taxes	t	t
	.	.	.
	.	.	.
	.	.	.
	m	—	—

domestic transactions, and transport, commerce and other distribution costs incurred due to its domestic use (dis^d). Finally, the cost to the domestic user may be expressed as

$$p^u = p^{fob} + s^x - dis^x + dis^d$$

$$p^u = p^{fob} + s^x - \Delta dis$$

and included in the input–output table as presented in Table 6.3.[14]

As in the case of the imported good, *spr*s for transport, commerce, other

---

14. If the good were subject to an export tax, its users' price would be $p^u = p^{fob} - t^x + t + \Delta dis$.

domestic distribution costs, and foreign exchange would allow the analyst to estimate the *spr* of an exported good using equation (6.3) without the need to include a cost structure in the matrix.

Produced Inputs

Marginally produced inputs are the *raison d'être* for using input–output techniques, which provide a way of estimating the effects of additional production throughout the output–inputs chain. Consider the case of an input with a perfectly elastic supply, as presented in Figure 6.1. Since an additional demand would be met in full by increasing production, its cost structure needs to be included in the matrix. To that effect, the long-run marginal cost structure should be examined in order to classify the inputs and assign them to the **A** or **F** matrixes. In so doing, care should be exercised in keeping the size of the matrix manageable. As a result, only the most important inputs should be separately included, while the remaining ones can be pooled in one or more groups of 'other produced inputs'.

Even fewer traded inputs would merit a column in the matrix. The cost of most traded inputs may be classified into exported and imported and aggregated into two composite inputs, as in the case of nontraded inputs. However, better estimates would be obtained by breaking down each input into its foreign exchange, transfers and produced-input components, adding each type of expenditure separately, and including each sum in the column under the headings foreign exchange, transport, commerce, and so on.

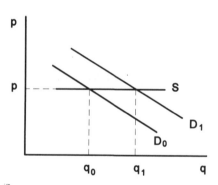

Figure 6.1 Marginally produced input

Chapter 8 and Appendix 8.1 describe the preparation of an input–output table for Colombia. Additional information on the Colombia study may be consulted in Cervini et al. (1990). Londero (1992) provides a detailed presentation on the preparation of input–output tables for this purpose.

Partially Produced Inputs

If the supply of an input is upwardly sloped (Figure 6.2); that is, the input is only partially produced at the margin, the fraction of the additional demand $(q_1 - q_d)$ that would be produced at the margin $(q_1 - q_0)$ needs to be estimated

and treated as explained for
marginally produced inputs. The
rest $(q_0 - q_d)$ would be withdrawn
from alternative uses that are not
willing to pay more than q_dBAq_0
for that quantity. This fraction
should be treated as an input in
fixed supply, implying that it
could be assigned to matrix **F** and
a conversion factor prepared
along the lines presented in
Appendix 6.1.

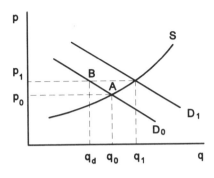

Figure 6.2 Partially produced input

Alternatively, if the market
price of the intermediate good is
considered a poor indicator of its efficiency value in alternative uses, if its
importance would merit the effort, and if the intermediate good were a direct
input to any consumption good, it could also be treated, although at a higher
cost, in the more specific manner presented in the Appendix 6.1 for the cases
of land and skilled labor.

Note that the split of the additional demand between increases in production
and reductions in consumption depends on demand and supply elasticities as
shown in Chapters 2 and 3. The more elastic the supply of q the smaller the
reduction in consumption would be. If supply is infinitely elastic, the good is
wholly produced at the margin. Conversely, if supply is totally inelastic the
additional demand is met fully by a reduction in alternative uses. This case was
presented in Chapter 4 in discussing land.

Partially Traded Inputs

An input is classed as partially traded when an additional demand for it is met
partially by increasing imports or reducing exports, and partially by increasing
its production or withdrawing it from alternative uses. This section will present
a few examples of partially traded goods and show how to treat them in the
input–output matrix. The presentation will ignore distributional aspects, since
they complicate the argument considerably. A more detailed presentation of
several examples of partially traded goods taking into account distributional
effects is provided by Londero (1996b).

Consider first the case of a profit-maximizing firm that is a monopolist in
the domestic market and a price taker in the international market. The
necessary condition for profit maximization is

$$y(q^d) = p^x = c(q^d + q^x)$$

where $y(q^d)$ is domestic marginal revenue, p^x is the export price received by the producer (export marginal revenue), and $c(q^d + q^x)$ is q's marginal cost.[15] Such is the case presented in Figure 6.3, where $LRMgC$ is the long-run marginal cost, p_0^d is the domestic price for demand D_0, p_1^d is the domestic price for demand D_1, and p^x is the export price. An additional demand $D_1 - D_0$ would result in a reduction in exports Δq^x and a withdrawal from alternative uses Δq^d due to the domestic price increase, fitting the definition of a partially traded good.

Note that in this case, even though it is a partially traded good, the domestic price at the margin does not depend on production costs, but on domestic demand and the export price. A cost increase would lead to a reduction in output without affecting the domestic price, which is determined by domestic marginal revenue and the export price. Also note that in this case the good is partially traded for demand increases, but exported at the margin for cost changes.

The input–output matrix needs to reflect both major effects. Ignoring the effects of the price change $p_1^d - p_0^d$ for the sake of simplicity, purchases by the project would be

$$\Delta q \, p^d = \Delta q^d \, p^d + \Delta q^x \, p^x + \Delta B$$

where $\Delta B = \Delta q^x \, p^d - p^x$ are normative excess profits. These expressions provide the information for preparing the column. First, $\Delta q^x \, p^x$ would be treated as if q were exported at the margin. Then, $\Delta q^d \, p^d$ would be treated as if q were an input in fixed supply, since this would also be a reallocation of domestic sales due to a price increase. Finally, normative excess profits ΔB are a transfer to the producer and would be assigned to the corresponding row in matrix **F**.

If the exported product were sold in a competitive domestic market, but producers faced an international demand that was less than infinitely elastic (Figure 6.3(b)), an increase in domestic demand $DD_1 - DD_0$ would result in a higher international price, and consequently in a higher domestic price as well. The additional domestic demand would be satisfied by reducing total consumption Δq^c and increasing domestic production Δq^s, where Δq^c is made up of a reduction in domestic consumption Δq^d and a reduction in exports $\Delta q^x = \Delta q^c - \Delta q^d$. In this case, the value of the additional purchases by the project may be presented as

$$\Delta q \, p = \Delta q^d \, p + \Delta q^s \, p + \Delta q^x \, p$$

---

15. Ferguson and Gould (1975, Ch. 9), and Henderson and Quandt (1971, Ch. 6) provide a more detailed analysis of profit maximizing conditions.

The additional domestic demand would also increase the international price, and thus the producers' export revenue in $\Delta p \ (q_0^x - \Delta q^x)$.[16] Therefore, the column should also include the additional foreign exchange revenue implicit in the additional export revenue

$$\Delta B = \Delta p \ (q_0^x - \Delta q^x)$$

which would be considered as additional exports, broken down accordingly,[17] and registered in the column with a negative sign. Finally, normative excess profits ΔB would be additional income for the producers. Thus, the column would reflect the expression

$$\Delta q \ p = \Delta q^d \ p + \Delta q^s \ p +$$

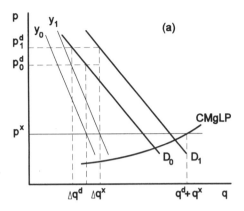

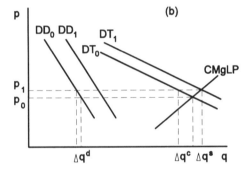

$\Delta q^x \ p - \Delta p \ (q_0^x - \Delta q^x) + \Delta B$ *Figure 6.3 Partially exported inputs*

and be made up of five transaction types: exported at the margin $\Delta q^x \ p$, produced at the margin $(\Delta q^s \ p)$, nonproduced at the margin $\Delta q^d \ p$, additional export revenue $[\Delta p \ (q_0^x - \Delta q^x)]$, and normative excess profits (ΔB).

The case of an imported good with a less than infinitely elastic international supply is similar (Figure 6.4). The additional demand $D_1 - D_0$ would bring about an increase in the international price, and consequently in the domestic one. The additional demand would be met by reducing domestic consumption Δq^d, increasing domestic production Δq^{sd}, and increasing imports $\Delta q^s - \Delta q^{sd}$. Each component corresponds to a different source and is thus associated with a different cost structure. Additionally, the demand increase raises the

---

16. Note that 'triangles' $\frac{1}{2} \Delta p \Delta q$ are ignored for the sake of simplicity.

17. Note that p is the price received by the producer, and it is therefore equal to the FOB price, minus export taxes and distribution costs.

domestic price by Δp. Part of this rise is an additional foreign exchange expenditure that may be included by recording the additional expenditure of consumers on imported goods

$$\Delta p \, (q_0^m - \Delta q^d - \Delta q^{sd})$$

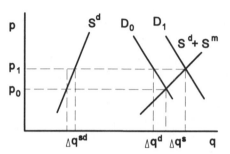

Consequently, the additional purchases by the project may be presented as

Figure 6.4 Partially imported input

$$\Delta q \, p = \Delta q^d \, p_1 - \Delta q^{sd} \, p_1 + \Delta q^m \, p_1 + \Delta p \, (q_0^m - \Delta q^d - \Delta q^{sd}) - \Delta B$$

where ΔB represents the transfer to those receiving the additional expenditure of the consumers. As in the preceding cases, the column in the matrix would record the five effects attributable to the additional demand. The first four have cost structures associated with them, while ΔB would be a transfer.

The case of the discriminating monopolist may be the most common case in practice. Partially traded goods resulting from an international demand or supply that is less than infinitely elastic may not be as common; the more elastic the international demand be (Figure 1.4), the smaller the effect on prices and the greater the share of the additional demand that would be met by reducing exports or increasing imports, respectively.

Finally, a domestically produced good may have very close substitutes that are traded, so that an increase in the demand for it brings about significant cross price effects that render the good partially traded. As a result, the additional demand may be met partially by an increase in its domestic production, and partially by an increase in imports (reduction in exports) of the close substitute. The ensuing column in the input–output table would thus indicate that an increase in demand is met by a weighted average of increasing production and imports (or reducing exports).

Conversion Factors

A conversion factor (cf) is the cost at shadow prices of providing a unit value of an additional basket of goods. Conversion factors may be calculated as a weighted average of the *spr*s of the goods making up the incremental basket, where the weights are the shares of each good q_i in the value (at users' prices p_i) of that basket; that is,

$$cf = \Sigma_i \, q_i \, p_i \, spr_i \quad (\Sigma_j \, q_i \, p_i = 1)$$

This approach assumes the availability of the spr_i, thus presenting two shortcomings: (1) it requires several calculations in addition to those needed to estimate the spr_i, calculations that increase with the number of cfs and with the number of goods comprising each basket; and (2) the existence of spr_i whose values depend on those of the cfs (such as those for investment and other nontraded intermediate goods) would require laborious iterative procedures in order to calculate both the sprs and the cfs. These complications may be avoided by including in the matrix a column that 'produces' the basket. Two alternative procedures may be used to that effect.

The first one consists of including in the matrix the cost structure for each of the goods comprising the basket, and an additional column, that of the cf, which demands inputs from the columns producing the goods according to the share of each good in the total value of the basket. Following the nomenclature used to define a cf, the elements of the column for the cf would be $q_i p_i = w_i$. For example, if additional investment in sector s consists of

Product	Value
Construction	0.20
Machinery	0.30
Equipment	0.40
Vehicles	0.10
Total	1.00

the matrix should include, for each of the four inputs, a column containing the corresponding cost structure. Say that numbers 7, 8, 9 and 10 correspond to the location of these columns (rows) in the matrix, then

$$w_{7s} = 0.20$$
$$w_{8s} = 0.30$$
$$w_{9s} = 0.40$$
$$w_{10s} = 0.10$$

would be the column for the investment cf for sector s. The main advantage of this method is in facilitating the updating of the cost structures of the goods included in the basket, as well as the composition of the basket. The main disadvantages are the manipulation of a larger matrix and the additional cost to prepare it.

The second method consists of including only one column for the cf containing the weighted average of the cost structures of products r comprising basket s, where the weights are the shares of each good in the value of basket s; that is, w_{rs}. The column for the cf may be expressed as vector

$$
\begin{vmatrix}
\Sigma_r \, w_{rs} \, a'_{1r} \\
\vdots \\
\Sigma_r \, w_{rs} \, a'_{nr} \\
\Sigma_r \, w_{rs} f'_{1r} \\
\vdots \\
\Sigma_r \, w_{rs} f'_{mr}
\end{vmatrix}
=
\begin{vmatrix}
a_{1s} \\
\vdots \\
a_{ms} \\
f_{1s} \\
\vdots \\
f_{ms}
\end{vmatrix}
\tag{6.10}
$$

where
a'_{ir}, f'_{hr} = value of inputs i or h used in producing a unit value of product r
a_{is}, f_{hs} = value of inputs i or h used in producing a unit value of basket s
Continuing with the example of the *cf* for sector s, assume that

		Construction $r = 7$	Machinery $r = 8$	Equipment $r = 9$	Vehicles $r = 10$
Input 4	a_{4r}	0.40			
Input 17	a_{17r}	0.05			
Input 18	a_{18r}		0.02	0.05	0.05
For. exchange	f_{1r}	0.05	0.98	0.95	0.80
Wages	f_{2r}	0.50			
Profits	f_{3r}				
Taxes	f_{4r}				0.15
Total		1.00	1.00	1.00	1.00

are the cost structures for the goods comprising the basket and

	Construction $r = 7$	Machinery $r = 8$	Equipment $r = 9$	Vehicles $r = 10$
w_{rs}	0.20	0.30	0.40	0.10

their respective weights. These data allow for the calculation of the column for the *cf* as:

	Construct.	Machinery	Equipment	Vehicles		cf_s
a_{4s}	0.20 × 0.40				=	0.080
a_{17s}	0.20 × 0.05				=	0.010
a_{18s}		0.30 × 0.02	0.40 × 0.05	0.10 × 0.05	=	0.031
f_{1s}	0.20 × 0.05 +	0.30 × 0.98 +	0.40 × 0.95 +	0.10 × 0.80	=	0.764
f_{2s}	0.20 × 0.50				=	0.100
f_{3s}						
f_{4s}				0 10 × 0 15	=	0.015
Σ	0.20	0.30	0.40	0.10	=	1.000

where a_{is} and f_{hs} represent the value of produced inputs i and nonproduced inputs h required to produce the unit investment basket of sector s. This method reduces the size of the matrix and the time to prepare it as long as data are processed by computer, but correcting and updating the matrix becomes difficult if there is not easy access to computing capacity.

6.5 NONPRODUCED INPUTS IN THE INPUT–OUTPUT TABLE

When an input–output table is available, total requirements of nonproduced inputs and transfers may be calculated as

$$\mathbf{F}^* = \mathbf{F} (\mathbf{I} - \mathbf{A})^{-1} \tag{6.11}$$

The results obtained by calculating (6.11) will look like data presented in Table 6.4. The first column may be considered representative of a marginally imported good, the second of a marginally produced good that is being subsidized (negative transfers) and that yields a by-product in fixed supply (negative entry for goods in fixed supply, i.e. a supply increase),[18] and the third one of a marginally exported good subject to an export tax.

The next step would be to revalue these total requirements at shadow prices; that is, to estimate vector $\mathbf{spr}^f$ and calculate $\mathbf{spr}^f \mathbf{F}^*$. That involves estimating *spr*s for foreign exchange, different types of labor, and goods in

---

18. For a discussion of by-products and their identification, see Londero (2001).

Table 6.4   Total unit-value requirements of nonproduced inputs and transfers

	Product		
Input	1	2	3
Foreign exchange	0.600	0.300	1.150
Trade taxes	0.200	0.030	-0.230
Indirect taxes	0.016	—	0.018
Other transfers	—	-0.050	—
Skilled labor	0.060	0.234	0.020
Unskilled labor	0.050	0.180	0.017
Goods in fixed supply	—	-0.014	—
Gross operating surplus at market prices	0.074	0.320	0.025
Total	1.000	1.000	1.000

fixed supply, as presented in Chapters 2, 3 and 4.[19] The resulting *spr*s would be the ratios of shadow to market prices, and each should correspond to the price to be corrected such that $spr_j \, p_j = sp_j$.

If the market price implicit in spr_j were to differ from p_j, we would not obtain shadow price sp_j as a result. Therefore, special care should be taken to ensure that relative prices in the matrix are (approximately) the same as the prevailing ones; that is, those prices used to value inputs and outputs in the financial statements of the projects. Otherwise, relative prices in the matrix would have to be corrected first. This subject will be considered in section 7.4.

Once the matrix is valued at the proper prices, attention should be focused on the spr_h^f, which should also correspond to the prevailing relative prices. Thus, estimates in the consumption numeraire require the *sprfe* to include possible differences between the prevailing and the equilibrium exchange rate. The real exchange rate implicit in the *sprfe* should be the same as the one implicit in the market prices of goods and services to be valued at shadow prices, and the same one used to value the transactions recorded in the matrix. Otherwise, the matrix would have to be revalued first in order to record

---

19. The issue of calculating and pricing fiscal effects is omitted for the reasons presented in Chapter 5.

transactions at the same real exchange rate implicit in the *sprfe* and in the market prices of goods and services to be valued at shadow prices. Section 7.4 provides an example of such repricing of the input–output table, and section 8.5 shows how it was done in the case of Colombia.

When foreign exchange valued at the official exchange rate – and for *given* taxes, subsidies and other trade restrictions or incentives – is used as the unit of account or numeraire, its *spr* is, by definition, equal to one. Here, attention should also be given to the matching between the prevailing real exchange rate and that implicit in the value of matrix transactions. If the official exchange rate differs from the equilibrium one, the shadow price ratio of foreign exchange used to express other shadow prices in the foreign exchange numeraire should include that effect, as shown by formulae (2.5) and (2.6). Otherwise, foreign exchange valued at the equilibrium exchange rate would be implicitly assumed as the numeraire, in which case total requirements $\mathbf{F}^*$ would have to be corrected for the ratio between the equilibrium and the exchange rate implicit in matrix transactions.[20]

Transfers are valued according to the interpersonal distributional value judgements and according to the assumption regarding the discount rate and the marginal rate of return at efficiency prices. In efficiency analysis, as long as the rate of discount equals the marginal rate of return at efficiency prices, the efficiency value of transfers is equal to zero, since someone's gain is somebody else's loss.

Skilled labor tends to be very scarce in developing countries. For that reason, it is normally assumed to be in fixed supply, and willingness to pay for such labor (cost to the employer) is taken as a good approximation for its opportunity cost at market prices. Thus, only those market prices need to be corrected. However, since skilled labor would be withdrawn from many different places, with *spr*s above and below one, opportunity cost at market prices may be taken as equal to opportunity cost at efficiency prices in the consumption numeraire (or equal to its market value divided by the *sprfe* in the foreign exchange numeraire). A similar approach may be followed with other widely used inputs in fixed supply, such as land. If willingness to pay is not deemed to be a good estimate of opportunity cost at efficiency prices (in the consumption numeraire), an *spr* may have to be estimated according to the lines presented in Appendix 6.1.

Unskilled labor markets are more likely to show significant differences between costs to the employer and opportunity costs at market prices, as well as differences between submarkets such as formal versus informal, and manufacturing versus agricultural, preventing the formulation of simple rules.

---

20. For an example, see Parot (1992) where the matrix was revalued in order to value transactions at the prevailing (equilibrium) exchange rate.

The analyst must start from an understanding of how these markets work and how they interrelate, for which the approach of Chapter 3 should be useful.

With regard to the gross operating surplus, for most sectors it may be accepted as approximately equal to the capital cost annuity as long as the investment rate is assumed to be the desired one; that is the rate of discount equals the efficiency marginal rate of return of investment and, consequently, shadow price ratios of investment are equal to one.[21] In such a case, total requirements of gross operating surplus may be revalued at shadow prices using an investment conversion factor, since it covers investment requirements in many different sectors.

There are situations in which the gross operating surplus should not be accepted as approximately equal to the capital cost annuity. That could be the case for public utilities such as water or electricity, where tariffs could be significantly below the long-run marginal costs at efficiency prices. Here, capital costs would have to be estimated and normative excess profits would have to be imputed as residuals, as represented by the example of Table 6.2. Section 8.3 shows how this approach was applied in the case of Colombia.[22]

In other cases the analyst may consider that the land annuity should be treated separately, along the lines presented in Chapter 4. A detailed approach to the treatment of land as a fully nonproduced and as a partially produced input is presented in Appendix 6.1.

Some elements of vector $\mathbf{spr}^f$ may in turn be a function of one or more spr_j, the values of which are themselves results of the calculation. This would be so, for example, for conversion factors that have been included as columns of the matrix and are also used to calculate an spr_h. In these instances, the system may be solved by iteration.[23] The system is initially solved for proxy values of the endogenous $sprf_h^c$ (e.g. those cf that are also elements of vector $\mathbf{spr}^f$), in order to obtain a first approximation to those $sprf_h^c$. These values are in turn used to replace the original proxies and the process is repeated until the results converge to a final vector $\mathbf{spr}$ when vector $\mathbf{spr}^f$ obtained in the solution equals that used in order to obtain it (see Londero and Soto, 1998).

---

21. When the assumption of optimal rates of investment is deemed to be incorrect, and consequently differences between the rate of discount and the efficiency rate of return are to be expected for most sectors, a different approach should be followed. As mentioned at the end of section 5.4, such an approach will not be considered here, since it has been discussed in detail in UNIDO (1972) and Londero (1987).

22. Also see Londero (1981, pp. 292-302), Flament (1987, Sections 3.6 and 3.7), and the case studies presented in Londero (1992).

23. For an alternative proposal, see Lucking (1993).

6.6   USING EXISTING INPUT–OUTPUT TABLES

The preparation of an input–output table specifically for microeconomic applications, including shadow prices, requires the availability of data to prepare the cost structures and a significant commitment of resources. For that reason, a number of studies have opted to use the columns of existing standard input–output tables. Let $\mathbf{A} = [a_{ij}]$ be the square coefficient matrix containing the transactions between domestic sectors, and $\mathbf{F} = [f_{hj}]$ the coefficient matrix registering the purchases of imported inputs (normally broken down into foreign exchange and trade taxes), payments to labor, and gross operating surplus.[24] The method consists of classifying the sectors in the matrix in produced (p) and traded (t) at the margin, and reordering them in a way that allows for the matrix to be partitioned as follows:

$$
\begin{vmatrix}
\mathbf{A}^{pp} & \mathbf{A}^{pt} \\
\mathbf{A}^{tp} & \mathbf{A}^{tt} \\
\mathbf{F}^{p} & \mathbf{F}^{t}
\end{vmatrix}
\tag{6.12}
$$

where superscripts ij indicate sales of sector type i to sector type j. Thus, $\mathbf{A}^{pp}$ contains the transactions between marginally produced sectors.

Three basic approaches may be followed starting from the partitioned matrix. The first approach would be to replace the cost structures of the domestically produced, but marginally traded goods by the composition of the equivalent import or export prices. Then, calculations would simply be made applying expression (6.7). The resulting **spr** vector would provide the shadow price ratios for both marginally produced and marginally traded sectors.

In order to prevent the project analyst from falling for the temptation of using these *spr*s of traded sectors to price traded inputs at the project level, a second approach may be followed. This consists of decomposing the value of the domestically produced, but marginally traded goods (elements of $\mathbf{A}^{tp}$) into foreign exchange, taxes, and domestic expenditures in marginally produced goods and services (e.g. commerce and transport margins). These costs could be aggregated by component and assigned to the corresponding columns in the

---

24. There are other methods of presenting input–output tables (e.g. a matrix for imported inputs), which can normally be transformed into that presented here. When the table does not distinguish between domestically produced and imported inputs, there may be problems with using it for calculating shadow prices, unless such a breakdown can be obtained from secondary sources.

A^{pp} and F^p matrixes in order to obtain matrixes $\widehat{A^{pp}}$ and $\widehat{F^p}$. Then, vector **spr** providing the spr_j for marginally produced goods can be calculated using expression (6.7); that is, $\mathbf{spr^p} = \mathbf{spr^f}\ \widehat{F^p}\ (I - \widehat{A^{pp}})^{-1}$.

The third approach consists of keeping matrix A^{tp} and calculating spr_i for the traded goods exogenously or through an iterative procedure. Starting from (6.12), the vector $\mathbf{spr^p}$ may be expressed as

$$\mathbf{spr^p} = \mathbf{spr^p}\ A^{pp} + \mathbf{spr^t}\ A^{tp} + \mathbf{spr^f}\ F^p \tag{6.13}$$

where $\mathbf{spr^t}$ is the vector containing the spr for the domestically produced but marginally traded inputs. From (6.13), the vector for the marginally produced goods may be calculated as

$$\mathbf{spr^p} = \mathbf{spr^t}\ A^{tp}\ (I - A^{pp})^{-1} + \mathbf{spr^f}\ F^p\ (I - A^{pp})^{-1} \tag{6.14}$$

Note that this is equivalent to defining matrix **B** and vector $\mathbf{spr^b}$

$$
B = \left|\begin{array}{c} A^{tp} \\ --- \\ F^p \end{array}\right|
\qquad
\mathbf{spr^b} = \left|\begin{array}{c} \mathbf{spr^t} \\ ---- \\ \mathbf{spr^f} \end{array}\right|
$$

and calculating

$$\mathbf{spr^p} = \mathbf{spr^b}\ B\ (I - A^{pp})^{-1} \tag{6.15}$$

The method for calculating individual spr'_i would depend on whether the original table is valued at producers' or at users' prices. If the table is valued at producers' prices, transactions in the A^{tp} matrix would be valued at prices equal to the corresponding import or export prices; that is,

$$p^m = oer\ p^{cif}\ (1 + t^m)(1 + t) \tag{6.16}$$

$$p^x = oer\ p^{fob}\ (1 - t^x - \delta^x)(1 + t) \tag{6.17}$$

where t^m and t^x are *ad valorem* trade-tax rates, t is the indirect tax rate on domestic transactions, and δ^x is the domestic export costs (e.g. transport from plant to export port, port handling) expressed as a proportion of the FOB price. Note that equation (6.17) assumes that export sales do not pay indirect taxes. The spr'_i for transactions a^{tp}_{ij} are calculated as the ratios of the shadow to the market prices. In the case of the imported goods, the *spr*s would be

$$spr_i^t = (spfe\ p^{cif}) / [oer\ p^{cif}\ (1 + t^m)(1 + t)]$$

$$spr_i^t = sprfe / [(1 + t_i^m)(1 + t)]$$

In the case of the marginally exported goods, it is normally assumed that the producer sells to the domestic and foreign markets at the same basic price; that is, receives the same net revenue per unit sold.[25] The basic price of the export sale would be

$$p^x = oer\ p^{fob}\ (1 - t^x - \delta^x)$$

The basic price for the domestic sale would be the producer price net of the indirect taxes affecting domestic transactions

$$p^b = p^p / (1 + t)$$

Therefore, if both prices are equal

$$p^p = oer\ p^{fob}\ (1 - t^x - \delta^x)(1 + t)$$

Consequently, the expression for the *spr* would be

$$spr_i^t = \frac{spfe\ p^{fob} - oer\ p^{fob}\ \delta^x\ spr_{dis}}{oer\ p^{fob}\ (1 - t^x - \delta^x)(1 + t)}$$

$$spr_i^t = \frac{sprfe - \delta^x\ spr_{dis}}{(1 - t^x - \delta^x)(1 + t)}$$

where spr_{dis} is the shadow price ratio for those distribution costs included in the FOB but not in the producers' price. Note that calculation of spr_i^t requires spr_{dis}, which would in turn be a result of calculating expression (6.15). This is an example where the iterative procedures referred to in section 6.5 would be used.

If the foreign exchange numeraire were to be used, the *spr* for the marginally traded goods would simply be

---

25. It may be argued that assuming that the producer sells at the same basic prices and that the gross operating surplus at market prices equals the capital cost annuity is inconsistent. Achieving consistency may require a review of the assumption regarding the capital cost annuity. See section 6.3.

$$spr'_i = 1 \, / \, [(1 + t'^m_i)(1 + t)]$$

$$spr'_i = \frac{1 - \delta^x \, spr_{dis}}{(1 - t^x - \delta^x)(1 + t)}$$

where spr_{dis} would also be calculated in that numeraire.

If the input–output table were valued at users' prices, the corresponding equivalent prices for the marginally imported and exported goods would be

$$p^m = oer \, p^{cif} \, [1 + t^m + \delta^m + (1 + t^m) \, t] \tag{6.18}$$

$$p^x = oer \, p^{fob} \, (1 - t^x - \delta^x)(1 + t) + oer \, p^{fob} \, \delta^d) \tag{6.19}$$

where δ^m and δ^d are the domestic distribution margins expressed as a fraction of the CIF and FOB prices, respectively.[26] In these cases, the corresponding *spr* in the consumption numeraire would be

$$spr'_i = \frac{sprfe + \delta^m \, spr_{dis}}{[1 + t^m + \delta^m + (1 + t^m) \, t]}$$

$$spr'_i = \frac{sprfe - (\delta^x - \delta^d) \, spr_{dis}}{(1 - t^x - \delta^x)(1 + t) + \delta^d}$$

and using foreign exchange as the unit of account it would be

$$spr'_i = \frac{1 + \delta^m \, spr_{dis}}{[1 + t^m + \delta^m + (1 + t^m) \, t]}$$

$$spr'_i = \frac{1 - (\delta^x - \delta^d) \, spr_{dis}}{(1 - t^x - \delta^x)(1 + t) + \delta^d}$$

where spr_{dis} would be also simultaneously obtained in the corresponding numeraire.

---

26. Note that distribution margins are normally available as a proportion of the producer price, rather than of the CIF or FOB price.

6.7   ESTIMATING *SPRS* WITHOUT AN INPUT–OUTPUT TABLE

When input–output techniques cannot be applied, the same logic implicit in the input–output method may still be used, although in a more limited manner, by decomposing the value of the inputs backwards. The method would require the cost structures of those inputs for which *sprs* are to be calculated, in order to classify the inputs as traded t, produced i and nonproduced h. Thus,

$$\Sigma_t \, a_{tj} + \Sigma_i \, a_{ij} + \Sigma_h f_{hj} \tag{6.20}$$

Traded inputs may be decomposed into foreign exchange, taxes and trade and distribution margins. Once all traded inputs have been decomposed, component totals may be obtained

$$\Sigma_t \, a_{tj} = \Sigma_t \, a_{tj} f_{ht} + \Sigma_t \, a_{tj} \, a_{it} \tag{6.21}$$

and substituted in expression (6.20) in order to obtain the cost composition of good j

$$\Sigma_t \, a_{tj} + \Sigma_i \, a_{ij} + \Sigma_h f_{hj} = \Sigma_i \, (a_{ij} + a_{it} \, a_{tj}) + \Sigma_h \, (f_{hj} + f_{ht} \, a_{tj}) \tag{6.22}$$

Then the foreign exchange component would be multiplied by the *sprfe*, taxes by zero, and marginally produced components by *sprs* calculated as explained below; that is,

$$spr_j = \Sigma_i \, (a_{ij} + a_{it} \, a_{tj}) \, spr_i + \Sigma_h \, (f_{hj} + f_{ht} \, a_{tj}) \, spr_h$$

In the case of inputs that are produced at the margin and for which there are significant differences between market prices and long-run marginal costs at efficiency prices, estimates of the composition of those long-run marginal costs would be desirable in order to estimate the corresponding normative excess profits, and allow for one round of backward cost decomposition.[27]

$$1 = \Sigma_i \, a_{ij} + \Sigma_h f_{hj} + b_j \tag{6.23}$$

Then, the above described procedure, synthesized by equation (6.22), may be used to transform this cost composition into a basket of inputs in fixed supply, foreign exchange, trade taxes, skilled and unskilled labor wages, gross operating surplus and marginally produced inputs. Normative excess profits would be multiplied by zero. Foreign exchange and trade taxes would be

---

27. In highly integrated industrial structures, more than one round of backward decomposition may be needed to obtain a good estimate.

priced as mentioned earlier for the case of traded goods, and those wages for which there are significant differences between the cost to the employer and the shadow price may be revalued by estimating the corresponding *sprs*. Finally, market values for the gross operating surplus, produced inputs, and the remainder of wages may be accepted as approximations for their shadow prices in the consumption numeraire.

This approximation may be used to calculate *sprs* and *cfs* for widely used marginally produced inputs, such as transportation, commerce, electricity, water, cement.[28] The gathering of data for this type of estimation would facilitate a later estimation using more sophisticated methods.

6.8   SOME EMPIRICAL RESULTS

This section provides information about the results of detailed studies for Colombia, Panama and Venezuela and compares the corresponding results. The comparison has the advantage that all three studies were based on preparing input–output tables specially for estimating shadow prices, followed the same methodology, and were conducted under a common direction (Londero, 1992), although differences in the available data and in the reading of that data by the individual authors are of course present.[29]

When input–output techniques are used, shadow price ratios are calculated as

$$spr_j = \Sigma_h \, spr_h^f f_{hj}^*$$

This formula shows the two main intermediate results to focus on: the composition of the total primary input content, and the shadow price ratios of those primary inputs. In order to provide an idea of the differences between countries, Table 6.5 summarizes these data for the countries being compared.

With regard to primary input content, the results have been grouped in a way that facilitates the comparison, since the classification used in each study was determined primarily by the nature of the primary input markets. As it would be expected, the foreign exchange content of Colombian manufactures is lower and the trade tax content higher. Venezuelan wage content is lower, reflecting its more capital intensive manufacturing sector.[30] Finally, the value for *Other* primary inputs in Venezuela is negative and relatively high due to

---

28. Mejía (1989) applied this approach in the Dominican Republic.

29. For a review of other input–output studies, see MacArthur (1994).

30. See Londero and Teitel (1996), and Parot (1998).

Table 6.5   Summary information on sprs *from three studies*

	Colombia	Panama	Venezuela
Average primary input content of manufactures[a]			
Foreign exchange	0.209 (0.083)	0.357 (0.118)	0.387 (0.110)
Trade taxes	0.074 (0.037)	0.035 (0.015)	0.022 (0.026)
Unskilled labor, rural	0.024 (0.045)	0.015 (0.036)	0.011 (0.025)
Unskilled labor, urban	0.154 (0.050)	0.101 (0.043)	0.100 (0.037)
Skilled labor	0.164 (0.054)	0.192 (0.064)	0.098 (0.027)
Gross operating surplus	0.386 (0.086)	0.255 (0.079)	0.470 (0.094)
Other	-0.011 (0.014)	0.045 (0.083)	-0.088 (0.046)
Shadow price ratios for primary inputs			
Foreign exchange	1.18	1.21	1.08
Unskilled labor, rural	1.00	0.60	1.00
Skilled labor, rural	1.00	1.00	1.00
Unskilled labor, urban	0.60 - 0.46[b]	0.60	0.55
Semiskilled labor, urban	0.49 - 0.41[b]	0.80	0.55
Skilled labor, urban	1.00 - 0.87[b]	1.00	1.00
Gross operating surplus[c]	0.87	0.97	1.00
Shadow price ratios for manufactured inputs[d]			
Average $(\bar{x})$	0.808	0.935	1.037
Dispersion (σ)	0.031	0.072	0.041
Coefficient of variation	0.038	0.077	0.040
Maximum	0.921	1.042	1.196
Minimum	0.720	0.619	0.917
$spr \le \bar{x} - \sigma$	28 12.6	9 13.4	6 8.7
$\bar{x} - \sigma < spr \le \bar{x} - \frac{1}{2}\sigma$	42 18.9	5 7.5	7 10.1
$\bar{x} - \frac{1}{2}\sigma < spr \le \bar{x}$	56 25.2	12 17.9	22 31.9
$\bar{x} < spr \le \bar{x} + \frac{1}{2}\sigma$	39 17.6	19 28.4	23 33.3
$\bar{x} + \frac{1}{2}\sigma < spr \le \bar{x} + \sigma$	25 11.3	15 22.4	4 5.8
$\bar{x} + \sigma < spr$	32 14.4	7 10.4	7 10.2
Number of cases	222 100.0	67 100.0	69 100.0

Notes: [a] Standard deviations in parentheses. [b] The lowest value corresponds to industries with high benefits (section 8.7). [c] Value of the investment conversion factor; for Colombia this is the investment conversion factor for manufactures. [d] In Venezuela it excludes oil refineries.

Source: Londero (1992).

the transfers implicit in public enterprise prices for energy sources and for oil-refined products used as inputs by other manufactures.

With regard to the *sprfe*s, the one for Panama is higher than that for Colombia, despite the average import taxes being lower. The apparent inconsistency is explained by the fact that in Colombia the average export subsidy is lower than the average import tax, and by the exclusion of exports from the calculation in Panama because most exports, particularly those of services, were considered to be very inelastic to price.[31] Two of the three *sprfe*s, those for Colombia and Venezuela, include a correction for differences between the prevailing and the equilibrium exchange rates, and in both cases these differences were of a significant magnitude.

Shadow prices for unskilled labor reflect employment and underemployment levels, the extent and nature of labor legislation, and union power. In Venezuela, rural unemployment is low and in certain areas labor was imported at the margin during peak periods. In Panama, rural unemployment and underemployment was higher, probably because high urban unemployment discourages rural–urban migration (Harberger, 1971); that, together with some effects of labor legislation on rural wages explains the low *spr*s. In Colombia, the large rural-urban migrations had already taken place, and in some rural areas there seems to be great competition for labor, particularly during peak periods; these characteristics and the fact that rural wages are market determined explain the high value of the *spr* for unskilled rural labor.

Due to the importance of oil for the level of economic activity and the composition of total output, in Venezuela there would be a set of long-run equilibrium prices (and thus efficiency prices) for each oil price level. Urban employment levels are directly linked to the value of oil exports, and an increase in that value would increase investments, urban unemployment would decline, and *spr*s would increase.

Differences in investment conversion factors are explained primarily by traded capital goods. In Venezuela and Panama, capital goods pay relatively low taxes, but in Venezuela a higher foreign exchange content of the conversion factor compensates for the lower *sprfe*.

The average *spr*s for manufactured goods are significantly different. The Venezuelan results are higher mainly due to the effect of high subsidies on energy sources and other oil derivatives used as inputs, as well as a higher conversion factor of investment used to value the total requirements of gross operating surplus. Panama's averages are higher than those of Colombia mainly due to higher *spr*s for foreign exchange and labor, as well as a higher

---

31. Since then, financial, trade and capital flows liberalization in many countries of Central and South America may have increased that elasticity.

conversion factor for investment.

Dispersions of *spr* values around the mean are relatively low, particularly in Colombia and Venezuela. These low dispersions may lead to the conclusion that it may not be necessary to derive detailed estimates by industries, and that it is sufficient to calculate an average conversion factor for manufactured inputs instead. A numerical example, however, shows that small differences in the values of *spr*s may have significant effects on project results.

Consider cost and benefit flows at shadow prices shown as *Flows A* in Table 6.6, and assume that average *spr*s for the inputs and outputs are both approximately equal to the average *spr*. The resulting internal rate of return is 10 percent, and the benefit–cost ratio for a 10 percent rate of discount is obviously equal to one. Assume now (*Flows B*) that the average *spr* for the inputs is 3.5 percent lower than that for the outputs, a difference perfectly possible from the results of Table 6.6. That seemingly small difference would lead to a 16 percent difference in the internal rate of return and an 8 percent difference in the benefit–cost ratio.

Table 6.6 *Hypothetical project flows valued at shadow prices*

	IRR	B/C	Year 0	1	2	3	4	5	6	7–11
Flows A										
Investments			-100.00	-90.00	—	—	—	—	-30.00	—
Current costs			—	—	-30.00	-70.00	-95.00	-100.00	-100.00	-100.00
Revenue			—	—	42.54	99.26	134.71	141.80	141.80	141.80
Balance	10.0%	1.00	-100.00	-90.00	12.54	29.26	39.71	41.80	11.80	41.80
Flows B										
Investments			-100.00	-90.00	—	—	—	—	-30.00	—
Current costs			—	—	-28.95	-67.55	-91.68	-96.50	-96.50	-96.50
Revenue			—	—	42.54	99.26	134.71	141.80	141.80	141.80
Balance	11.6%	1.08	-100.00	-90.00	13.59	31.71	43.04	45.30	15.30	45.30

APPENDIX 6.1 INPUTS IN FIXED SUPPLY AND PARTIALLY PRODUCED GOODS

Say that skilled labor (s) and land (N) are deemed to be in fixed supply, and the analyst wants to price them specifically. There are two classical solutions. The first is to treat these inputs as being in fixed supply; that is, assign the coefficient to matrix **F**, create a column for a conversion factor prepared along the lines described below, and solve the system iteratively (Londero and Soto, 1998). A second solution would be to treat skilled labor and land *as if* they were produced at the margin by assigning their coefficients to the **A** matrix, opening a row for consumption in matrix **F**, and building columns containing the cost compositions of each of the specific conversion factors.

The cost compositions of these conversion factors may be calculated starting from a consumption conversion factor prepared according to (6.10), and presenting the value of the fixed supply coefficients, say skilled labor and land, as

$$a_{sc} = 1 - \Sigma_{i \neq s}\, a_{ic} + \Sigma_{h \neq s,N} f_{hc}$$

$$a_{Nc} = 1 - \Sigma_{i \neq N}\, a_{ic} + \Sigma_{h \neq s,N} f_{hc}$$

(6.A1)

where c represents the consumption basket, and the index i now includes land and skilled labor. In words, withdrawing a_{sc} of skilled labor reduces consumption in one unit, but releases other produced inputs by $\Sigma_{i \neq s}\, a_{ic}$ (including the land coefficient) and other nonproduced inputs by $\Sigma_{h \neq s,N} f_{hc}$. Therefore, from (6.A1) the cost structures of skilled labor and land when treated as fully in fixed supply would be

$$\Sigma_i\, a_{is} + \Sigma_h f_{hs} = (1/a_{sc}) - \Sigma_{i \neq s}\, a_{ic}\,/\,a_{sc} + \Sigma_{h \neq s,N} f_{hc}\,/\,a_{sc} = 1$$

$$\Sigma_i\, a_{iN} + \Sigma_i f_{hN} = (1/a_{Nc}) - \Sigma_{i \neq N}\, a_{ic}\,/\,a_{Nc} + \Sigma_{h \neq s,N} f_{hc}\,/\,a_{Nc} = 1$$

(6.A2)

where coefficients $1/a_{sc}$ and $1/a_{Nc}$ are assigned as demands to the consumption row in matrix **F** to indicate the consumption loss. When estimates are based on the consumption numeraire, the consumption row will be multiplied by an *sprf*$_h$ of one; when working in the foreign exchange numeraire its *sprf*$_h$ would be equal to $1/sprfe$.

If land were partially produced, as suggested in section 4.2, the land coefficient will represent a demand from a column containing the cost structure of producing and withdrawing land from alternative uses,

$$(dN_a\,/\,dN)(\Sigma_i\, a_{iN} + \Sigma_h f_{hN}) + (dN_{fs}\,/\,dN)$$

(6.A3)

where dN_a is the share of additional demand met by incorporating additional land, dN_{fs} is the share withdrawn from alternative uses ($dN_a + dN_{fs} = dN$). Coefficient dN_{fs} / dN is assigned to the row in matrix $\mathbf{F}$ that will be converted to efficiency prices using the conversion factor by solving the system iteratively (Londero and Soto, 1998).

Alternatively, if the additional demand for land is partially met by incorporating new land and partially by withdrawing land from alternative uses, the land coefficient a_{Nj} would have to be split in two according to the shares of the two sources in meeting the additional demand. The first coefficient would demand from a column containing the cost of incorporating land, and this column would be similar to the cost structure of any produced good. The second coefficient would demand from a column prepared according to equation (6.A2) in order to represent the withdrawal of land from alternative uses.

Equations (6.A2) and (6.A3) are specific to skilled labor and land, with the underlying idea that it is very different to affect the production of land intensive goods than it is to affect the production of skilled-labor intensive ones. However, there may be cases when there are other inputs in fixed supply and only a general conversion factor for withdrawing inputs in fixed supply is desired. In that case, a cf to correct the willingness to pay for these inputs could be calculated. As in the preceding case, the demand for the inputs in fixed supply could be assigned to matrix $\mathbf{F}$ and the system solved iteratively, or assigned to matrix $\mathbf{A}$ and demand from a column registering the loss of consumption and the value of the released resources resulting from the reduction in the supply of the input in fixed supply. Say that the cost composition linking the market value of one additional unit of consumption and its long run marginal cost is

$$1 = \Sigma_{i \in fs}\, a_{ic} + \Sigma_{i \notin fs}\, a_{ic} + \Sigma_h f_{hc} \qquad (6.A4)$$

where inputs in fixed supply $i \in fs$ are specified separately from the produced inputs and the other nonproduced inputs that have been assigned to matrix $\mathbf{F}$. Then, the value of the inputs in fixed supply would be

$$\Sigma_{i \in fs}\, a_{ic} = 1 - \Sigma_{i \notin fs}\, a_{ic} + \Sigma_h f_{hc} \qquad (6.A5)$$

and the cost structure for the conversion factor would be

$$1 = (1/\Sigma_{i \in fs}\, a_{ic}) - \Sigma_{i \notin fs}\, a_{ic} / \Sigma_{i \in fs}\, a_{ic} + \Sigma_h f_{hc} / \Sigma_{i \in fs}\, a_{ic} \qquad (6.A6)$$

where the coefficient $1/\Sigma_{i \in fs}\, a_{ic}$ would be assigned to the consumption row in matrix $\mathbf{F}$.

Either one of these approaches may also be used in the case of partially produced goods presented in section 6.4, where an additional demand for the input was partially met by withdrawing units from other uses, while the other part was met by increasing production.

7. Using and Updating Shadow Prices

7.1 PRICING PROJECT OUTPUTS

An investment project may be conceived of as a flow of additional input uses in order to obtain a certain output flow. Outputs are generally few and their markets are usually analyzed in greater detail during project preparation. For these reasons, their pricing is often done by applying cost–benefit methods at the level of each individual output.[1] In this section, a brief presentation will be provided on pricing project outputs under different scenarios, with emphasis on the use of existing *sprs*.

Traded Outputs

If the project substitutes for imports, it is important that the substituted imports are valued on a comparable basis with domestic production. The methodologically correct approach is to conduct the analysis at the prices actually paid by the users. In such a case, both domestic and import prices may have to be complemented by the corresponding distribution margins in order to estimate the net effect attributable to the substitution. The users' price of the imported product may be represented by

$$p^{mu} = p^{cif} + t^m + t + dis^m \tag{7.1}$$

where p^{cif} is the CIF price, t^m is the import tax, t is the indirect tax on domestic sales, and dis^m is the domestic distribution cost. The corresponding price for the domestic production would be

$$p^u = p^f + dis \tag{7.2}$$

where superscript f indicates the factory-gate price and dis is the distribution costs for the domestically produced good. If domestic and import users' prices are equal, from (7.1) and (7.2) the factory-gate price would be

$$p^f = p^{cif} + t^m + t + dis^m - dis \tag{7.3}$$

---

1. See, *inter alia*, Gittinger (1982), Londero (1987, Chs. 4 and 7), and Mishan (1988).

Thus, the efficiency value of the per unit resource savings attributable to the substitution of imports, or efficiency price of the substituted import, would be

$$sp^m = p^{cif} sprfe + (dis^m - dis) spr_{dis}$$

the efficiency value of the foreign exchange savings, plus that of any net distribution cost savings. The *spr* for these distribution cost savings can normally be obtained from a study on shadow prices. Even though users' prices are the appropriate level for comparison, in practice incremental costs ($dis^m - dis$) are frequently ignored on the assumption that they are insignificant.

When the project exports directly, and as long as transportation and other export related costs, such as port handling or trading services, have been charged to the project, the efficiency price would be the FOB price multiplied by the *sprfe*. If export costs have not been charged to the project, the output would be valued at factory-gate prices, in which case the corresponding efficiency price would be

$$sp^{xf} = p^{fob} sprfe - oc^x spr_{oc}$$

where oc^x is the transportation and other export costs.

When the project sells its output in the domestic market, but it is expected that other producers will increase their exports by an equivalent amount without affecting the domestic price, the factory-gate price to the exporters would be

$$p^{xf} = p^{fob} - t^x - oc^x \tag{7.4}$$

where it is implicitly assumed that export sales do not pay indirect taxes. The corresponding domestic price would be

$$p^{xu} = p^{xf} + dis^x = p^{fob} - t^x - oc^x + t + dis^x \tag{7.5}$$

where *t* is the indirect taxes levied on domestic sales, and dis^x is distribution costs associated with sales to the domestic market. The project would sell to domestic users at price

$$p^u = p^f + dis^d \tag{7.6}$$

Thus, as long as the domestic price remains unaffected ($p^u - p^{xu} = 0$), from equations (7.5) and (7.6) the factory-gate price would be

$$p^f = p^{fob} - t^x - oc^x + t + dis^x - dis^d \tag{7.7}$$

and the corresponding efficiency price would be

$$sp = p^{fob}\, sprfe - oc^x\, spr_{oc} + \Delta dis\, spr_{dis} \qquad (7.8)$$

That is, the efficiency value of the additional foreign exchange, minus the export costs, plus the net saving of domestic distribution costs. Normally, Δdis would be close to zero and the efficiency value would equal the case where the project exports directly. However, for example, if reductions in transportation costs are expected ($\Delta dis > 0$) – for example due to the location of the project – the benefits associated with transport cost savings should be included and valued at their efficiency price using the corresponding spr.

Nontraded Outputs Treated as Traded

There are cases in which the project's output is not exported directly, but the additional supply results in additional exports in a readily identifiable manner. For example, cattle are normally not exported, but refrigerated beef may be. In such a case, the preferred approach for pricing cattle would be to start from the FOB price of beef and work backwards to the farm-gate price of cattle, which may be represented as the FOB price of beef, minus the export tax, minus all the processing slaughtering costs, plus the value of all other joint products:

$$\text{farm-gate price of cattle} = p^{fob} + ojp - t^x - slg - oc$$

where t^x is export taxes, ojp is other joint products of the slaughterhosue, slg is slaughtering and refrigerating costs, and oc is transport, commerce and other export related costs. The efficiency price would then be

$$\frac{\begin{array}{l} p^{fob} \times sprfe \\ + spr_{ojp} \times ojp \\ - spr_{slg} \times slg \\ + spr_{oc} \times oc \end{array}}{\text{farm-gate } sp \text{ for cattle}}$$

where spr_{ojp}, spr_{slg} and spr_{oc} are, respectively, the shadow price ratios for the other joint products, the slaughtering and refrigeration costs, and the other export costs.

If refrigerated beef were imported, its domestic users' price p^{mu} would be

$$p^{mu} = p^{cif} + t^m + t + rs + dis^m$$

where p^{cif} represents the CIF price, t^m the tariff, t the indirect tax on domestic sales, *rs* the refrigerated storage, and *dis^m* the other distribution costs. The corresponding users' price for domestically produced beef would be

$$p^u = p^c + slg - ojp + dis$$

where *p^c* is the domestic price of cattle, *slg* is the slaughtering cost, *ojp* is the value of the other joint products, and *dis* is the distribution cost. If prices for imported and domestically produced beef are equal (i.e. $p^{mu} = p^u$), then

$$p^c = p^{cif} + t^m + t + rs + dis^m - slg + ojp - dis$$

Consequently, the shadow price of cattle at the farm-gate level would be

$$
\frac{
\begin{aligned}
& sprfe \times p^{cif} \\
& + spr_{ojp} \times ojp \\
& + spr_{rs} \times rs \\
& - spr_{slg} \times slg \\
& + spr_{dis} \times (dis^m - dis)
\end{aligned}
}{\text{farm-gate } sp \text{ for cattle}}
$$

since not only would there be foreign exchange savings due the substitution of imports of refrigerated beef, but also an additional supply of joint products, refrigerated storage would be saved, additional slaughtering costs would have to be incurred, and there would be net transport, commerce and other distribution costs.

In practice, it is unlikely that the *spr* for slaughtering, refrigeration or the joint products would be known. Estimates of shadow prices very seldom reach such a level of detail. However, these *spr*s may be estimated following the method proposed in section 7.3.[2]

Strictly Nontraded Outputs

In practice, it is often the case that some agricultural and industrial by-products are in fixed supply. For example, it is likely that an increase in the demand for hides would have no effect on slaughtering, which is primarily determined by the price of beef (see Londero, 2001). As a result, the most likely impact of an additional demand for hides would be an increase in price that would redistribute the available quantity among competing uses. If the project

---

2. If many projects involving the same outputs or inputs are expected to be appraised, the possibility of preparing sector-specific *spr*s may be considered.

increases the supply of a consumption good in fixed supply – $(f_1 - f_0)$ in Figure 7.1(a) – the efficiency value of the additional supply would be simply the willingness to pay for the additional quantity.[3]

If the project increased the supply of an intermediate good in fixed supply, it would be consumption of other goods that use this intermediate good as an input that would increase – $(a_1 - a_0)$ in Figure 7.1(b). The value of these additional consumption goods, minus the corresponding incremental costs (excluding the input in fixed supply), all at shadow prices, would be the shadow value for the input in fixed supply. For example, if the good represented in Figure 7.1(b) were a consumption good, the *spr* for the input in fixed supply would

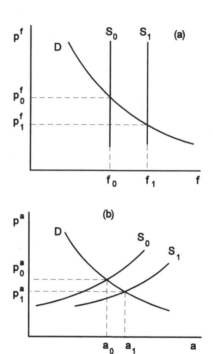

Figure 7.1 Increase in the supply of an input in fixed supply

have, in the denominator, the consumers' willingness to pay for the additional consumption $a_1 - a_0$, minus the market value of the additional resources used (other than the input in fixed supply), and in the numerator the corresponding value at shadow prices.[4] If the industries using inputs in fixed supply are few and easily identifiable, it may be practical to calculate a *cf* to correct the willingness to pay for $f_1 - f_0$. A method to that effect was presented in Appendix 6.1.

In the great majority of cases where input–output techniques are used, goods and services are assumed to be in perfectly elastic or totally inelastic supply, which is a result of the complexities associated with capturing both production and reallocation effects. If the supply of the project's output is upwardly sloped (Figure 7.2), the efficiency value of the project's additional supply $q_1 - q_s$ would be the sum of the efficiency values of the resource

3. Or that willingness to pay divided by the *sprfe* in the case of the foreign exchange numeraire.

4. Only a sector-specific input–output table would allow such detailed pricing.

savings of the replaced production $q_0 - q_s$ (area below S_0 between q_s and q_0) and the additional availability $q_1 - q_0$. Resource savings associated with $q_0 - q_s$ may be priced using a *cf* reflecting the ratios of efficiency to market prices of the saved resources. If the project produces a consumption good, the additional availability $q_1 - q_0$ would be valued at the corresponding willingness to pay; if it were an intermediate good, instead, the preferred conversion factor would

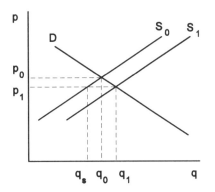

Figure 7.2 Increase in the supply of a nontraded good

be one similar to that described for the case of inputs in fixed supply.

7.2   PRICING PROJECT INPUTS

The number of project inputs would normally exceed that of project outputs by a considerable margin, and feasibility studies generally would not include market studies for project inputs because of three main reasons. First, the difference between market and efficiency prices of an individual input would normally not have a decisive role in the final result of the appraisal. Second, because of the artificial separation between project preparation and project appraisal, since often the information for the main project inputs is available or it has been gathered as part of the preparation process. Finally, because of the cost of doing those market studies.

Traded Inputs

Traded inputs are normally not included in studies for estimating shadow prices. This is to avoid an unmanageably large input–output table but, more importantly, because traded inputs are easily priced following the approach presented in the preceding section for traded outputs once the structure of the domestic price is known and *spr*s for foreign exchange and domestic distribution costs are available. For example, if equation (7.1) describes the composition of the users' price of an imported input, its efficiency price would be

$$p^e = p^{cif} \, sprfe + dis \, spr_{dis}$$

where *sprfe* and spr_{dis} are the shadow price ratios for foreign exchange and distribution margins, respectively. Therefore, the *spr* for the imported input would be

$$spr = \frac{p^e}{p^u} = \frac{p^{cif} \, sprfe + dis \, spr_{dis}}{p^{cif} + t^m + t + dis} \tag{7.9}$$

The same approach would allow the formulation of an *spr* for the users' price of an exported input. From equations (7.7) and (7.8), that *spr* would be

$$spr = \frac{p^{fob} \, sprfe - oc^x \, spr_{oc} + \Delta dis \, spr_{dis}}{p^{fob} - t^x - oc^x + t + \Delta dis} \tag{7.10}$$

Nontraded Inputs

Pricing inputs is simple when market prices used to value inputs are the same as those used to calculate the *spr*. If input *i* purchased by project *k* (Q_{ik}) is valued at market price p_i, so that total purchases are $A_{ik} = Q_{ik} \, p_i$, the corresponding value at shadow prices is obtained by multiplying the value of the purchase by the corresponding *spr*; that is,

$$A_{ik} \, spr_i = Q_{ik} \, p_i \, \frac{sp_i}{p_i} = Q_{ik} \, sp_i$$

In practice, the correspondence between the market price that needs to be corrected and the available *spr* may not be perfect; that is, it may not be the same price. This is due not only to aggregation discrepancies between shadow price studies and project detail, but also to differences in the distribution margins included. However, detailed estimates like the one presented in Chapter 8, where the input–output table was tailor-made to the needs of estimating *spr*s, would provide *spr*s that can be used at project level because they are very specific and because distribution margins would not differ substantially from those included in feasibility studies. Nevertheless, methods of correcting for different distribution margins are presented in section 7.3.

Using Conversion Factors

Many studies on shadow prices provide estimates of *conversion factors*. Recalling from Chapter 6, a conversion factor (*cf*) is the ratio between the value of a basket of goods at shadow prices and the value of the same basket at market prices. For example, an investment conversion factor is the quotient of the shadow price value of a basket of investment goods – normally comprising construction, machinery, and equipment – and the value of that basket at market prices. The composition of the basket is normally defined by the analyst based on the expected use of the *cf* either in the estimation itself, or in project work. For example, in some studies the investment conversion factor is used to convert *total* requirements of gross operating surplus from market to shadow prices (see section 8.8). Therefore, the conversion factor should reflect the average composition of investment in those sectors. Due to their lack of specificity, *cf*s should be avoided as much as possible at the project level, since their use may lead to results significantly different from those obtained using a more detailed, item by item, valuation.

7.3 USING SHADOW PRICES TO CALCULATE MORE

The *spr* required by the project analyst may not always be available. That may be due to the coverage of the existing study (it is impossible to include all goods), to lack of specificity in the case of an input representing a high share of total cost, or to significant differences between the distribution margins assumed in the study and those paid by the project. In those cases, a good *spr* study should provide the analyst with the critical inputs required to produce his or her own estimate. This section will address these situations.

Aggregation Problems

Despite all efforts at producing input–output tables with the lowest possible level of aggregation, and consequently highly specific *spr*s, these *spr*s would inevitably refer to a basket of products. This lack of specificity is due to the existence of secondary production, to the constraints imposed by the 'statistical confidentiality' of the data, and to the fact that there are limits to matrix size imposed by resource availability.[5] As a result, a specific spr_j may correspond to a basket that is not sufficiently specific for a very important input. In such a case, if the input cost structure is available, a more specific *spr* may be calculated as

$$spr_j = \Sigma_i \, spr_i \, a_{ij} + \Sigma_h \, spr_h f_{hj} \qquad (7.11)$$

where the spr_i and the spr_h would be obtained from the original study. The same procedure may be used when a better approximation to the desired cost

---

5. It is normally expected, however, that products making up the basket would have similar cost structures.

structure becomes available after the main study has been completed.

When equation (7.11) needs to be applied to a large number of products, simple matrix procedures may be used. Say that there are k products not included in the original study for which *sprs* are needed. The cost structures of these k products may be arranged in matrix form so that their rows are the same as the original matrix. Say that matrix

$$\left| \begin{array}{c} \mathbf{C} \\ -- \\ \mathbf{U} \end{array} \right.$$

contains these cost structures. Then

$$\mathbf{spr}^k = \mathbf{spr\ C} + \mathbf{spr}^f\ \mathbf{U} \qquad (7.12)$$

would provide the *sprs* of the additional products. This matrix procedure may be extended if further insight into the sources of the differences between market and shadow prices is desired. From expressions (6.7) and (7.12)

$$\mathbf{spr}^k = \mathbf{spr}^f\ \mathbf{F}^*\ \mathbf{C} + \mathbf{spr}^f\ \mathbf{U} = \mathbf{spr}^f\ (\mathbf{F}^*\ \mathbf{C} + \mathbf{U}) \qquad (7.13)$$

where matrix $(\mathbf{F}^*\ \mathbf{C} + \mathbf{U})$ provides the total requirements of nonproduced inputs and transfers for the k additional products. A computer program to implement this method is provided by Londero and Soto (1998). The approach represented by equation (7.13) may also be used to reduce the size of the matrix that needs to be inverted, by excluding products that are not inputs of those that are included. A practical application is shown in section 8.2.

Same Costs, Different Prices

It is common for certain inputs to have different prices for different buyers, despite the fact that costs are equal. In such a case, it is not necessary to increase the size of the matrix in order to include the two (or more) cost structures for the same input. Starting from the *spr* for one of the prices, $spr^1_j = sp_j\,/\,p^1_j$, the *spr* for the other prices may be obtained by multiplying the former by the ratio between the prices; that is

$$spr^2_j = spr^1_j\ \frac{p^1_j}{p^2_j} = \frac{sp_j}{p^1_j}\ \frac{p^1_j}{p^2_j} \qquad (7.14)$$

It may be concluded that it is very important for the original estimate to specify the price used to prepare the cost structure.

Different Distribution Costs

Most input–output estimates of *sprs* would refer to users' prices; that is, those including indirect taxes associated with selling the output as well as distribution costs required to reach the purchaser. When estimates are based on existing input–output tables, the analyst is constrained by the price level used to prepare the table. Tailor-made input–output tables, on the other hand, tend to be priced at the wholesale level and register average margins, since that is how transactions between establishments would be valued in the cost structures. This is probably also how most inputs would be valued in project accounts.

At project level, however, there may be cases when distribution margins differ considerably from those implicit in the *sprs*. For example, the project may purchase inputs at factory-gate prices and transport these inputs with its own trucks, situations that would require *sprs* at producers' prices. This is considered in the following section. It may also be the case that access to the project site is difficult, as a result of which transport costs differ significantly from those implicit in the *sprs*. Moreover, it may be that the mode of transportation to be used will be different. In such cases, it may be advisable to adjust the existing *spr*. Two alternative ways may be followed to that effect.

One approach would be to decompose project purchases into producers' prices and distribution margins. Then existing *sprs* may be revalued at producers' prices and used to value project inputs net of distribution costs, which would be priced separately. The next section discusses the revaluing of *sprs* from users' to producers' prices.

The second approach consists of calculating a new *spr* at the project-specific users' prices. Defining the new users' price p''_j as

$$p''_j = p^u_j - dis^u_j + dis''_j \tag{7.15}$$

where dis^u_j is the old distribution margin and dis''_j is the new one, the new *spr''*_j would be[6]

$$spr''_j = \Sigma_i (p^u_j/p''_j) \, a_{ij} \, spr_i + \Sigma_h (p^u_j/p''_j) f_{hj} \, spr_h -$$

$$spr^u_{dis} \, dis^u_j/p''_j + spr''_{dis} \, dis''_j/p''_j \tag{7.16}$$

---

6. For a demonstration see Appendix 7.1.

An analytical understanding of the sources of the difference between spr''_j and spr''_j would allow the economist to determine whether the cost of effecting the correction is justified. Defining

$$spr''_{dis} = spr''_{dis}(1 + ß)$$

the ratio between the *spr*s yields

$$\frac{spr''_j}{spr''_j} \cdot \frac{p''_j}{p''_j} = -[1 + \frac{(p''_j - p''_j)\, spr''_{dis}}{p''_j} \cdot \frac{ß\, dis''_j}{spr''_j} + \frac{ß\, dis''_j}{p''_j} \cdot \frac{spr''_{dis}}{spr''_j}] \qquad (7.17)$$

If the product's *spr* equals that of the distribution margin, which in turn equals the *spr* of the new margin ($ß = 0$), the ratio between the spr_j would be equal to one. Finally, if both spr_{dis} are equal (i.e. $ß = 0$), and therefore the difference is just one of the size of the margin, the ratio of the two *spr*s would depend only on the ratio of spr''_{dis} to spr''_j, and it would be greater the greater the ratio between the margins.

Shadow Price Ratios at Users', Producers' and Basic Prices

In most cases, *spr*s calculated at users' prices would be used. There may be situations, however, where *spr*s at producers' prices may be needed. To that effect, this section shows how to calculate producers'-price-based *spr*s from a set of *spr*s that were calculated at users' prices. Say that p''_j is the users' price of j and p''_j its producers' price. Then,

$$p''_j = p''_j + tra_j + com_j \qquad (7.18)$$

where tra_j and com_j are j's transport and commerce margins, assumed to be the only sources of difference between producers' and users' prices. Then, the spr_j at users' prices would be

$$spr''_j\, p''_j = spr''_j\, p''_j + spr_{tra}\, tra_j + spr_{com}\, com_j$$

where
spr''_j = shadow price ratio of j at users' prices
spr''_j = shadow price ratio of j at producers' prices
spr_{tra} = shadow price ratio for transport
spr_{com} = shadow price ratio for commerce

Finally, spr^p_j may be obtained as[7]

$$spr^p_j = \frac{spr^u_j - spr_{tra}\,(tra_j/p^u_j) - spr_{com}\,(com_j/p^u_j)}{p^p_j/p^u_j} \tag{7.19}$$

From a practical point of view, it is important to know when the effort to change the base for calculating the *spr* is justified. To that effect, equation (7.19) allows for the ratio between both *spr*s to be calculated. Then, replacing p^p_j by expression (7.18) gives

$$\frac{spr^p_j}{spr^u_j} = \frac{1 - spr_{tra}/spr^u_j\,(tra_j/p^u_j) - spr_{com}/spr^u_j\,(com_j/p^u_j)}{1 - (tra_j/p^u_j) - (com_j/p^u_j)} \tag{7.20}$$

The impact of changing the base for calculating an *spr* from users' to producers' prices depends on the ratio between the *spr* of the product and those of the distribution margins, and it would be smaller the smaller those margins are.

In contrast with the change from users' to producers' prices, in the case of *spr* at efficiency prices, moving from producers' to basic prices does not affect costs, but only the reference price.[8] Thus, following expression (7.14), the *spr* at basic prices would be $spr^b_j = spr^p_j\,(p^p_j\,/\,p^b_j)$; that is,

$$spr^b_j = \frac{spr^u_j - spr_{tra}\,(tra_j/p^u_j) - spr_{com}\,(com_j/p^u_j)}{p^b_j/p^u_j} \tag{7.21}$$

Expressing the basic price of *j* with reference to its users' price

$$p^b_j = p^u_j - t_j - tra_j - com_j$$

the ratio between the *spr*s at basic and users' prices would be

$$\frac{spr^b_j}{spr^u_j} = \frac{1 - spr_{tra}/spr^u_j\,(tra_j/p^u_j) - spr_{com}/spr^u_j\,(com_j/p^u_j)}{1 - (t_j/p^u_j) - (tra_j/p^u_j) - (com_j/p^u_j)} \tag{7.22}$$

---

7. Londero and Soto (1998) provide a computer program for converting a total requirements matrix **F** from one price level to the other.

8. This statement assumes a shadow price ratio of public funds equal to one. See Chapter 5.

The preceding expression shows that in this case the ratio between the two *spr*s would also depend on the indirect tax rate (net of subsidies) as a proportion of the users' price (t_j/p_j^u). Thus, a moderately high tax rate would be enough to justify a significant difference between the *spr* at users' (or producers' prices) and that at basic prices. This is important, since in some countries the government purchases at prices net of indirect taxes.

7.4   UPDATING THE ESTIMATES

As time goes by, estimates of shadow prices for produced goods become less accurate due to changes in *physical* input–output coefficients originating in changes in operational efficiency and technical change, changes in basic relative prices (e.g. the wage-to-exchange-rate ratio), changes in the prices of goods and services determined by the public sector – and, consequently, subject to policy induced changes – changes in the traded or nontraded classification of products due to import substitution or the initiation of exports at the margin or, finally, due to changes in commercial policy that drastically alter the classification between traded and nontraded goods. This section will be devoted to analyzing the effects of these events on the matrix and the approaches that may be used to try to correct for such effects.

Changes in Physical Coefficients

Changes in physical coefficients take place slowly over time. The most important changes are those originating in the introduction of new production techniques that significantly change the input structure, such as the case of substitution of machines for labor, or of plastic for metallic parts. These effects are less significant in a conventional I–O table based on average costs, since the effects of technical change are diluted by the averaging with other existing establishments using the traditional techniques. A matrix to estimate shadow prices, instead, may be significantly affected since it is based on *marginal* costs. From an analytical point of view, however, the solution to changes in physical coefficients is clear: whenever the accumulated changes reach the point of significantly affecting the results, a new matrix has to be prepared. From a practical point of view, until a new matrix is available, the best solution is to keep the old matrix as it is, and for those products most affected to calculate new *spr*s using the new cost structure. This would avoid errors in projects that use such inputs directly.

Changes in Basic Relative Prices

Changes in basic prices, for example an increase in the wage-to-exchange-rate ratio, would affect relative prices between traded and nontraded goods, as well as the relative prices between nontraded goods, increasing those with a higher labor to output ratio. If price indexes for all activities in the matrix are available, and assuming that physical coefficients are not affected, the matrix may be price-updated by calculating

$$\mathbf{A}^n = \hat{\mathbf{z}} \, \mathbf{A} \, \hat{\mathbf{z}}^{-1}$$

$$\mathbf{F}^n = \hat{\mathbf{z}}^f \, \mathbf{F} \, \hat{\mathbf{z}}^{-1}$$

(7.23)

where superscript n indicates the new relative prices, $\mathbf{z}$ is the vector containing the price indexes for matrix activities (columns), $\mathbf{z}^f$ is the vector containing the price indexes for the nonproduced inputs and transfers, and the circumflex indicates that vectors have been transformed into diagonal matrixes. Then, spr_h estimates would be reviewed to adjust them to the new relative price situation, and a new spr could be calculated as

$$\mathbf{spr}^n = \mathbf{spr}^{fn} \, \mathbf{F}^n \, (\mathbf{I} - \mathbf{A}^n)^{-1}$$

(7.24)

It is important to review estimates of spr_h^f when basic relative prices change. The relative price change may be due to a temporary appreciation of the domestic currency; that is, a prevailing exchange rate that is below the equilibrium real exchange rate for a given protection level. In such a case, the *sprfe* should incorporate the new ratio of the equilibrium to the current exchange rate. Otherwise, it would underestimate the true one since market prices would correspond to the current exchange rate (see section 2.3).

In practice, however, sectoral price indexes will rarely be available for most sectors of the matrix, making it necessary to use an alternative procedure. If price indexes for nonproduced inputs are available, the input–output price model may be used to estimate vector $\mathbf{z}$ in equation (7.23) assuming that physical coefficients remain unchanged and cost changes are transferred through prices maintaining a constant gross operating surplus coefficient. These assumptions allow for z_j to be expressed as

$$z_j = \Sigma_i z_i \, a_{ij} + \Sigma_h z_h^f f_{hj} + z_j \, g_j$$

(7.25)

where z_j (z_i) is the price index for good j (i), and g_j is the fixed gross operating surplus coefficient in the production of j. Price indexes for all goods $j = i$ may be expressed as

$$\mathbf{z} = \mathbf{z} \, \mathbf{A} + \mathbf{z} \, \hat{\mathbf{g}} + \mathbf{z}^f \, \mathbf{F}$$

where $\hat{\mathbf{g}}$ is the diagonal matrix containing the fixed gross operating surplus coefficients calculated as a proportion of price. From this equation, endogenous vector z containing the price indexes may be calculated as a function of exogenous price indexes for the nonproduced inputs z^f as

$$z = z^f \, F \, (I - A - \hat{g})^{-1} \qquad (7.26)$$

Once an estimate of vector z is available, the A matrix may be price-updated by using expression (7.23), and then recalculating vector spr^n using expression (7.24). To that effect, the already mentioned need to revise spr^f_h estimates should be kept in mind.

Changes in Prices Fixed by the Government

Consider a hypothetical example in which the government increases the prices of goods and services provided by public utilities. Specifically, assume that electricity tariffs increase by 30 percent, that this is the only price change affecting our matrix since the date to which it corresponds, and that the matrix columns for electricity are the result of relating long-run marginal costs to tariffs and allocating any difference to normative excess profits.

There would be two effects of the tariff increase in the short run. First, it would affect the row corresponding to electricity purchases, and consequently all sectors consuming electricity. That, in turn, would lead to successive rounds of price changes until a new 'equilibrium' was reached. Second, it would also affect the electricity column, increasing normative excess profits. In the longer run, a sustained increase in the relative price of electricity may affect physical coefficients (reductions in the kWh per unit of output) if production techniques were originally selected with reference to the lower price.

If producers are expected to substitute for the more expensive electricity, value coefficients may be affected only marginally if price increases compensate quantity reductions (see Klein, 1953). But, if most techniques are expected to have been selected for a price of electricity higher than the one that is being updated, it is possible to update the matrix for price changes under the assumption of fixed physical coefficients. If some substitution takes place in sectors that selected their production techniques based on the lower price, the price adjustment assuming fixed physical coefficients would overestimate electricity coefficients and underestimate those of the electricity substitutes.

The matrix may be price-updated using the input–output price model, which allows for the effects of the price increase on the prices of all other goods to be estimated. Starting from the original matrix

$$\left| \begin{array}{c} \mathbf{A} \\ -- \\ \mathbf{F} \end{array} \right|$$

the row containing electricity purchases may be moved to the **F** matrix, and the corresponding column be eliminated. Thus, a new matrix is obtained

$$\left| \begin{array}{c} \mathbf{B} \\ -- \\ \mathbf{V} \end{array} \right|$$

From this new matrix, an input–output price model similar to expression (7.25) may be formulated

$$z_j = \Sigma_i \, z_i \, b_{ij} + \Sigma_h \, z_h^f \, v_{hj} + z_j \, g_j \tag{7.27}$$

The model for all sectors $j = i$ may be then expressed as

$$\mathbf{z} = \mathbf{z} \, \mathbf{B} + \mathbf{z} \, \hat{\mathbf{g}} + \mathbf{z}^v \, \mathbf{V}$$

where $\hat{\mathbf{g}}$ is the matrix containing the fixed gross operating surplus coefficients. From this equation, vector **z** containing the sectoral price indexes may be calculated as a function of exogenous price indexes $\mathbf{z}^v$, which include that of electricity (1.30 in the example),

$$\mathbf{z} = \mathbf{z}^v \, \mathbf{V} \, (\mathbf{I} - \mathbf{B} - \hat{\mathbf{g}})^{-1} \tag{7.28}$$

Vector $\mathbf{z}^v$ would have 1.0s in all positions except the one corresponding to electricity, since in this hypothetical example the price of electricity is the only one that changes.

An estimate of the changes in the prices of goods i allows for the price-updating of matrix **B**. Using expression (7.23) the new matrixes would be

$$\mathbf{B}^n = \hat{\mathbf{z}} \, \mathbf{B} \, \hat{\mathbf{z}}^{-1}$$

$$\mathbf{V}^n = \hat{\mathbf{z}}^v \, \mathbf{V} \, \hat{\mathbf{z}}^{-1}$$

Then, matrixes **A** and **F** may be reassembled by relocating the electricity row in **A** and the corresponding column. For the column to refer to the same price level, input coefficients would have to be multiplied by the corresponding price indexes, the value of output by 1.3, and normative excess profits would absorb the difference. Thus, if the column before the adjustments was

$$1 = \Sigma_i\, a_{ij} + \Sigma_h f_{hj} + \gamma_j$$

where γ_j is normative excess profits, the new column would result from price-adjusting the coefficients

$$z_j - \Sigma_i\, z_i\, a_{ij} + \Sigma_h\, z_h f_{hj} = \gamma_j^n \qquad\qquad (7.29)$$

where γ_j^n is the normative excess profits corresponding to the new prices. In this example, the new coefficients would result from

$$1.3 - \Sigma_i\, z_i\, a_{ij} + \Sigma_h\, z_h f_{hj} = \gamma_j^n$$

The new value for γ_j^n would depend not only on the tariff increase, but also on its effects on the prices of all inputs purchased by the electricity sector. If the tariff is below marginal cost, γ_j would be negative; thus γ_j^n would now be greater (smaller in absolute value if it continues to be negative) indicating a reduction in the transfer to electricity users.

The preceding example assumes that the column was based on a marginal cost estimate, and consequently on estimated capital costs, where normative excess profits capture the difference between price and marginal cost. The original cost structure, however, may have been based on current costs, implicitly (and incorrectly) assuming that the gross operating surplus at market prices was equal to the capital cost annuity. In such a case, the whole effect of the tariff increase (net of the cost increase, equation (7.29)) could be allocated to the gross operating surplus, so bringing it closer to the true capital cost.

A More General Model for Price Changes

In practice, the analyst would face a combination of the cases discussed above. There would be changes in prices that are exogenous to the input–output model – since they are not determined based exclusively on costs (like public services) – as well as changes in the prices of nonproduced goods, altering all relative prices. Price indexes for some produced goods may be available, and they are preferable to estimates based on expression (7.28). In such a case, the preceding method could be used following essentially the same procedure – treating all activities for which a price index is available as exogenous, and using expression (7.28) to estimate only the remainder. First, all rows that will be adjusted exogenously are removed from matrix **A** and transferred to **F**, also removing the corresponding columns. The resulting **B** and **V** matrixes are next used to calculate vector **z**, and then matrixes $\mathbf{B}^n$ and $\mathbf{V}^n$. The columns for the exogenously updated activities are updated as described in equation (7.29), and finally matrixes $\mathbf{A}$ and $\mathbf{F}$ are reassembled, removing from $\mathbf{V}^n$ the rows of the exogenously updated inputs, placing them back in the transactions matrix, and reinserting the updated columns.

An example would help in clarifying the procedure. Assume that a devaluation exceeding the nominal wage increase has taken place, together with an increase in the price of electricity. As a result, a decision is made to modify the input–output matrix presented in Table 7.1. Further assume that the price changes are the following:

1. a 25 percent increase in the nominal exchange rate;
2. a 15 percent increase in the nominal wage;
3. a 35 percent increase in the price of electricity; and
4. a 20 percent increase in agricultural prices.

All activities for which a price index is available will be treated as exogenous. Such is the case of electricity and agricultural goods. Thus the modified input–output table is prepared (Table 7.2) and used to estimate price indexes for the remaining produced activities using expression (7.28). The resulting matrixes are

$$
\mathbf{B} = \begin{vmatrix}
0 & 0.05 & 0 & 0 \\
0.2 & 0.17 & 0.15 & 0.1 \\
0.09 & 0.01 & 0 & 0 \\
0 & 0.15 & 0 & 0
\end{vmatrix}
$$

$$
\mathbf{V} = \begin{vmatrix}
0 & 0.08 & 0 & 0 \\
0.06 & 0.02 & 0 & 0.05 \\
0 & 0.2 & 0.45 & 0.08 \\
0 & 0.02 & 0.05 & 0.02 \\
0.25 & 0.14 & 0.1 & 0.35
\end{vmatrix}
$$

$$
\hat{\mathbf{g}} = \begin{vmatrix}
0.4 & 0 & 0 & 0 \\
0 & 0.16 & 0 & 0 \\
0 & 0 & 0.255 & 0 \\
0 & 0 & 0 & 0.4
\end{vmatrix}
$$

$$
\mathbf{z}^f = \begin{bmatrix} 1.20 & 1.35 & 1.25 & 1.25 & 1.15 \end{bmatrix}
$$

Table 7.1   Original input–output table

	(1)	(2)	(3)	(4)	(5)	(6)
(1) Agriculture	0.030	—	0.080	—	—	—
(2) Mining	—	—	0.050	—	—	0.020
(3) Industry	0.150	0.200	0.170	0.150	0.100	0.350
(4) Transport	0.020	0.090	0.010	—	—	0.030
(5) Commerce	0.100	—	0.150	—	—	—
(6) Electricity	—	0.060	0.020	—	0.050	—
(7) Foreign exchange	0.100	—	0.200	0.450	0.080	0.650
(8) Trade taxes	0.050	—	0.020	0.045	0.020	—
(9) Wages	0.150	0.250	0.140	0.100	0.350	0.120
(10) Gross oper. surplus	0.400	0.400	0.160	0.255	0.400	—
(11) Norm. excess profits	—	—	—	—	—	−0.170

Table 7.2   Modified input–output table

	(2)	(3)	(4)	(5)
(2) Mining	—	0.050	—	—
(3) Industry	0.200	0.170	0.150	0.100
(4) Transport	0.090	0.010	—	—
(5) Commerce	—	0.150	—	—
(1) Agriculture	—	0.080	—	—
(6) Electricity	0.060	0.020	—	0.050
(7) Foreign exchange	—	0.200	0.450	0.080
(8) Trade taxes	—	0.020	0.045	0.020
(9) Wages	0.250	0.140	0.100	0.350
(10) Gross oper. surplus	0.400	0.160	0.255	0.400
(11) Norm. excess profits	—	—	—	—

Note that in z^f foreign exchange and trade taxes are updated by the same coefficient, since these are *ad valorem* taxes. Substituting in expression (7.28), vector z becomes

$$z = [1.20159 \quad 1.20948 \quad 1.22842 \quad 1.19325]$$

This vector allows the calculation of matrixes B^n and V^n using expression (7.23). The results are:

$$B^n = \begin{vmatrix} 0 & 0.0497 & 0 & 0 \\ 0.20131 & 0.17 & 0.14769 & 0.10136 \\ 0.092 & 0.0102 & 0 & 0 \\ 0 & 0.14799 & 0 & 0 \end{vmatrix}$$

$$V^n = \begin{vmatrix} 0 & 0.0794 & 0 & 0 \\ 0.0674 & 0.0223 & 0 & 0.0566 \\ 0 & 0.2067 & 0.45791 & 0.0838 \\ 0 & 0.0207 & 0.0458 & 0.021 \\ 0.23927 & 0.13312 & 0.0458 & 0.021 \end{vmatrix}$$

The *Agriculture* and *Electricity* columns are updated using the price indices in vectors z and z^f, obtaining the gross operating surplus and the normative excess profits, respectively, as a residual. The resulting coefficients are presented in Table 7.3, where $a''_{ij} = a_{ij} z_i/z_j$ and $f''_{hj} = f_{hj} z_h/z_j$.

Finally, rows for agriculture and electricity are moved from V^n to B^n and the corresponding updated columns are also incorporated. Thus, the updated matrix showed in Table 7.4 is obtained. There it may be observed that increasing the electricity tariff by more than the increase in the cost of inputs results in an increase in normative excess profits. It also may be observed that the resulting real depreciation increases the foreign exchange coefficients and reduces the wage coefficients.

Import Substitution

Consider a substitution of imports that transforms the product from imported to nontraded at the margin, which takes place without changing the import tariff, and where existing protection is just enough to make domestic production possible; that is, the price of the domestic good is approximately equal to that of the imported good. Thus, the substitution takes place without

Table 7.3 Exogenously updated columns

Inputs	(1) Agriculture		(6) Electricity	
	$a_{i1} \times z_i$ and $f_{h1} \times z_h$	a_{i1}^n and f_{h1}^n	$a_{i6} \times z_i$ and $f_{h6} \times z_h$	a_{i6}^n and f_{h6}^n
(1) Agriculture	$0.030 \times 1.20000 = 0.03600$	0.03000	—	—
(2) Mining	—	—	$0.020 \times 1.20159 = 0.02403$	0.01780
(3) Industry	$0.150 \times 1.20948 = 0.18142$	0.15119	$0.350 \times 1.20948 = 0.42332$	0.31357
(4) Transport	$0.020 \times 1.22842 = 0.02457$	0.02047	$0.030 \times 1.22842 = 0.03685$	0.02730
(5) Commerce	$0.100 \times 1.19325 = 0.11933$	0.09944	—	—
(6) Electricity	—	—	—	—
(7) Foreign exchange	$0.100 \times 1.25000 = 0.12500$	0.10417	$0.650 \times 1.25000 = 0.81250$	0.60185
(8) Trade taxes	$0.050 \times 1.25000 = 0.06250$	0.05208	—	—
(9) Wages	$0.150 \times 1.15000 = 0.17250$	0.14375	$0.120 \times 1.15000 = 0.13800$	0.10222
(10) Gross operation surplus	0.47868	0.39890	—	—
(11) Excess profits	—	—	-0.170	-0.06274
Total	1.20000	1.00000	1.35000	1.00000

Table 7.4 Updated input–output table

	(1)	(2)	(3)	(4)	(5)	(6)
(1) Agriculture	0.030	—	0.079	—	—	—
(2) Mining	—	—	0.050	—	—	0.018
(3) Industry	0.151	0.201	0.170	0.148	0.101	0.314
(4) Transport	0.020	0.092	0.010	—	—	0.027
(5) Commerce	0.099	—	0.148	—	—	—
(6) Electricity	—	0.067	0.022	—	0.057	—
(7) Foreign exchange	0.104	—	0.207	0.458	0.084	0.602
(8) Trade taxes	0.052	—	0.021	0.046	0.021	—
(9) Wages	0.144	0.239	0.133	0.094	0.337	0.102
(10) Gross oper. surplus	0.399	0.400	0.160	0.255	0.400	—
(11) Norm. excess profits	—	—	—	—	—	-0.063

affecting other prices. In this case, the new *spr* may be calculated using equation (7.11) if a cost structure is available. Since this is a recent event, the investment project leading to the substitution may be available and allow for the cost structure to be based on marginal costs.

It would be more difficult, however, to correct the matrix in order to incorporate the new column, since the demand for this input would have been decomposed into foreign exchange, trade taxes, transport and other costs, and each component allocated to the corresponding row. It would be necessary to return to the original data and specify this intermediate demand for all columns, which would be costly. Thus, it is likely that the best feasible approach would be using equation (7.11) to correct the spr_j of those products for which this input is a high proportion of total cost.

If in order to achieve the complete substitution, protection for this product was increased so as to allow for a higher domestic price, the problem to be solved would not be just that of a new cost structure, but also that of the effect of the ensuing price increase on the prices of the other goods. This situation is similar to that of the price of electricity considered above. Since redoing cost structures is costly, the preceding solution for the case when price does not change may be the only practicable one.

However, if intermediate demands for the substituted input could be identified, and the different costs making up its price (foreign exchange, taxes, transport, etc.) could be deducted from the respective rows, a new row for the substituted import may be created in matrix **A**, moved to **F**, and the matrixes could then be updated for the exogenous increase in the price of the input following the method presented earlier in this section. Then, the updated row could be reinserted into matrix **A** and the new column prepared with the corresponding cost data.

Changes in Trade Policy

The most important effect of changes in trade policy is to switch products between traded and nontraded at the margin categories. A reduction in protection, for example, would have two principal effects. First, to reduce the prices of previously nontraded goods and make some become traded at the margin. Second, to change relative prices between nonproduced inputs, in particular the exchange-rate-to-wage ratio, and some transfers (e.g. trade taxes).

The effects of reducing protection may be incorporated in an *approximate* manner. First, all intermediate demands of previously nontraded inputs that would now be supplied at the margin by imports or by the reduction of exports are relocated to matrix **F**. Then, the matrixes are adjusted by the relative price changes originated by the reduction in protection, taking into account both those originated in previously nontraded goods and those resulting from changes in the prices of nonproduced inputs and transfers. To these effects, one of the methods presented in the preceding sections may be followed.

Once the new B^n and V^n matrixes have been obtained, the rows corresponding to the new traded goods currently in V^n are broken down into foreign exchange, taxes, transport, and so on, and allocated to the corresponding rows. Thus, matrixes A^n and F^n are obtained and used to calculate the new **spr**^{n} vector.

This type of updating is necessarily approximate, since changes in protection lead to significant changes in relative prices and in the classification of goods as traded or nontraded at the margin. The method may be used as a temporary measure to allow the use of the existing *spr* until the economy reaches a new 'equilibrium' position and new data reflecting the effects of the policy changes may become available, allowing for a new matrix to be built.

The use of approximations may be feasible for reductions in protection, where the most important effect on the sources of input supply is the conversion of nontraded into traded goods, and those previously nontraded goods are specified in the matrix. On the other hand, in the case of increases in protection – that is, when marginally traded goods are converted into nontraded – previously traded inputs are not specified in the matrix, making the updating practically impossible for the reasons discussed when considering import substitution.

APPENDIX 7.1 DERIVATION OF EXPRESSIONS (7.16) AND (7.17)

Say that the users' price is

$$p_j^u = \Sigma_i a_{ij} p_j^u + \Sigma_h f_{hj} p_j^u \tag{7.A1}$$

where $[a_{ij}; f_{hj}]$ is j's cost structure in the input–output matrix at users' prices. In order to incorporate the effects of the new unit distribution margin dis_j^n, the old unit margin dis_j^u is subtracted and the new one is added to both sides of (7.A1). Thus, the following expression is obtained

$$p_j^n = p_j^u - dis_j^u + dis_j^n = \Sigma_i a_{ij} p_j^u + \Sigma_h f_{hj} p_j^u - dis_j^u + dis_j^n \tag{7.A2}$$

Note that dis_j^u is *not* the coefficient in the input–output table (i.e. one a_{ij}) multiplied by p_j^u, since transport and trade coefficients would include those of the traded inputs. Coefficients with respect to p_j^n may be calculated from expression (7.A2), allowing for spr_j^n to be calculated as

$$spr_j^n = \Sigma_i (p_i^u/p_j^n) a_{ij} spr_i + \Sigma_h (p_h^u/p_j^n) f_{hj} spr_h -$$

$$spr_{dis}^u dis_j^u/p_j^n + spr_{dis}^n dis_j^n/p_j^n \tag{7.16}$$

In order to find the ratio between the two spr_j, define

$$spr_{dis}^n = spr_{dis}^u (1 + \beta)$$

and rewrite expression (7.16) as

$$spr_j^n = \Sigma_i (p_i^u/p_j^n) a_{ij} spr_i + \Sigma_h (p_h^u/p_j^n) f_{hj} spr_h +$$

$$spr_{dis}^u (dis_j^n - dis_j^u)/p_j^n + \beta spr_{dis}^u dis_j^n/p_j^n \tag{7.A3}$$

From expression (7.A2)

$$(dis_j^n - dis_j^u)/p_j^n = (p_j^n - p_j^u)/p_j^n \tag{7.A4}$$

Substituting (7.A4) in expression (7.A3) and regrouping yields

$$spr_j^n = \Sigma_i (p_i^u/p_j^n) a_{ij} spr_i + \Sigma_h (p_h^u/p_j^n) f_{hj} spr_h +$$

$$+ spr_{dis}^u (p_j^n - p_j^u)/p_j^n + \beta spr_{dis}^u dis_j^n/p_j^n \tag{7.A5}$$

Then, factoring expression (7.A5) yields

$$spr_j^n = (p_j^u/p_j^n) \left[\Sigma_i \, a_{ij} \, spr_i + \Sigma_h f_{hj} \, spr_h + \right.$$

$$\left. spr_{dis}^u (p_j^n - p_j^u)/p_j^u + \beta \, spr_{dis}^u \, dis_j^n/p_j^u \right] \tag{7.A6}$$

The ratio of this expression for spr_j^n to the original spr represented by (7.15) yields expression (7.17) presented in the text.

8. Shadow Prices for Colombia[1]

8.1 INTRODUCTION

This section provides a brief summary of the main characteristics and evolution of the Colombian economy up to 1987, two years before this study was completed. No effort has been made to update it, and major changes took place in Colombia during the 1990s. The presentation, however, is aimed at informing the reader of the economic environment in which the study took place.

Colombia occupies some 1 141 748 km² and in 1985 had a population of 29.3 million inhabitants growing at an annual rate of approximately 1.9 percent. This growth rate was considerably smaller than rates registered during the 1964–73 (3.4 percent) and 1951–64 (3.5 percent) periods. The population under 15 years of age, both in absolute as well as relative terms, remained almost constant. In contrast, the population above that age was growing at a faster rate than the total population. In the 1950s the population was overwhelmingly rural, but the accelerated urban growth that occurred after that time meant that by 1985 only two thirds of the population lived in rural areas. Thirty percent of Colombia's total population, and 44 percent of its urban population lived in the four main cities of Barranquilla, Bogotá, Cali and Medellín, and their metropolitan areas. By 1987, the global participation rate (i.e. the economically active population as a proportion of total population of working age) in those cities had reached 57.8 percent, while 10 years before it had been 50 percent on average, the highest since censuses were carried out. This increase in the participation rate was explained by the increase in female workers and child labor, as well as part-time workers.

In the 1970s, the growth in the demand for labor began to decline, resulting in an ever increasing labor force surplus, the proliferation of marginal occupations, and the deterioration of working conditions. During the 1980s, the number of underemployed persons accepting precarious subsistence options outside any legal framework considerably increased. The most obvious manifestation of Colombia's employment problem was its urban unemployment. The high economic growth of the 1970s was accompanied by

---

1. By Professor Héctor Cervini, Universidad Autónoma Metropolitana, Azcapotzalco, Mexico, DF.

177

unemployment rates of around 9 percent, and by the beginning of the 1980s unemployment rates increased in the four principal cities, reaching a maximum of 15 percent in 1986. However, the 1986–87 unemployment rate fell, reaching 11.7 percent in 1987. Unemployment was primarily associated with the formal market. In the informal sector, wages and working time adjusted the labor market.

Urban and rural real wages in the private sector showed an increasing long-term trend, although subject to fluctuations. During the 1980s, the real minimum wage also showed an increasing trend. At the same time permanent jobs were lost, as temporary contracts became more common, particularly for unskilled labor covered by the minimum wage. This resulted in a deterioration of the quality of available jobs, as well as in notorious wage differences between sectors and occupations.

Colombia had a mixed economy dominated by the private sector. The public sector was responsible for public services and transportation infrastructure, and owned the country's mineral resources. The dominant characteristic of Colombia's economic policy during the 1960s, 1970s and 1980s was that of gradualism and continuity, reflected in the persistence of economic policies and the way in which they were carried out.

The GNP's high growth rate, at around 5.4 percent per annum between 1961 and 1980, was attained while following a development strategy that combined import substitution with export promotion. According to data from the Departamento Nacional de Planeación, between 1980 and 1987 per capita income in 1975 US dollars rose from 989 to 1 249.

The share of agriculture in GNP decreased from 40 percent in 1945 to around 23 percent in the mid-1980s. However, agriculture employed about a third of the labor force and produced more than two thirds of the country's export revenue. Coffee was the principal agricultural product, and Colombia was second only to Brazil as a world supplier. Furthermore, the country was the world's fourth largest supplier of bananas, and second, after Holland, of fresh flowers. Cotton, sugar, tobacco, cocoa and cattle exports were also important.

Mining, which traditionally represented a very low percentage of GNP, grew fast starting in 1983, due to increased production and exports of petroleum, coal and gold, reaching approximately 4 percent of the GNP in 1987. The manufacturing sector generated about 22 percent of GNP, with consumer goods making up approximately 49 percent of gross value of production, intermediate goods a further 40 percent, and capital goods accounting for 11 percent. Construction represented close to 3.5 percent of GNP and more than 40 percent of gross capital formation; public construction accounted for roughly half the sector's value added.

At the beginning of the 1980s, the Colombian economy suffered a recession that lasted until the middle of 1983. During this period a sharp deficit in the balance of payments and increased unemployment developed as a result of a deteriorating fiscal situation, an import liberalization policy with an overvalued local currency, and the effects of the debt crisis on trade between countries. The crises in Ecuador and Venezuela were especially important for Colombia's foreign trade, because these countries increased protection and depreciated their currencies, resulting in a noticeable reduction of imports of manufactures from Colombia.

In 1983 and 1984, new adjustment programs aimed at achieving monetary and fiscal discipline, depreciating the overvalued local currency and rationalizing the external sector, were put in place. Results were seen as from 1984, especially in import-substituting industries. That same year GNP grew 3.4 percent. However, the positive effects of this policy were not felt until 1985, when improvements in the fiscal and external sectors were registered; even though the GNP only grew by 3.1 percent.

At the end of 1984, the low level of international reserves threatened a currency crisis. As part of the measures taken to solve the situation, the peso was devalued by a record almost 50 percent. As the real exchange rate came closer to an equilibrium level, the situation reversed. Service revenues began to increase and the deterioration of the capital account stopped. As the situation improved in 1986, service revenue and capital inflows increased noticeably.

The difficult situation in the international markets at the beginning of the 1980s, as well as the overvaluation, led the government to modify its export incentives in order to improve international competitiveness. Throughout 1985, higher rates of depreciation were accompanied by the elimination of some of these incentives. For example, tax reimbursements were reduced for a great number of tariff items, dispersion was also reduced, and differential rates according to destination were eliminated.

From 1982 to the end of 1984, protection was increased by using both tariff and nontariff barriers. The majority of imports were also subjected to import licenses, thus reversing the tendency of previous years. In addition, in 1984, import prohibitions, that had not been used since the 1960s, were established. During that same year, 78 percent of imports required import licenses. The remaining 22 percent mostly corresponded to raw materials, and inputs that did not compete with domestic production (or supplemented insufficient domestic supply), as well as to imports through a special export promotion plan (Plan Vallejo).

Despite the effectiveness of import controls, foreign reserves continued to decline. As a result, the emphasis of economic policy switched to reducing public spending and increasing the real depreciation. The new policy allowed for a reduction in trade barriers, and in 1985 a gradual and selective liberalization of imports began with significant reductions in both import licenses and prohibitions (World Bank, 1989).

8.2 METHODOLOGICAL APPROACH

This estimation follows an input–output approach, as described in Chapter 6. Since an input–output table with the desired level of detail was not available, one was prepared specifically for this study. This section and Appendix 8.1 provide a brief account of its preparation.[2]

The process started with selecting the most frequently used inputs by manufacturing industries, assuming that these same inputs would be the ones most frequently used by investment projects to be subject to a cost–benefit analysis. In order to select these inputs, especially those of manufacturing origin, the share of each one in the total value of inputs used by the manufacturing sector as a whole, as well as their importance for each individual industry, were taken into account. Similar criteria were used for the selection of the remaining inputs. Thus, the analysis took place along the rows of the matrix, allowing for an efficient processing of the available data by computer.

This procedure also allowed the identification of a subsystem of goods with three common characteristics: (1) not being important current inputs of any industry, (2) shadow prices for these goods were desired, and (3) their production depended on inputs from other industries for their production (e.g. capital goods). The *spr*s for these goods were calculated using expression (7.13) after calculating the *spr*s corresponding to the goods included in the matrix (those that were interrelated by way of their input demands).

The more specific an input is, the easier it is to determine how additional demand would be met. On the contrary, when an input is defined as an aggregate of various goods it is more difficult to identify the impact of an increase in its demand, and subsequently to classify it. In this study, the analysis was conducted at the lowest level of aggregation allowed by the data, that is 8-digit ISIC[3] as defined by the Colombian Statistical Office (DANE). However, even at this level of aggregation an 8-digit code may still correspond to products of different characteristics. For example, 8-digit ISIC codes that group 'parts and accessories' normally include different products.

Inputs were classified taking into account their origin (national or imported), as declared in the *Annual Manufacturing Survey* (DANE, 1985a), and their domestic production levels, complemented by data on imports and exports provided by trade statistics. This information, together with the opinion of experts for each input, led to the final classification of inputs as either nontraded, imported or exported.

---

2. Cervini (1992) and Cervini et al. (1990) provide a more detailed presentation.

3. International Standard Industrial Classification of all Economic Activities. See United Nations (1969).

The criteria for classifying inputs was applied at the same time as the selection process was carried out, requiring some simplifying assumptions in order to concentrate efforts on the most important inputs. Thus, for example, the decision to create baskets of manufactured inputs with minor importance in total costs, was concomitant with the assumption that these inputs were imported for the part declared as such in the *Annual Manufacturing Survey*, and nontraded for the part declared to be of domestic origin.

Valuation

The matrix used in this study was prepared at users' prices. The choice was largely determined by the availability of data, in particular data on the value of inputs purchased by manufacturing establishments. According to the *Annual Manufacturing Survey* these expenditures were valued at acquisition prices, including transportation and trade margins, but excluding sales taxes. Outputs were valued at factory gate, and did not include indirect taxes. In order to arrive at a uniform valuation, the value of the inputs had to be completed by the corresponding indirect taxes, and the value of the outputs with the indirect taxes and the distribution margins. This method of valuation was used for preparing all cost structures in the matrix.

Valuation at user prices may result in a small error, since it assumes that distribution margins are equal irrespective of the input's destination. First, it presumes that the margins are the same irrespective of the distance between seller and producer, and ignores whether some establishments buy the input directly at factory-gate prices, while others obtain them from distributors that have already added on transportation and trade margins. Second, the method also presumes that distribution margins are the same, irrespective of whether the product is used as an intermediate or a consumption good. This latter type of error, however, was not important for this study, since the matrix includes almost exclusively the cost structures of the most important inputs. Also, with the exception of the investment and the consumption conversion factors, trade margins for the outputs were assigned at the wholesale level, since the matrix registers intermediate transactions.

The Transactions Matrix

The matrix is schematically described in Table 8.1. The submatrix A_{11} contains the intermediate demands of the manufacturing industries to those same industries, the submatrix A_{21} includes the demands of manufacturing industries to nonmanufacturing industries, and submatrix F_1 the payments for primary inputs made by manufacturing industries. Thus, the first column of the table represents the cost structures of manufacturing industries, while the second represents those of the nonmanufacturing ones.

With regard to conversion factors, each basket of goods may be treated as originating in an 'industry' that produces it, demanding the required inputs. Alternatively, the conversion factor may be calculated as a weighted average of the *sprs* of the goods that make up the said basket (see section 6.4). In this study, both procedures were used. An additional distinction that should be borne in mind is that some conversion factors supplied the intermediate demands of industries, while others did not provide inputs to any. The conversion factors in the first group were treated as any other input and included under manufacturing or nonmanufacturing industries, depending on their particular nature. Those in the second group make up the third column of Table 8.1, and they did not satisfy the intermediate demands of any sector.

Table 8.1   Scheme of the matrix

	Manufacturing industries	Nonmanufacturing industries	Conversion factors
Manufacturing industries	A_{11}	A_{12}	A_{13}
Nonmanufacturing industries	A_{21}	A_{22}	A_{23}
Conversion factors	0	0	0
Primary inputs and transfers	F_1	F_2	F_3

The matrix was constructed by blocks. The cost structures of the manufacturing industries were prepared first, identifying and classifying their inputs. In order to follow uniform criteria throughout the process, columns of the nonmanufacturing goods were prepared, taking aggregations and classifications done in the previous stage into account.

The submatrix A_{11} contains the transactions between manufacturing industries. The value of each transaction was obtained from the 1985 *Annual Manufacturing Survey*. Appendix 8.1 presents the criteria used for selecting and classifying these inputs, as well as the procedures followed in order to construct the corresponding cost structures. Marginally traded inputs (imported or exported) used by each industry were broken down in foreign exchange, taxes, and transport and commerce margins, and assigned to the corresponding rows. These break-downs were based on import and export price structures prepared according to the method shown in Appendix 8.1.

The submatrix A_{21} corresponds to the demand for nonmanufactured inputs by manufacturing industries. Most of this information was obtained from the

Annual Manufacturing Survey. Inputs were classified as traded or nontraded at the margin, and treated in the matrix following the same criteria applied in the case of inputs of manufacturing origin.

Matrix F_1 corresponds to purchases of primary inputs made by manufacturing industries, and was also prepared with data coming primarily from the *Annual Manufacturing Survey*. These purchases were broken down into labor costs, fixed-supply inputs, foreign exchange, indirect taxes, and gross operating surplus. Labor costs were in turn broken down according to the type of labor employed – foreign, professional, administrative, skilled, or unskilled labor – in accordance with the analysis of labor markets presented in section 8.7. Also, for each of these types, with the exception of foreign labor, two different subclassifications (and consequently shadow prices) were made: one for those activities where benefits (leave, social security, severance, training, etc.) were considerably above those of other sectors, and another for those with benefits close to the average, (see section 8.7). Thus, two different rows were created in matrix F for each labor type, leading to the following nine types of labor costs: Professional; Professional, high benefits; Administrative; Administrative, high benefits; Skilled workers; Skilled workers, high benefits; Unskilled; Unskilled, high benefits; and Foreign. The data on 'Foreign exchange' came from breaking down the cost of marginally imported and exported inputs. The gross operating surplus is the difference between the value of production at users' prices and total current costs, and is thus valued at market prices (see Appendix 8.1).

The submatrixes A_{12} and A_{22} correspond to the demands for inputs of manufacturing origin by nonmanufacturing sectors, and the demands for nonmanufacturing inputs by these same sectors. The procedure used in order to prepare some of these columns is presented in sections 8.3 and 8.4. The submatrix F_2 contains the payments made by nonmanufacturing activities for primary inputs. The demands for unskilled labor by agricultural and mining activities were grouped into a separate row in matrix F. As a result, labor costs occupy 10 different rows: the nine previously identified, plus unskilled labor in the primary sectors (agriculture and mining, see Table 8.2). This further classification is required by the different *spr*s resulting from the functioning of labor markets (see section 8.7). The gross operating surpluses of the mining and manufacturing industries were assigned to a single row, while those of the agricultural, services and transportation ones were given separate rows. The treatment of the gross operating surpluses is consistent with that of the conversion factors used to express them at shadow prices (see section 8.8). Two other items were included: land and normative excess profits. Land represents the opportunity costs of areas with hydroelectric developments. Normative excess profits capture the difference between price and long-run marginal cost. In those activities where the cost structures were based on the marginal costs of expanding production, present values of the sales and cost

Table 8.2   Matrix of nonproduced inputs and transfers

Nonproduced input or transfer	Manufacturing industries	Nonmanufacturing industries	
		Agriculture and mining	Services
Wages	—	—	—
Professional	X	X	X
Professional, high benefits	X	—	—
Administrative	X	X	X
Administrative, high benefits	X	—	—
Skilled workers	X	X	X
Skilled workers, high benefits	X	—	—
Unskilled	X	—	X
Unskilled, high benefits	X	—	—
Unskilled primary sector	—	X	—
Foreign	X	X	X
Fixed supply inputs	X	X	—
Foreign exchange	X	X	X
Indirect taxes	X	X	X
Gross operating surplus	X	X	X
Manufacturing and mining	X	X	—
Agriculture	—	X	—
Services	—	—	X
Transportation	—	—	X
Land	—	—	X
Normative excess profits	—	—	X

Note: The Xs indicate the existence of transactions.

flows were calculated at a rate of 12 percent. The difference between the present value of sales and the present value of long-run marginal costs, all valued at market prices, was assigned to normative excess profits (see section 6.3).

In the majority of cases, capital costs were not assigned separately. The gross operating surplus at market prices, which is approximately equivalent to the capital cost annuity plus the normative excess profits, was used in its place (see section 6.3). In other cases, part of the capital cost annuity was separately estimated and assigned as an intermediate demand in matrix **A**. For example, in determining the cost structures of inputs of agricultural origin, the capital cost annuity of tractors and combines was estimated and deducted from the operating surplus. The rest of the operating surplus was assumed to be made up of other unidentifiable factor costs. Capital cost annuities (CCA) were estimated using the following expression

$$CCA = \frac{PVK \, d}{1 - (1 + d)^{-n}} \qquad (8.1)$$

where PVK is the present value of capital costs, d is the annual discount rate (equal to 12 percent), and n is the useful life of the asset, in years. Lastly, when long-run marginal costs were estimated and the price charged did not cover such costs, the difference was assigned to normative excess profits. This was the case for drinking water and electricity, for which capital costs were assigned as an intermediate demand, while the difference between tariff and costs was assigned to normative excess profits. The methodology for preparing the cost structures of these two goods is presented in section 8.3, since it is likely to be of special interest to the applied economist.

Those inputs judged to be 'relatively insignificant' were aggregated into 'baskets', and a cost structure was given to each. Thus, 'relatively insignificant' inputs of manufacturing origin were aggregated at the 2-digit ISIC level, and their cost structures were prepared on the basis of aggregating the respective cost structures. The 'relatively insignificant' inputs of agricultural and mining origin were treated in a similar fashion.

In the case of road transportation, four different types were identified, and a cost structure was associated with each of them. However, from the viewpoint of intermediate demand, it was only possible to identify the aggregate demand for transportation. Therefore, a transportation conversion factor was included using the first approach described in section 6.4. This conversion factor sells transportation services to the other industries and purchases from the four transportation types in accordance with their respective participation in the sector as a whole. In turn, the column of a transportation type contains the corresponding cost structure, and the respective row only includes the participation of that mode of transport in the transportation conversion factor. This transaction is at the intersection with the column of the said conversion factor. Detailed explanation for the different forms of transportation and the conversion factor is not reported in this chapter, but may be consulted in Cervini (1992).

Investment and consumption conversion factors were also estimated according to criteria summarized in section 8.4. The matrix includes four investment conversion factors, which correspond to the investment in industry, agriculture, transport and services. Each one of these conversion factors has different proportions of diverse capital goods, which in turn make up baskets of investment goods with similar destinations. Lastly, a consumption conversion factor was included, whose column is the aggregation of cost structures corresponding to industries which primarily produce consumer goods, plus an allowance for imported consumption goods.

The resulting matrix, outlined in Table 8.3, consists of 276 industries (columns) and 295 inputs (rows), 19 of which correspond to the primary inputs detailed in Table 8.2. The 276 industries making up the matrix of interindustrial transactions are presented, with the final results, at the end of this chapter (Table 8.31). An additional 67 cost structures corresponding to manufactures that were not used as common inputs in any industry were also prepared, although not reported in this chapter, and used for calculating the respective shadow price ratios, in accordance with expression (7.3).

Table 8.3   Size and composition of the matrix

Type of industries	Number
Inputs of manufacturing origin	222
Inputs of agricultural origin	22
Inputs of mining origin	7
Other inputs	11
Commerce	1
Transportation	5

Conversion factors[a]
   Agricultural machinery
   Office equipment
   Transport equipment
   Manufacturing investment
   Agricultural investment
   Investment in transport
   Investment in services
   Consumption
	8

Total	276

Note: [a] Only those that do not appear as an intermediate demand.

Reference Year

The selection of a reference year is the result of technical and practical considerations, which are frequently difficult to reconcile. For instance, it is desirable that the data used correspond to a year of 'equilibrium prices', that is, a year in which relative prices of produced and nonproduced goods reflect a long-run equilibrium situation. Such might be the case if the economy does not experience high inflationary pressures, presents a 'normal' growth rate, and relative prices of primary inputs – particularly the wage-to-exchange-rate ratio – are not under or overvalued. On the other hand, it is important that the data used correspond to the same year, and that this year is the most recent possible. In this way, cost structures will not correspond to different relative prices and will better reflect the techniques being used.

An effort was made to take full advantage of data sources, evaluating their reliability, level of aggregation and availability, and reconciling these different aspects. Cost and output data for manufacturing industries were taken from the 1985 *Annual Manufacturing Survey*, which was available for processing from the start of the study. Foreign trade data were obtained from the magnetic tape corresponding to that same year. Cost structures for agricultural inputs were also obtained from surveys conducted during 1985. However, the columns for drinking water, electricity, mining products and transportation were prepared from 1987 data obtained directly from the producing companies. Lastly, the columns corresponding to communications, insurance and commerce were based on the input–output matrix of the national accounts (DANE, 1985b).

The vast majority of data used correspond to 1985, when a significant real depreciation of the currency took place. Taken at the year's average, however, the peso was still overvalued. The wage-to-exchange-rate ratio began to decline in 1985, and this continued in 1986 and 1987, a process that certainly contributed to restoring equilibrium to the current account of the balance of payments in 1986 and 1987. These events led to the judgement that it was necessary to price update the matrix in order to better reflect the conditions prevailing in 1987. The updating, presented in section 8.5, was done using the method described in section 7.4.

8.3 THE USE OF MARGINAL COST ESTIMATES

The generation of electricity was predominately carried out by public enterprises. With the aim of planning the expansion of the system, and achieving greater efficiency, *Interconexión Eléctrica SA* (ISA) was set up in 1970 to interconnect the system and administer the grid. Electricity was not traded at the margin. Even though the possibility of exporting it had been considered, no project existed which could be viewed as feasible in the short or medium term.

Hydroelectricity was the principal form of electricity in Colombia. Throughout the 1980s the participation of hydroelectricity grew so as to account for 78.5 percent of all electricity by 1987. The generation of thermal plants decreased as a consequence of less investment in new plants, as well as the limited availability of the existing ones. The majority of the thermal units used natural gas or coal, which in 1986 represented 68 percent and 30 percent, respectively, of energy sources used by thermal generation.

The prices charged for electricity differed according to the user. Three possible sectoral destinations were considered in this study: manufacturing, agriculture, and services. A row for each one was prepared – which registered the value of electricity consumed by each industry – and a column, which contained the corresponding cost structures. The consumption of electricity by each one of the manufacturing industries was provided by the *Annual Manufacturing Survey*. The consumption of electricity by agricultural activities was determined during the preparation of each column. The intermediate demand for electricity by services includes that of commerce, communications, insurance, and other services. From the viewpoint of cost structures, electricity for manufacturing industries is a weighted average of the cost structures corresponding to the different voltage levels in accordance with the procedure described further on. The cost structure of the electricity for services activities, on the other hand, corresponds only to that delivered in low voltage. The agricultural sector also purchased in low voltage, but at a different tariff, which meant that the appropriate cost structure had to be different.

The incremental cost of supplying electricity to the grid was estimated by ISA, using the average incremental long-run cost approach (AILRC), which may be expressed as follows,

$$\text{AILRC} = \frac{\Sigma_t \, [C(q_t) - C(q_0)] \, (1 + d)^{-t}}{\Sigma_t \, (q_t - q_0) \, (1 + d)^{-t}} \tag{8.2}$$

where $C(q_t)$ is the cost of generating q units in period t, $C(q_0)$ is the cost of generating q units in the base period $(t = 0)$, d is the discount rate, and $(q_t - q_0)$ is the increase in consumption. The 1989–99 expansion plan, primarily based on hydroelectric plants, was used to estimate the long-run incremental cost for the interconnected system, including the investments required for transmission, subtransmission, and distribution, both primary and secondary. The cost structure for the overall interconnected system was calculated taking into account losses and demands at the different voltage levels, and assuming a 0.65 load factor. The resulting unit costs are presented in Table 8.4.

The expansion plan includes the value of the investments on a project basis, differentiating between local and foreign currency expenses, but does not

Table 8.4   Average incremental long-run cost of electricity at different levels (at 1987 prices)

Level	$/kWh
Generation and interconnection	10.69
Transmission	11.95
Subtransmission	13.28
Distribution:	
primary	14.50
secondary	17.81

Source: ISA (1987).

include the demand for specific inputs generated by these investments. An estimated break-down of the domestic expenditures by industry of origin for each one of the projects contemplated by the expansion plan was obtained from ISA for dam construction and civil engineering. The break-downs for the remaining broad investment categories were obtained from various sources. Since no information on the input composition was available for each of the projects contemplated by the expansion plan, the cost structure of the San Carlos I project, which was already completed, was used (Perfetti, 1987). Investments in the Guavio project were not included as the cost of civil engineering works was considered atypical.

No data on the cost of acquiring the land were available on a project basis. Thus, a value of land per unit cost of infrastructure calculated from the Guavio project was used. The resulting land cost was assigned to the row 'Land' in the matrix of nonproduced inputs **F**, assuming that for the majority of the hydroelectric projects, the land to be bought would have an opportunity cost at market prices equal to its market value. Finally, the foreign exchange component was estimated based on the San Carlos I project.

Cost structures for investments in transmission, subtransmission and distribution were not available. They were estimated with the help of an electrical engineer and using the cost structure of the transmission and distribution investments carried out during 1983 (Perfetti, 1987).

The cost structure of electricity for the service activities was calculated as a weighted average of the cost structures for the generation, transmission, subtransmission and distribution, such that $a_{ij} = \sum_k \beta_k X_{ijk}$, where a_{ij} is the technical coefficient of the input i in the delivery of one kWh, x_{ijk} is the share of input i in the total investment of process k (k = generation, transmission, subtransmission and distribution), and β_k is the share of process k in total

Table 8.5   *Average incremental long-run cost of electricity for services and*
            manufacturing industries (December 1987 pesos/kWh)

Inputs	Services	Manufactures
Machinery and equip. for road construction	2.9171	2.9546
Electromechanical equipment		
Generators	0.1271	0.1291
Transformers	2.2510	1.2769
Bars	0.0224	0.0228
Lightning rods and condensers	0.0002	0.0002
Multiple switchboards	0.0329	0.0334
Cables	0.2608	0.2648
Mechanical equipment		
Turbines	0.4477	0.4546
Gates	0.0889	0.0903
Iron dikes	0.1445	0.1468
Transporter bridges	0.0476	0.0483
Others	0.0388	0.0343
Tools	0.0061	0.0062
Materials		
Cables ACSR	0.4035	0.3770
Steel structures for towers	0.4552	0.4295
Concrete posts	0.3388	0.1250
Porcelain insulators	0.1322	0.1248
Cramp-irons (suspension and tying)	0.1848	0.1292
Control and measuring equipment	1.0781	0.4598
Aluminum screen bars	0.0371	0.0350
Galvanized steel cables	0.0318	0.0300
Vibration shock absorbers	0.1511	0.1425
Cement	0.6130	0.6433
Steel	0.4956	0.4995
Fuels (diesel)	0.3052	0.3061
Coal	0.2636	0.2639
Dynamite	0.0784	0.0796
Electrical installations	0.0817	0.0830
Wood	0.0169	0.0172
Others	0.6185	0.4631
Land	0.2523	0.2527

Sources: ISA (1987) and Junta Nacional de Tarifas.

Inputs	Services	Manufactures
Insurance	0.0471	0.0473
Labor		
Skilled, domestic	4.9506	3.9332
Skilled, foreign	0.6091	0.6187
Unskilled, domestic	0.2976	0.3022
Long-run incremental cost (ISA)	**17.8100**	**14.8248**
Normative excess profits	0.2900	-1.7648
Average tariff for service industries	**18.1000**	**13.0600**

incremental cost. The results thus obtained are presented in Table 8.5.

The demand for electricity by the agricultural sector originated primarily in pumping for irrigation, a high proportion of which consumes low voltage electricity. The cost of producing that electricity was similar to that of electricity for services, and only the tariff needed to be modified. Since there was no published data on the average agricultural tariff for each electricity company, it was estimated at 80 percent of the average manufacturing tariff based on information provided by the Junta Nacional de Tarifas, and experts from the Corporación Eléctrica de la Costa Atlántica and the Empresa de Energía Eléctrica de Bogotá.

The manufacturing sector consumes electricity at different voltages (high, medium and low), and the cost structure for each of these voltage levels is different. Since no information was available on the tariff paid by each manufacturing industry, a weighted average of the cost structures of the three voltage levels was used. The weights were the consumption by manufacturing industries at each of the voltage levels, as a proportion of total manufacturing consumption.

The cost structure for potable water was prepared in a similar manner; that is, comparing the tariff and an estimate of the long-run marginal cost of supplying that water. No estimates for long-run marginal costs were available, and no detailed information was available for large scale projects. Thus, marginal costs were estimated based on two projects designed for satisfying the medium-run demand expansion in small cities. Both projects corresponded to complete systems, and thus included the intake, transmission pipeline, grit chamber, water treatment plant, storage tanks, distribution network, connections, and meters.

In order to prepare the cost structure, the present values of expenditures in each input to be used in the construction, operation and maintenance of the aqueduct were calculated, and then classified by the 8-digit ISIC according to origin (national or foreign). Traded inputs were broken down accordingly (foreign exchange, taxes, transportation and commerce margins) and nontraded inputs were assigned to their respective columns. Those present-value costs were compared with the present value of sales at the prevailing tariff, and the normative excess profit was calculated as the difference between the present value of all costs and the present value of water sales. The results, reported in Table 8.6, were used to prepare the final column.

8.4   INVESTMENT AND CONSUMPTION CONVERSION FACTORS

Nontraded Investment Goods

The matrix includes five groupings of nontraded investment goods: industrial machinery and equipment, agricultural machinery, transportation equipment, office equipment, and industrial construction. The cost structures corresponding to the first four were prepared by aggregating the cost structures of the industries producing the corresponding goods. The column for the last grouping was based on cost structures for the building of large-scale social housing projects, since specific data for industrial construction were not available.

From the point of view of intermediate demand, the 'Industrial machinery and equipment' row supplies the leasing of machinery and equipment, as well as demands originated in the conversion factors for manufacturing and investment services. The intermediate demand for 'Agricultural machinery' comes exclusively from the agricultural investment conversion factor. The intermediate demand for 'Transportation equipment' originates in the investment conversion factors for manufacturing, agriculture, transportation and services. Lastly, the intermediate demand for 'Office equipment' originates in the investment conversion factors for manufacturing, transportation and services.

Fixed Gross Investment Conversion Factors

Four sectoral investment groups were defined: manufacturing, agricultural, transportation, and services. For each group, goods were classified as traded or nontraded. Traded goods were broken down into foreign exchange, taxes, transportation and commerce margins, in accordance with their corresponding import price structures. Nontraded investment goods were grouped according to the five types of nontraded investment goods mentioned above. The results obtained are presented in Table 8.7.

Consumption Conversion Factor

The matrix includes a consumption conversion factor, used exclusively for shadow pricing the consumption expenditure of foreign labor. Detailed

*Table 8.6   Present value of the costs of constructing, operating and
maintaining an aqueduct (thousands of 1987 pesos)*

	Domestic	Foreign	Total
Operating and maintenance	**168 625.42**	**12 324.45**	**180 949.90**
Stationery	9 092.00	—	9 092.00
Lime	2 709.00	1 161.40	3 870.40
Heating	26 494.00	—	26 494.00
Gaseous chlorine	12 983.70	—	12 983.70
Others	39 096.72	4 344.08	43 440.80
Materials for repairs	15 910.90	6 818.97	22 729.90
Energy	11 242.30	—	11 242.30
Unskilled labor	35 767.70	—	35 767.70
Skilled labor	15 329.10	—	15 329.10
Investment costs	**316 564.92**	**32 495.38**	**349 060.30**
Tar and other sealing	1 145.60	—	1 145.60
PVC pipes	20 490.90	—	20 490.90
PVC accessories for pipes	2 112.30	—	2 112.30
Double baked brick walls	1 477.20	—	1 477.20
Rough stone drainage pipes	174.50	—	174.50
Rough stone accessories	5.40	—	5.40
Delivered concrete	27 650.40	—	2 7650.40
Simple concrete drainage	159.70	—	159.70
Asbestos-concrete pipes	84 716.20	—	84 716.20
Asbestos-concrete accessories	11 733.40	—	11 733.40
1/2" grate bars	77.40	—	77.40
Forged iron for floor plates	4 257.70	—	4 257.70
Water purification plants	67 760.00	29 040.00	96 800.00
High pressure floats	766.66	31.94	798.60
Valves	2 441.85	2 441.85	4 883.70
Wall coverings/facings	845.7	—	845.70
Accessories for metal pipes	9 815.80	—	9 815.80

Sources: Authors' elaboration based on investment projects provided by DNP.

	Domestic	Foreign	Total
Lateral gates	484.00	—	484.00
Forged iron circular lids	50.80	—	50.80
Paint for pipes and iron	12.20	—	12.20
Control and measuring	2 130.38	112.13	2 242.50
Water measuring instruments	3 477.84	869.46	4 347.30
Unskilled labor	52 345.30	—	52 345.30
Skilled labor	22 433.70	—	22 433.70
Total costs	**485 190.34**	**44 819.83**	**530 010.20**
Normative excess profits	—	—	−379
Present value of sales	—	—	**150 324.30**

Table 8.7   Composition of investment conversion factors

Conversion factor	Manufactures	Agriculture	Transport	Services
Industrial machinery and equipment	0.1610	—	—	0.0480
Agricultural machinery	—	0.2590	—	—
Transportation equipment	0.0440	0.0660	0.6270	0.1320
Office equipment	0.0320	—	0.0350	0.4200
Industrial construction	0.2170	—	—	—
Commerce	0.0487	0.0620	0.0270	0.0317
Transport	0.0051	0.0020	0.0002	0.0015
Taxes	0.0977	0.0980	0.0900	0.1108
Foreign exchange	0.3945	0.5130	0.2208	0.2560
Total	1.0000	1.0000	1.0000	1.0000

Source: Authors' elaboration.

information on the composition of the consumption basket of these families, and of the sectoral origin of the goods they included, was not available. Thus, a simple approximation of aggregating the cost structures of consumption goods was used. The input–output matrix (DANE, 1985b) was used to obtain the composition of private consumption according to sector of origin. Private consumption of domestic origin was accounted for in the column by including the aggregate of all cost structures of industries of the matrix producing these goods. The private imported consumption was broken down into foreign exchange, taxes, commerce and transport, and added to the domestic component.

8.5   UPDATING THE MATRIX

Changes in Relative Prices, 1985–87

The domestic currency appreciated in Colombia after 1975 until 1983 (see Table 8.9). In this period, the wage/exchange rate ratio increased in approximately 13 percent, the merchandise account of the balance of payments went from 2 to −3 percent of GNP, and the current account balance from −1 to −7 percent (see Table 8.9). Concomitantly, the external debt increased from 27 to 30 percent of GNP, interest payments jumped from 7 to 19 percent of exports of goods, and import restrictions were increased. The real depreciation of the peso began in 1983 and lasted until late 1987. During this period, the index of the real exchange rate calculated by *Banco de la República* (1984, 1988) increased by more than 50 percent, and the wage/exchange rate ratio fell by 40 percent. In 1983, together with the devaluation, advance deposits for importing were eliminated and partially compensated for by another type of deposit, especially from 1986 on (see Table 8.11). As from 1985, import taxes increased, and quotas were reduced (see Tables 8.12 and 8.18).

The data used for preparing the matrix primarily corresponds to 1985, the year during which the most important real depreciation took place. Between January and December of that year the index of the real exchange rate of the Colombian peso increased by 30 percent and the wage/exchange ratio fell by 32 percent. Later on, the peso continued to depreciate, but at a much slower rate. In 1987 the index of the real exchange rate of the Colombian peso was only 5 percent higher than that of December 1985. This real depreciation was sufficient to balance the 1985 merchandise account and to obtain surpluses in the 1986 and 1987 current accounts (see Table 8.9). The exchange rate that existed during these last two years was higher than that of 1975, reflecting the additional depreciation required to compensate for the larger debt service (see Table 8.9). Finally, the real exchange rate stabilized during 1987.

Given that the matrix corresponds to a year in which the adjustment of relative prices was still taking place, that relative prices seemed to have stabilized in 1987, and that a certain consensus existed in Colombia for these relative prices to prevail in the medium term, it was decided to bring the prices in the matrix up to date with those existing in 1987.

Updating Methodology

The procedure presented in Chapter 7 was used to revalue the matrix at the new relative prices, taking several factors into account. First, some columns of the matrix were already constructed with data corresponding to 1987, so it was not necessary to update these. The corresponding rows were evaluated at 1985 prices, so it was necessary to adjust the corresponding prices. Second, price indexes with an aggregation level comparable to that of the matrix – vector z of the equation (7.23) – were not available. The government, however, determines the prices of some of these inputs; consequently, reliable price indexes could be constructed. Finally, there were price indexes for the nonproduced inputs (elements of the matrix F), except for the gross operating surplus. For these reasons, equation (7.28) was used to estimate the vector containing the 1987 prices of the produced goods (z).

Inputs whose prices were determined by the government and those whose columns already corresponded to 1987, had prices determined exogenously. In other words, they were the ones eliminated from matrix A in order to obtain matrix B and that were incorporated into F in order to obtain V. Also, the gross operating surplus was assumed to be a constant proportion of the price; vector $\hat{g}$ contains in its diagonal the respective coefficients. Lastly, land and normative excess profits only appeared in the cases of water and electricity, whose cost structures corresponded to recent data, so they were removed from F in passing from A to B. Table 8.8 presents the price indexes used for updating the nonproduced inputs and transfers, as well as the indexes used for exogenously updating specific inputs.

Once vector z of price indexes for produced goods was estimated, the matrixes corresponding to the new prices were calculated as $B^n = \hat{z} \, B \, \hat{z}^{-1}$ and $V^n = \hat{z}^v \, V \, \hat{z}^{-1}$. These matrixes, however, differed from A and F in that B^n omitted two types of goods that had been assigned as rows in the V^n: (1) those with cost structures that already corresponded to 1987; (2) those that were indexed exogenously. In order to reconstruct matrixes A^n and F^n, those rows corresponding to cost structures already at 1987 prices were taken out of matrix V^n and put, together with their respective columns, into matrix B. The exogenously updated rows were reassigned to matrix A. In order to reincorporate the corresponding columns, it was taken into account that these were constructed using 1985 data, and that their prices were considered as exogenous. For this reason, it was necessary to update the cost structures, and recalculate the gross operating surplus, so it would correspond to the

Table 8.8   Exogenously determined input-price indexes, 1987 (1985 = 100)

Inputs	Index	Source
Nonproduced		
Unskilled urban labor	140.86	Monthly salary of manufacturing industry workers (DANE, *Boletín Mensual de Estadística*).
Unskilled rural labor	157.23	Monthly agricultural wage (DANE, *Boletín Mensual de Estadística*).
Skilled labor	141.08	Monthly salary of manufacturing industry employees (DANE, *Boletín Mensual de Estadística*).
Foreign exchange	185.14	Wholesale price index, imported inputs (Banco de la República, 1988)
Import taxes	185.14	Ibid.
Fixed supply inputs	158.82	Wholesale price index, intermediate goods (Banco de la República, 1988)
Government administered		
Coffee	215.0	Resolutions by Ministries and relevant enterprises
Sesame	158.8	Ibid.
Rice	151.3	Ibid.
Corn	138.6	Ibid.
Sorghum	157.1	Ibid.
Soy bean	136.7	Ibid.
Sugar	158.2	Ibid.
Cotton fiber	164.1	Ibid.
Fertilizers	127.8	Ibid.
Milk	144.2	Ibid.
Cement	152.8	Ibid.
Tires	167.2	Ibid.
Communications	166.1	Ibid.
With updated cost structures		
Mineral coal	166.3	Resolutions by Ministries and relevant enterprises

Inputs	Index	Source
Industrial sands	168.0	Wholesale price index, intermediate goods (Banco de la República, 1988)
Calcium stone	168.0	Ibid.
Sand and gravel	168.0	Ibid.
Natural gas	177.8	Resolutions by Ministries and relevant enterprises
Unpurified marine salt	174.7	Ibid.
Electricity (manufactures)	166.8	Ibid.
Electricity (services)	172.1	Ibid.
Electricity (agriculture)	166.8	Ibid.
Drinking water	192.0	Ibid.
Gas pipeline	177.8	Ibid.
Industrial construction	152.0	GNP implicit price index (DANE, 1987b)
Transport (all types)	170.0	Ibid.

exogenous prices. The coefficients of these columns were updated using vectors z and z^v, and the coefficients for the gross operating surpluses were obtained as residuals. Matrixes A^n and F^n were completed with the inclusion of these columns and eventually used to calculate the shadow price ratios.

8.6   FOREIGN EXCHANGE

Introduction

No reliable estimates of price elasticities of exports and imports were available for Colombia. Therefore, in this study the shadow price ratio of foreign exchange, at efficiency prices, was calculated according to expression (2.16).

Given that (2.16) should be calculated with reference to the equilibrium exchange rate, the taxes (or *ad valorem* equivalent of other restrictions) on, and subsidies to foreign trade, included in T_m and T_x, should be those that form part of the long-run commercial policy. In the case of Colombia, the import duties, gasoline subsidy, advance deposits, CAT and CERT export incentives,[4] and PROEXPO financing were considered part of this commercial policy. The

---

4. Acronyms for negotiable tax reimbursement certificates usable to pay taxes.

following sections of this chapter deal with the estimation of expression (2.29) for the period 1982–87.

The Equilibrium Exchange Rate

An approximation of the equilibrium exchange rate (*eer*) may be obtained by estimating a parity exchange rate (*per*), defined as one that equalizes the domestic and world values of a basket of goods; that is to say,

$$\mathbf{q}_0' [1 \hat{+} \tau_0] \mathbf{p}_0^w \, per_0 = \mathbf{q}_0' \mathbf{p}_0^d \tag{8.3}$$

where per_0 is the parity exchange rate in year zero, $\mathbf{q}_0'$ is the row vector of the basket chosen for year zero, $\mathbf{p}_0^i$ is a column vector of the prices of the basket in the market i (w = world, d = domestic) in year zero, and $[1 \hat{+} \tau_0]$ is a diagonal matrix whose diagonal elements are equal to one plus the *ad valorem* equivalent rates of those incentives or restrictions to foreign trade that were considered part of the long-run commercial policy. Similarly, the value of the baskets in year t would be

$$\mathbf{q}_0' [1 \hat{+} \tau_t] \mathbf{p}_0^t \, per_t = \mathbf{q}_0' \mathbf{p}_t^d \tag{8.4}$$

Thus, from expressions (8.3) and (8.4) an index of the parity exchange rate (*IPER*) may be defined as

$$IPER_t = \frac{per_t}{per_0} = \frac{\mathbf{q}_0' \mathbf{p}_t^d / \mathbf{q}_0' \mathbf{p}_0^d}{\mathbf{q}_0' [1 \hat{+} \tau_t] \mathbf{p}_0^t / \mathbf{q}_0' [1 \hat{+} \tau_0] \mathbf{p}_0^w} \tag{8.5}$$

Then, if the exchange rate prevailing at moment k may be considered as an 'equilibrium' one, the *eer* in period t may be approximated by $eer_t = eer_k$ ($IPER_t / IPER_k$). That is, long-run equilibrium would require the real exchange rate between periods t and k to compensate for the differential rates of inflation, discounting for the effects of those changes in incentives and restrictions to foreign trade that are considered as part of long-run policy. Even if the theoretical argument for considering the *per* as the *eer* has been criticized by various authors, it is considered useful for providing an approximation for the direction of long-term fluctuations of the *eer*, although not necessarily its magnitude (Balassa, 1964).[5]

The *Banco de la República* (1984, 1988) calculated an IPER based on a basket of currencies from the United States, Germany, Japan, France, the

---

5. Officer (1976) provides a review on parity exchange rates.

United Kingdom, Spain, Venezuela and Ecuador. This index only reflects the appreciation, or depreciation, of the peso with respect to price changes. It did not take into account the changes in trade incentives and restrictions that were part of the long-run policy, nor the differential evolution of relative productivities. The formula used was

$$IPER(BR)_t = \frac{\Pi_j (er_{jt})^{w_j}}{\Pi_j (er_{j0})^{w_j}} \quad \frac{\Pi_j (er_{jt} P_{jt} / P_{dt})^{w_j}}{\Pi_j (er_{j0} P_{j0} / P_{d0})^{w_j}} \qquad (8.6)$$

in which er_{jt} is the nominal exchange rate of the Colombian peso with respect to the currencies of each one of the countries j, P_{jt} is country j's wholesale price index in month t (1975 = 100), P_{dt} is Colombia's wholesale price in month t (1975 = 100), w_j is country j's participation in Colombia's foreign trade.

The results obtained by the *Banco de la República* for the basket of foreign currencies, as well as the US parity exchange rate calculated according to expression (8.5) only in relation to the US dollar, are presented in Table 8.9. The reference year (1975) may be considered as a year of relative 'equilibrium'. The current account deficit was small, and the coffee bonanza had not begun (Table 8.9). In 1975, an almost uninterrupted fall of the real exchange rate began, lasting until 1983. From then on the real exchange rate began to increase, and during 1985 recovered to its 1975 level. During this period of the peso's overvaluation, and despite the coffee bonanza at the end of 1985, and 1986, foreign debt increased considerably. These reasons, coupled with the reduction of export incentives in 1986, may justify treating the 1987 real exchange rate as an equilibrium one even though it is 11 percent above that of 1975. Also, a consensus seemed to exist among Colombian economists that a real exchange rate 10 percent above that of 1975 might be considered as a reasonable approximation to the *eer* for the level of foreign trade interventions prevailing at that time; that is, it would have maintained the current account of the balance of payments in equilibrium. In this study, the level of the real exchange rate during 1987 and 1988 was considered to be an 'equilibrium' one.

Import Taxes

Imports of goods were subject to numerous duties, as indicated in Table 8.10. A significant import subsidy was also identified. Gasoline is imported at the margin and its users' price is below marginal cost (CIF price plus domestic distribution costs). The unit subsidy, estimated as the difference between these two amounts, was multiplied by the gasoline imports and taken into account for calculating the *sprfe*. The estimated amount of the subsidy is also given in Table 8.10.

Table 8.9 Real exchange rate and balance of payments indicators

Year	Real exchange rate indexes			Balance of payments (% of GNP)		
	Banco de la República[a]	US dollar[b]	Wage/exchange rate[c]	Current account	External debt	Interest paid
1975	100.00	100.00	100.00	−0.01	27.27	6.95
1976	95.40	93.78	90.99	0.01	24.41	4.90
1977	85.74	82.10	90.73	0.02	19.68	5.34
1978	85.50	81.25	99.71	0.01	17.45	5.45
1979	81.71	76.79	100.98	0.02	18.98	6.71
1980	83.50	81.64	104.19	0.00	19.33	7.12
1981	81.59	83.22	106.01	−0.05	23.41	12.73
1982	75.63	80.37	110.97	−0.07	26.35	19.27
1983	73.58	84.47	113.30	−0.07	29.58	19.02
1984	79.86	93.84	103.18	−0.05	32.29	18.35
1985	91.40	113.05	82.26	−0.05	40.37	23.27
1986	108.46	114.44	70.72	0.01	43.44	18.24
1987	111.17*	113.32	68.04	0.00	43.28	22.90

Notes: * Provisional. [a] See expression (8.6). [b] (Nominal exchange rate index × US wholesale price index)/Colombian wholesale price index. [c] Nominal wage index divided by the nominal exchange rate index.

Sources: Revista del Banco de la República, December 1988, and author's calculations from *International Financial Statistics*, IMF, 1987, and *Boletín Mensual de Estadística*, DANE.

Table 8.10 Import tax revenue and subsidies (in millions of pesos)

	1982	1983	1984	1985	1986	1987
Custom duties	33 645	34 716	39 754	53 887	79 915	108 716
Law 68/83 (2% CIF)	3 007[a]	3 193	3 789	6 690	10 160	1 501
Law 50/83 (8% CIF)	—	—	—	23 453	38 715	5 400
Stamp tax	17	46	21	8	11	43
Cigarettes	4	3	—	—	—	—
Law 74/86	—	—	—	—	—	113 039
Export Promotion Fund	9 940	10 485	12 013	16 225	26 303	3 512
Custom duties paid with CAT or CERT	760	927	768	1 584	1 391	2 872
Other fees and fines	672	755	727	794	1 996	2 748
Sales tax	21 282	21 358	25 827	40 758	62 743	91 219
Total import tax revenue	69 327	71 483	81 899	143 399	221 234	329 119
Gasoline subsidy	5 357	2 790	2 726	16 020	655	4 825

Note: [a] Corresponds to Decree 237/4/74, immediate precedent of Law 68/83.

Source: Informe de Recaudos, Ministry of Finance, 1982–87.

Advance Import Deposits

In 1976, the Junta Monetaria instituted that deposits had to be made in advance as a requirement for access to foreign exchange for the payment of imports. These deposits were modified several times after their introduction, principally regarding the percentage of the value of imports required, and were eliminated at the end of 1983. The deposits were an implicit *ad valorem* cost for the importer due to the opportunity cost of the funds deposited. The cost to the importer of the advance deposit (*cad*) was calculated as the difference between the future (terminal) value of the deposit when invested in the financial market for the deposit period, minus the sum effectively received back from the deposit. According to the rules, the deposit was returned adjusted for any possible devaluation during the stipulated period. Thus, the present value (PV) of the *cad* was calculated as[6]

$$\text{PV}(cad) = \frac{\alpha \, cif \, (1 + r)^n - \alpha \, cif \, (1 + d_n)}{(1 + r)^n} \tag{8.7}$$

where α is the percentage rate of the advance deposit, *cif* is the CIF value of the imported good, n is the number of months the deposit is retained, r is the nominal monthly rate of interest, and d_n is the total devaluation during the n months. Since the opportunity cost of the deposit was probably greater than the interest rate, this calculation may have underestimated the real cost of the advance deposit. This deposit was abolished in 1984.

In addition to the advance deposits, in 1977 the *Junta Monetaria* created the 'payment deposit', which was later subject to various modifications. That same year the Colombian government initiated an adjustment process, and the payment deposit was used as an import control instrument, since it also implied a financial cost to the importer. In order to calculate the cost of the payment deposits, equation (8.7) was also used, taking into account that n now means the number of days that funds were deposited. It was assumed that the opportunity cost of the deposit would be determined by the marginal cost of financing the importer's working capital, estimated by the bank lending interest rate, since during the period 1982–87 that rate was freely determined by the financial market. The total cost was estimated under the assumption that between 1982 and 1984 all imports were subject to the advance deposit. The results are presented in Table 8.11.[7]

---

6. The formula corresponds to that used by Clavijo (1982), but incorporating the adjustment for devaluation.

7. In 1986 and 1987 approximately 10 percent of imports were exempt.

Table 8.11 Cost of the advance deposit (in percentages and millions of current pesos)

Year	Lending interest rate	Devaluation rate[a]	CIF value of imports of goods		Cost of advance deposit
			Total	Subject to the advance deposit	
1982	40.53	19.00	382 032	328 032	19 584
1983	39.97	26.30	364 423	364 423	14 504
1984	40.23	28.30	419 040	419 040	2 011
1985	42.26	51.20	513 468	531 468	–1 488
1986	39.07	27.18	690 450	621 405	2 921
1987	39.90	20.41	966 368	869 731	7 306

Note: [a] Calculated using the average exchange rate for December of each year.

Sources: *Revista del Banco de la República, Anuario de Comercio Exterior* (DANE), and author's own calculations.

Quantitative Restrictions

The use of import licenses and other quantitative restrictions, including import prohibitions, has been frequent in Colombia since the 1950s (World Bank, 1989). Their use was intensified in 1982–84, in response to persistent current account deficits. As a result, by the end of 1984, binding constraints on imports consisted almost exclusively of import licenses and import prohibitions. From 1985 on, the depreciation of the Colombian peso was accompanied by an increase in import taxes (seeTable 8.10) and a reduction in quantitative restrictions, which were maintained until 1988. Information about the degree to which the remaining licenses were binding constraints determining domestic prices was not available; nevertheless, it could be said that this was more likely in the case of consumer goods than for intermediate and capital goods, and for goods which directly competed with domestic production than for others.

Following Londero and Remes (1989) and Londero, Remes and Teitel (1998), in order to approximate the effects of quantitative restrictions, an index of the ratio of users' (wholesale) to producers' prices of imports was prepared

Table 8.12 Effects of quantitative restrictions on the domestic price of imports (indexes, 1970 = 1)

Year	(1) CIF prices in pesos	(2) Import tax rates $(1 + t_m)$	(3) Wholesale prices	(4) (3)/(1) × (2)
1970	1.000	1.000	1.000	1.000
1971	1.073	0.978	1.124	1.071
1972	1.191	0.988	1.400	1.190
1973	1.471	0.997	1.931	1.317
1974	2.219	0.966	2.663	1.242
1975	2.801	0.990	3.201	1.154
1976	3.230	0.953	3.875	1.259
1977	3.728	0.997	4.084	1.099
1978	4.090	0.997	4.949	1.214
1979	5.176	1.014	5.969	1.137
1980	6.745	1.008	7.377	1.085
1981	8.003	1.011	9.033	1.116
1982	9.188	1.013	10.705	1.150
1983	10.723	1.012	13.212	1.218
1984	13.244	1.006	17.913	1.344
1985	18.303	1.040	23.849	1.253
1986	23.101	1.084	28.969	1.157
1987	30.670	1.098	36.798	1.093

Sources: (1) DANE, *Cuentas Nacionales de Colombia*; (2) Ministerio de Hacienda; and (3) *Revista del Banco de la República*.

(Table 8.12). The increased incidence of these restrictions during the period 1982-84 can be observed, as well as their reduction from 1985 on. By 1987, the index had reached its lowest level since 1971. The estimated *sprfe* did not include the effect of the quantitative restrictions. Therefore, if they were binding, the *sprfe* would have been underestimated.

Coffee Exports

Coffee exports were not included in estimating the *sprfe* despite the fact that they represented around 50 percent of Colombia's total exports. This decision was based on an analysis of how coffee prices were determined, and it was concluded that an additional demand for foreign exchange would not have affected its production, or its domestic consumption because: (1) Colombia belonged to the International Coffee Organization, so the corresponding exports were determined exogenously by a quota system; and, (2) the country used specific instruments (the coffee retention, and the *ad valorem* tax) in order to suppress the effects of exchange rate variations on the domestic price of coffee (Lanzetta, 1986). In conclusion, it was assumed that the adjustment to an additional supply or demand of foreign exchange would be done by changing all exports except coffee, or by increasing imports. For that reason, coffee exports were not included in the calculation of the *sprfe*.

Export Incentives

The data on tax-credit certificates to promote exports, CAT or CERT, were taken from the *Informe de Recaudos* of the Ministerio de Hacienda, where the certificates issued, redeemed, and still in circulation are reported. Those issued during a certain year were used to estimate the incentive provided to the exporters in that year (Table 8.13).

The subsidy implicit in PROEXPO export financing was taken from the study by Fernández Rivas et al. (1985). The subsidy per peso lent results from dividing the difference between the value of the loan received and the present value of the repayment flows, by the loan's nominal value. The result is then multiplied by the proportion of the value of the exports financed by PROEXPO (0.8) in order to obtain the subsidy per peso exported. Finally, assuming that the financing is received six months before exporting, the subsidy per peso exported is expressed in present value at the shipping date. This procedure showed that, in 1985 the average subsidy implicit in the PROEXPO credit was between 7.5 and 9.5 percent of the value of the exports eligible for this incentive (Table 8.13). Estimates were done using a single rate of 8.5 percent for all the years during the period 1982–87, excluding ineligible exports.

Calculating the Shadow Price Ratio of Foreign Exchange

The shadow price ratio of foreign exchange was calculated according to expression (2.29), omitting the indirect taxes on the domestic sales of

Table 8.13 CERTs and CATs (in millions of pesos)

Year	CERTs and CATs			PROEXPO credit	
	Issued	Redeemed	In circulation	Exports	Subsidy[b]
1982	5 318.6	5 650.6	1 299.5	72 590	6 170
1983	5 875.9	5 888.5	1 371.6	86 159	7 324
1984	9 572.3	5 269.5	4 273.7	116 255	9 882
1985	18 430.9	17 662.9	5 070.0	172 268	14 643
1986	19 741.8	16 534.6	8 251.0	278 712	23 691
1987	21 495.6	20 744.2	8 594.0[a]	411 879	35 010

Notes: [a] Preliminary figures. [b] Calculated as 8.5 percent of the total exports' value, excluding coffee, coal, oil and its derivatives, precious stones, and hides.

Source: *Informe de Recaudo*, Treasury, and author's calculations.

marginally exported goods, and using the data reported in Tables 8.14 and 8.15. Since the exchange rate prevailing during 1987 was assumed to be the equilibrium one, the *sprfe* for the said year would simply be,

$$sprfe(1987) = \frac{1\ 124\ 119 + 331\ 600 + 1\ 085\ 463 + 56\ 606}{1\ 124\ 119 + 1\ 085\ 463} = 1.18$$

Instead, in 1986 the real exchange rate was slightly below its 'equilibrium' level. Therefore, using the estimate for *eer/oer* from Table 8.16 and the remaining data from Tables 8.14 and 8.15, the resulting *sprfe* was

$$sprfe(1986) = \frac{111.17}{108.46} \quad \frac{814\ 106 + 223\ 500 + 662\ 443 + 43\ 406}{814\ 106 + 662\ 443} = 1.21$$

The greater value obtained in 1986 and before was fundamentally due to the then larger export subsidies (Table 8.15), as well as to the effect of the correction made to the *oer*. The results for the period 1982–87 are reported in the second column of Table 8.16. The third column corresponds to a *sprfe* calculated without correcting for the ratio of the equilibrium to the current exchange rate. These results show that omitting this correction may lead to a severe underestimation of the *sprfe*, especially if, as it is often the case, it is

Table 8.14 Estimated value of total import restrictions (in millions of current pesos)

Year	Taxes	Gasoline subsidy	Advance deposits	Total restrictions	Total imports	Average rate (%)
1982	69 327	−5 357	19 584	83 554	379 363	22.0
1983	71 483	−2 790	14 504	83 197	404 377	20.6
1984	82 899	−2 726	2 011	82 184	480 683	17.1
1985	143 399	−16 020	−1 488	125 891	625 993	20.2
1986	221 234	−655	2 921	223 500	814 106	27.5
1987	329 119	−4 825	7 306	331 600	1 124 119	29.5

Sources: Tables 8.10 and 8.11, and DANE, *Cuentas Nacionales*.

Table 8.15 Estimated value of total export incentives (in millions of current pesos)

Year	CERT or CAT	PROEXPO credit	Total incentives	Total exports (excl. coffee)	Average rate (%)
1982	5 319	6 170	11 489	163 196	7.0
1983	5 876	7 324	13 200	188 361	7.0
1984	9 572	9 882	19 454	261 979	7.4
1985	18 431	14 643	33 074	427 783	7.7
1986	19 715	23 091	43 406	662 443	6.6
1987	21 496	35 010	56 506	1 085 463	5.2

Sources: Table 8.13 and DANE, *Cuentas Nacionales*.

Table 8.16 Estimated values of the sprfe

Year	Based on the *eer*[a]	Based on the *oer*[b]
1982	1.73	1.18
1983	1.75	1.16
1984	1.59	1.14
1985	1.40	1.15
1986	1.21	1.18
1987	1.18	1.18

Notes: [a] Includes the effect of the *eer/oer* ratio, in 1987 *eer* = *oer*. [b] Does not include the effect of the *eer/oer* ratio.

Sources: Tables 8.9, 8.14 and 8.15.

not possible to estimate the *ad valorem* equivalents of quantitative restrictions that frequently accompany overvaluation.

8.7 LABOR

The estimation of shadow prices of labor requires an understanding of the sources that would satisfy an additional demand for labor. The task was approached by area of origin and skill level, since these are the characteristics determining the conditions individuals face in the labor market. Based on information about labor demand and average wages in the different sectors, labor was classified into: (1) skilled labor in all sectors, comprising professional, administrative and other skilled subgroups; (2) unskilled urban; and (3) rural labor. Each subgroup of skilled labor and the unskilled labor were in turn divided in two according to the level of benefits received: those receiving high benefits, and those receiving normal benefits. For each one of these groups an effort was made to determine the alternative occupations available to a worker hired in the formal labor market. The following subsections present the principal characteristics of the urban and rural labor markets, as well as the calculation of the shadow price ratios for each labor group.

Urban Labor Markets

According to the Misión de Empleo (1986), two types of factors determined employment levels in Colombia.[8] The first is related to the cyclical character of economic activity and its influence on the demand for labor. The second refers to the labor supply, and to the characteristics provided by demographic and educational changes.

Since the end of the Second World War, labor markets had been affected by: the decline of the participation of the agricultural sector in total production and employment, and the increase of manufacturing and services; rapid urbanization (Table 8.17); reductions in mortality and fertility rates; and a considerable increase in educational levels (Table 8.18). These changes generated a supply of labor that the cities could not absorb. Urban unemployment increased (Table 8.17) and tended to be systematically greater for workers with intermediate schooling levels – such as administrative staff with high school education – and less so for those educated to university level (Table 8.18).

The small absorption of the labor force in the cities was reflected in the growth of the so called 'informal sector'. According to the DANE this informal sector was made up of self employed that were not independent professionals, domestics, employees of firms with fewer than 10 workers, and family helpers (FEDESARROLLO, 1984; and DANE, 1987a, Stage 44). According to this definition, DANE (1987a) reports that 56.5 percent of total urban employment was informal in 1984.

Workers seemed to use small firms for entering the market. With little experience, they would join these firms at low wages, until they found more attractive and stable opportunities in larger establishments. Small businesses could pay these lower wages, because to an extent they operated outside labor legislation, avoiding registration and evading the law. Also, the law required a minimum of 25 workers to form a union. In contrast, the larger companies were more supervised and more affected by labor legislation. In particular, firms of 25 workers or more set wages and benefits in accordance with union agreements, not necessarily because a union existed in the establishment (union membership is low in Colombia), but in order to reduce the probability that one was formed.

The worker protected by labor legislation enjoyed greater stability of his employment, since he or she could not be fired without severance payment unless there was 'just cause'. Also, during the worker's employment with the establishment, his or her nominal wage could not be reduced. In summary,

---

8. The 'Misión de Empleo', or 'Chenery Mission', was a study group created by the President of Colombia and directed by Professor Hollis Chenery. See Ocampo and Ramírez (1987).

Table 8.17 Urban population and employment indicators (in percentages)

Year	Share in total	Total	Working age	Unemployment rate
		Growth rates		
1978	62.92	—	—	8.1
1979	63.63	3.09	3.96	9.1
1980	64.31	2.98	3.88	10.0
1981	64.96	2.88	3.72	8.7
1982	65.59	2.78	3.58	9.3
1983	66.20	2.67	3.44	11.0
1984	66.79	2.57	3.29	13.2
1985	67.36	2.46	3.14	12.5
1986	67.92	2.36	2.95	14.5
1987	68.46	2.26	2.90	—
1988	68.99	2.16	2.84	—

Source: Flórez et al. (1987), and Misión de Empleo (1986).

Table 8.18 Labor force and unemployment rates, by educational level (in percentages)

Education level	1976	1980	1984	Composition of 1976–84 growth	Average unemployment rate 1975–85
None	4.5	3.9	3.4	1.4	6.0
Primary	45.7	40.4	36.0	18.3	6.5
Secondary	38.3	41.0	44.8	56.6	12.7
Tertiary	11.6	14.7	15.8	23.7	7.0
Total	100.0	100.0	100.0	100.0	n.a.

Sources: DANE (1987a) and Misión de Empleo (1986).

labor laws and the possibility of setting up a union resulted in lower turnover and higher wages among larger firms. Smaller businesses, instead, were affected very little by union negotiations or by labor legislation, all of which resulted in a more unstable situation for the worker.

Londoño (1987) has argued that the type of contract is the factor determining how the labor market functions. He observed that nonsalaried workers in the informal sector and salaried workers confronted the economic cycle in a different manner. The former seemed to have been able to isolate themselves from the effects of the economic cycle, while salaried urban employment grew in a pro-cyclical manner (Table 8.19).

Table 8.19 GNP and urban employment growth rates (in percentages)

| | | Urban employment | |
Period	GNP	Salaried	Nonsalaried
1976–80	5.5	6.8	6.1
1980–85	2.1	2.0	6.1

Sources: Londoño (1987), and DANE (1985b).

Correlations between the GNP and the different segments of salaried and nonsalaried employment, support the hypothesis of the independence of nonsalaried sectors with respect to the rhythm of economic activity (Londoño, 1987). A weak relationship between the economic cycle and employment creation was obtained when salaried and nonsalaried markets were taken as an aggregate. A more detailed approach, however, allowed three different types of behavior to be identified. First, salaried employment maintained a close association with the level of economic activity, although somewhat delayed in its effects. Second, the level of independent employment (both freelance, bosses, and workers) were less related to activity levels. Lastly, working as a domestic and in a family business was inversely related to the economic cycle.

Nonsalaried workers joined the labor force when economic conditions compelled them to do so, and could be conceived of as a reserve labor force that supplied, in the last instance, the additional demands for urban labor. Sánchez (1988) suggested that domestics and family helpers moved to formal jobs in periods of economic boom, and 'returned' in periods of crisis or reduction in labor demand in the formal sector.

Rural Labor Markets

In the rural sector, demographic, educational and economic changes took place at a slower pace. Rural mortality and fertility rates had declined more slowly

Table 8.20 Composition of the population of more than five years of age by educational level (in percentages)

Educational level	Urban	Rural	Total
Primary	56.7	87.8	65.6
Secondary	37.6	11.7	30.2
University	5.5	0.3	4.0
Other	0.2	0.2	0.2
Total	100.0	100.0	100.0

Sources: DANE (1987a, Stage 31), and Misión de Empleo (1986).

and were approximately twice the urban ones, and schooling levels continued to be lower than those of the urban population (Table 8.20). Rural employment (associated with the primary sector) decreased as a share of total employment. In agriculture, this was due to the reduction in the total cultivated land area, and to the increase in commercial agriculture.[9] In the mining sector, it was due to the increase in medium- and large-scale mining, which were less labor intensive than traditional mining.

During the period 1978–84, employment in the coffee sector and the modernized agricultural sector decreased at annual rates of 4.4 and 4.1 percent, respectively (Reyes, 1987). During this period, rural labor markets adjusted to the reduction in the demand for labor in three ways: (1) increasing underemployment in peasant agriculture; (2) reducing real wages in modern agriculture; and (3) accelerating rural migration to urban areas, which tended to increase urban unemployment and employment in the marginal urban sector.

Wages in modern agriculture grew noticeably during the 1960s and were higher than the legal minimum wage from 1965 until 1983. However, as from 1981 the real wage diminished continuously, to the point where it was below the legal minimum wage, and the average wage in the marginal urban sector. Conversely, starting in 1970, real wages in traditional agriculture 'show a tendency to increase . . . indicating the possibility of increasing scarcity of labor in areas of traditional agriculture . . . as a result of the large accumulated emigrations of the last decades to urban areas and bordering countries' (Reyes, 1987).

---

9. According to estimates of the Ministry of Agriculture, from 1980 to 1984 the total area cultivated with traditional crops declined by 9.6 percent, and that with permanent crops declined by 5.6 percent.

The preceding considerations indicate that fluctuations in agricultural wages and in underemployment reflected the fluctuations in the demand for agricultural labor. Direct consultation with farmers confirmed that the daily pay to agricultural workers was affected by the seasonal demand for labor, although no data were available. Also, since the efficacy of government intervention in rural labor markets was low, benefits and the minimum rural wage were normally not paid. Therefore, the agricultural daily wage may be considered a good estimate of the market value of labor's marginal product and used as such in order to estimate the corresponding shadow price ratio.

There were no studies on workers' mobility, or alternative occupations in the other rural labor markets, in particular of mining workers. In the absence of better information, employment in traditional agriculture was assumed to be the most likely alternative employment for mining workers.

From here on, reference will be made to remunerations that may, or may not include benefits for the worker. In order to distinguish between them, the term 'wage' will be reserved for the basic wage, which does not include benefits. In contrast, the term 'cost to the employer' will be used for the sum of the basic wage and benefits.

Rural Labor

The skilled rural labor force may be classified in two subgroups: professionals, and skilled operators of agricultural and mining machinery. Rural markets for professionals were similar to urban ones. For professionals, working in the rural sector seemed to be the result of personal preference and available opportunities. There seemed to be great mobility between rural and urban areas, there were low levels of professional unemployment, and no statistically significant differences between the average salaries of the rural and urban professionals were found.[10] For these reasons, professionals working in the primary sector were considered together with skilled urban labor and a single shadow price ratio was calculated for both.

In the case of the skilled operators, the tasks for which they had been trained were limited to the primary sector, making them as subject to market fluctuations as less skilled workers. Also, they received no benefits, nor were they organized into unions. For these reasons, skilled rural operators were grouped with unskilled rural labor.[11]

---

10. Strictly speaking, the data did not support the conclusion that there were no differences between the average salaries, since information on rural salaries was limited to those individuals who, although working in the countryside, kept an urban home. For further details, see Cervini (1992).

11. Agricultural labor costs were arranged accordingly in matrix **F**.

Considering that emigration to the cities led to a relative scarcity of labor in the rural areas and increases in real rural wages, and that regional wage differences were considered to reflect imperfect mobility and differences in labor abundance, it was assumed that an additional demand for labor in the rural areas would lead, at least in part, to a reallocation of workers between competing agricultural activities. In other words, its opportunity cost included the reduction in the production of certain agricultural goods. Similarly, an increase in the demand for mining labor would have reduced the supply of labor in agriculture, which was the source of unskilled mining labor at the margin.

For small, medium, and subsistence mining the labor market was competitive. There were neither barriers to entry, nor effective labor legislation. According to interviewed miners, the difference between mining and agricultural wages was the amount required in order to induce workers to endure the tougher work, longer working days, and health risks.

In the case of large-scale mining, labor markets were less competitive, since there were unions and labor negotiations. The average wage, however, when adjusted for productivity, was not above that of subsistence mining. This higher productivity was attributed to a more capital intensive mining, which required more skilled workers. For this reason, it was assumed that the higher wage reflected the more skilled labor needed, and the decision was made to use an *spr* for mining labor equal to one.[12]

Urban Labor

The main source of wage data for the different labor groups was the *National Household Survey*. It was complemented by other similar surveys and the *Annual Manufacturing Survey*, which provided data on benefits for different labor groupings. With respect to the sectoral classification, average hourly wages for the different occupations, by sector, were based on the 1987 *National Household Survey*. With few exceptions, t-tests could not reject the hypothesis that the difference between the average wage for each occupation and sector and the overall average for the occupation, was nil. Significant average wage differences between industries could still be observed. Cervini, et al. (1990, pp. 10.36–10.39) showed, however, that these differences were due to different compositions of the labor force between industries, and not to different average wages for similar occupations. Therefore, no reasons were found for calculating the *spr* for labor at a sectoral level. The same cannot be said, however, for the cost to the employer, since differences in benefits received by workers in different industries made it necessary to calculate

---

12. In matrix **F**, mining wages were included with agricultural wages.

separate *sprs* for labor employed in industries with higher benefits.

Given its great heterogeneity, labor in urban centers was classified by occupational groups, and an *spr* was calculated for each group. Groups were defined by looking for homogeneity in training or experience, negotiating power with respect to the employer, unemployment levels, and employment alternatives. It should be noted that using the same *spr* for the group does not mean that each member had the same cost to the employer. It is sufficient that the ratios of each shadow price to the respective cost to the employer are equal. The following occupational groups were defined: professional, administrative, skilled workers and unskilled workers.[13]

Professionals

This category includes professionals, executives and technicians with professional appointments. According to the data, more than 70 percent of those interviewed and that declared they had professional jobs, had completed a university career. Unemployment among university educated people was considerably below average, and labor markets for professionals were quite competitive. Table 8.21 shows that differences in average professional salaries between small and large establishments were not statistically significant, nor were those between professionals affiliated to a social security scheme (salaried work) and nonaffiliated ones (nonsalaried), or between permanent and temporary jobs (Table 8.22). For this reason, the hourly shadow price of professional labor (consumption numeraire) with normal benefits was assumed to be equal to the employer's hourly cost, so that its *spr* was equal to one.

Benefit coefficients for professionals were calculated with data for executives and national technicians from the *Annual Manufacturing Survey*, 1985. Three-digit ISIC sectors of chemicals (351), rubber (355), oil refining (353), cement (369), iron and steel (371), beverages (313), and paper (341) showed higher benefits than the other industries, thus raising the average considerably.[14] The average benefit coefficient for executives and national technicians, excluding the industries just mentioned, was 73.2 percent. The same coefficient in industries with high benefits was estimated at 98.8 percent.

---

13. The list of occupations included in each category may be consulted in Cervini et al. (1990) and Cervini (1992).

14. Industries showing high benefits were: malt drinks and malt (3133); nonalcoholic drinks and soft drinks (3134); sawdust, paper and cardboard (3411); packaging, paper and cardboard boxes (3412); articles of pulp, paper and cardboard nec. (3419); basic industrial chemical substances, except fertilizers (3511); fertilizers and pesticides (3512); synthetic resins, plastic materials and artificial fibers, except glass (3513); oil refineries (3530); tires (3551); rubber products nec (3559); cement, lime and plaster (3692); and basic iron and steel industries (3710).

Table 8.21 Hourly average professional salary, by sector and establishment (in 1984 pesos)

Occupation	Manufactures		Services	
	Fewer than 10 employees	More than 10 employees	Fewer than 10 employees	More than 10 employees
Architect, engineer	325.23	313.95	280.39	349.93
Architect, technician	250.00	203.61	193.00	188.63
Economist	250.00	401.97	188.80	254.08
Accountant	232.64	253.50	266.11	285.31
Executive	287.76	441.41	297.92	375.13
Biologist, agronomist	303.61	211.23	204.61	246.09
Nurse	—	—	312.42	159.90

Note: In no case could the hypothesis of equality between the average wages for both size intervals be rejected at the 5 percent level.

Sources: DANE (1987a, Stage 44) and authors' own elaboration.

Table 8.22 Hourly average professional salary, by work permanency and affiliation to social security (in 1984 pesos)

Occupation	Permanent	Temporary	Affiliated	Not affiliated
Architect, engineer	358.33	300.30	359.76	320.79
Architect, technician	181.98	171.56	188.27	139.71[b]
Economist	320.91	559.72	321.57	429.62
Accountant	272.39	209.00	270.64	257.49
Executive	369.89	769.67[a]	368.94	555.65[b]
Biologist, agronomist	238.87	333.33	243.44	217.23
Nurse	173.07	143.26	179.58	171.90

Notes: [a] The difference between the two averages is statistically significant at the 1 percent level. [b] The difference between the two averages is statistically significant at the 5 percent level.

Sources: DANE (1987a, Stage 44) and authors' own elaboration.

In these industries, production was concentrated in a few, relatively isolated, big establishments, where unions were particularly strong. Here, benefits were considered more of a reflection of the power of the unions than of opportunity cost. For that reason, these industries were excluded from the calculation of the normal benefits coefficient and treated separately.[15]

The opportunity cost of hiring a professional in industries with high benefits was assumed to be the cost to the employer in industries with normal benefits. So, their *spr* in the consumption numeraire would be

$$spr = 1.732 / 1.988 = 0.87$$

The average salaries of professionals in the different industries (calculated on the basis of hourly salaries) varied between $121.5 and $491.8, without adjusting for social benefits. These differences in average salaries were explained by the differences in composition of the professionals occupied in the different industries. Hourly shadow prices were different by sector, but there was no a priori reason for thinking that the *spr*s were different.

Administrative Workers

The administrative workers include those defined as such by the DANE,[16] 68 percent of whom stated they had completed only secondary education, 26 percent a higher level than that, and 6 percent a lower one (Table 8.23). According to the Misión de Empleo (1986), unemployment for this subgroup of workers was above 25 percent. Also, their educational profile coincides with that of workers with the highest unemployment rates. The average hourly salary, calculated on the basis of data from the *National Household Survey*, shows that permanent administrative workers employed in medium- and large-scale manufacturing, earned $128.16 per hour. This salary is intermediary between the professionals and the skilled workers.

The unemployment levels among administrative workers allowed for the opportunity cost of employing one of them in the formal sector to be estimated by the average remuneration of temporary administrative workers. On the one hand, there were no barriers to entry for anyone attempting to do this type of unsalaried work, which means that all administrative workers saw it as an alternative to a stable job. On the other hand, the market for temporary

---

15. Union negotiations normally affect all personnel. When establishments pay higher benefits because of geographical isolation, personnel working in the urban centers receive the same benefits.

16. The DANE definition corresponds to codes 30–39 of the International Standard Classification of Occupations (ILO, 1969).

Table 8.23 Administrative employees by educational level completed (in percentages)

Survey	None	Primary	Secondary	University
National Household, 1984	0.38	9.80	71.28	18.54
National Household, 1987	0.40	9.40	67.60	22.60
Income and Expenditure, 1985–86	0.00	5.17	68.39	26.44
Employment and Housing, 1987	0.24	8.03	69.26	22.07

Source: Authors' elaboration.

workers was not subject to labor legislation. The salary of the temporary employees in the establishments with fewer than 10 workers was used, which amounted to only 60 to 80 percent that of the permanent workers in the large establishments (Table 8.24). The average value (70 percent) was used, and given the average hourly salary of $128.16 for the medium, and large scale industry, the opportunity cost was $89.71.

These values should be adjusted, taking into account benefits paid to permanent and temporary administrative workers. The average benefits reported for 'Employees' (excluding sectors with high benefits) in the *Annual Manufacturing Survey* was 75 percent. Workers employed in temporary jobs and in microenterprises interviewed by the *Housing and Employment Survey in Bogotá* (CEDE, 1987) were considered the most likely candidates for entry into a formal job. This survey showed that benefits to temporary workers were minimal (Table 8.25), and that benefits paid to workers in microenterprises were also low, but considerably more widespread than for temporary workers. According to Ocampo (1987), the average benefit coefficient for all sectors amounts to some 48.6 percent (Table 8.25), with large variations depending on the size of the establishment, and the sector.[17] On the basis of the data in Table 8.25, the temporary workers and those of small establishments were estimated to receive, on average, 28.47 percent of the benefits (see Cervini et al., 1990, pp. 10.50-10.52). With these data, the hourly cost to the employer of the administrative workers in the medium and large establishments was calculated as

$$\$128.16 \times 1.75 = \$224.28$$

---

17. Despite the variation in the benefits coefficient, the manufacturing average was used in order to calculate the *spr*. Therefore, the denominator of the *spr* was estimated on the basis of a cost to the employer calculated according to the overall manufacturing sector. In the numerator, the benefits coefficient was calculated as a percentage of the manufacturing average.

Table 8.24   Average hourly salary of administrative personnel (in 1984 pesos)

Occupation	Temporary	Permanent	Temporary/ permanent
Messenger	63.83	79.58	0.80
Accountant	82.92	136.73	0.61
Secretary	77.08	112.66	0.60

Source: DANE (1987a, Stage 44).

Table 8.25   Main nonsalary labor costs (in percentages)

Non salary cost	Share of workers receiving the benefit		All sectors	
	Temporary workers	In small establishments	Average percentage over base salary	Share in total benefits
Leave	[a]	47.5[d]	6.7	13.8
Social security	7.7	32.0	13.3	27.4
Family subsidy	0.0[b]	9.5[b]	4.3	8.8
Unemployment	7.0	43.5	13.3	27.4
Service premium	7.1	47.5	8.9	18.3
Training (SENA)	[c]	[c]	2.1	4.3
Total	n. a.	n. a.	48.6	100.0

Notes: [a] Assumed equal to zero, since in order to have the right to some leave payment, the worker must have worked for at least six months. [b] Percentage of temporary workers affiliated to the *cajas de compensación familiar* (institutions in charge of paying the subsidy). [c] Assumed equal to zero. [d] Assumed equal to the service premium.

Sources: Percentage of temporary workers who receive benefits: authors' calculations based on the *Housing and Employment Survey*, 1987. Weighted data: Ocampo (1987).

and for the temporary workers, and those in small establishments the hourly cost to the employer was

$$\$128.16 \times 0.7 \times (1 + 0.75 \times 0.2847) = \$108.87$$

Since the opportunity cost of administrative workers was assumed equal to the cost to the employer of temporary workers or the cost in small establishments, the *spr* for skilled administrative labor would be

$$\$108.87 / 224.28 = 0.49$$

For administrative workers in sectors with high benefits the benefit coefficient was estimated as 108 percent, which resulted in an hourly cost to the employer equal to

$$\$128.16 \times 2.08 = \$266.57$$

In this case, it was also assumed that the opportunity cost of this type of labor was the cost to the employer of temporary workers and of small enterprises. For this reason their *spr* was calculated as

$$\$108.87 / 266.57 = 0.41$$

Skilled Workers

Skilled workers presented an educational level considered average, since 50 percent of them completed only secondary education (Table 8.26). No data on their unemployment level was available, but it was suspected to be high because unemployment among people with this educational level was also high. The average hourly salary, calculated on the basis of information from the *National Household Survey* (1984) was 102.71 in 1984 pesos. Benefits for blue-collar workers, estimated from the *Annual Manufacturing Survey* (1985), were 70.7 percent on average, which excluded the following broad industries: beverages (313), paper (341), chemicals (351), oil refining (353), rubber (355) and steel (371). As a result, the hourly average cost to the employer was:

$$\$102.71 \times 1.707 = \$175.33$$

These workers frequently acquire their skills in temporary jobs, or in small enterprises, where they develop their skills for jobs in the formal sector. Thus, the opportunity cost of a worker who enters the formal market could be considered equal to the marginal product in these less desirable occupations. Considering that there was mobility of skilled workers between temporary

Table 8.26 Skilled workers according to educational level completed (in percentages)

Survey	None	Primary	Secondary	University
National Household, 1984	2.01	45.61	46.18	6.20
National Household, 1987	3.28	41.10	49.12	6.50
Income and Expenditure,1985–86	1.79	36.16	54.91	7.14
Employment and Housing, 1987	2.48	46.04	48.62	2.86

Source: Authors' elaboration.

jobs and jobs in small establishments, salaries for these workers in these submarkets were compared to salaries in permanent jobs. Based on the results of these comparisons, presented in Table 8.27, an approximate ratio of 0.85 was used, so that the salary in temporary and microenterprise occupations would be

$$0.85 \times \$102.71 = \$87.30$$

Benefits were calculated applying the same criteria used for administrative labor. Skilled workers with temporary contracts, or employees in small establishments were estimated to receive 28.47 percent of the benefits received by their colleagues in the formal market, that is

$$0.2847 \times 0.707 = 0.2013$$

This coefficient results in a cost of employing workers temporarily or in small enterprises of $104.87. The *spr* in consumption numeraire for skilled workers was calculated as the ratio of the two costs

$$\$87.30 \times 1.2013 / \$175.33 = 0.60$$

For skilled workers in sectors with high benefits, a benefits coefficient of 120 percent was estimated, and the *spr* in consumption numeraire would be equal to

$$\$104.87 / (\$102.71 \times 2.2) = 0.46$$

Table 8.27 Hourly salary of skilled workers (in 1984 pesos)

| Occupation | Temporary | Small establishments | Medium and large establishments | Relative salaries | |
	(a)	(b)	(c)	(a)/(c)	(b)/(c)
Worker, metallurgical	68.73	73.80	77.83	0.88	0.94
Worker, wood, paper	53.67	57.34	86.67	0.62	0.66
Worker, chemical	172.28	71.17	112.55	1.53	0.63
Worker, fur tanning and dyeing	52.08	67.80	73.82	0.71	0.92
Tailor	62.90	66.19	68.24	0.92	0.97
Spinner	75.63	61.27	94.34	0.80	0.65
Glass worker	56.44	56.20	79.74	0.71	0.70
Machine operator	68.33	n.a.	79.99	0.85	n.a.
Fine furniture maker	71.83	71.52	80.49	0.89	0.89

Source: DANE (1987a, Stage 44).

Unskilled Urban Labor

Unskilled labor registered low educational levels. All the surveys analyzed during the course of this study (Table 8.28) indicate that between 55 and 60 percent of unskilled workers had only primary education or less. No data exist about unskilled labor unemployment; however, it is expected to be average since that is the unemployment rate for the educational level attained by the majority of these workers. Using the data of the *National Household Survey* (1984), the hourly salary of unskilled permanent workers in an establishment of 11 or more workers was estimated at $86.993. The benefits coefficient was calculated from the category 'Workers', of the *Annual Manufacturing Survey*, giving a result of 0.707. Therefore, the cost to the employer would be equal to

$$1.707 \times 86.993 = \$148.50$$

In the case of unskilled labor no significant difference was found for salaries paid to different occupations and industries.

At the margin, the supply of unskilled workers to the formal sector of the economy could come from four possible sources: unemployed, temporary workers, workers in microenterprises, or rural migrants. Even though rural–urban migration had slowed down in Colombia, it continued to exist. Social and political pressures, low living standards, and low salaries in the countryside encouraged migration, but migrants did not go directly to formal employment. Flórez et al. (1988) showed that Colombia's migratory pattern followed a path from the countryside to a small town, from there to a medium-sized town, and only afterwards to a big city. During this process the migrant went through a formative cycle doing temporary or nonsalaried work, and working in microenterprises – costs that are not included in the opportunity cost of the rural migrant. Therefore, it was unskilled workers with temporary

Table 8.28 Unskilled workers according to educational level completed (in percentages)

Survey	None	Primary	Secondary	University
National Household, 1984	5.08	56.56	36.51	1.85
National Household, 1987	5.60	52.30	39.40	2.70
Income and Expenditure,1985–86	4.45	50.00	42.62	2.93
Employment and Housing, 1987	5.32	55.62	36.93	2.13

Source: Authors' elaboration.

contracts or employed in microenterprises who were assumed to supply the formal market at the margin.

The opportunity cost of the temporary unskilled workers, and that of those occupied in small enterprises, was estimated by the respective cost to the employer, since these markets operate freely and unaffected by labor legislation. The average ratio between temporary or microenterprise wages, and those paid in medium and large establishments was 0.85 (Table 8.29). Thus, the hourly shadow salary, without adjusting for benefits, was

$$0.85 \times \$86.99 = \$73.94$$

The corresponding benefit coefficient was calculated as equal to that of the skilled workers, resulting in an hourly cost to the employer of

$$\$73.94 \times 1.2013 = \$88.82$$

and a shadow price ratio of unskilled labor of

$$\$88.82 / \$148.50 = 0.60$$

For industries with high benefits, a benefits coefficient of 120 percent of the salary was calculated from the 'Workers' category of the *Annual Manufacturing Survey* for the corresponding sectors. Thus, the hourly cost to the employer would be equal to

$$\$86.99 \times 2.2 = \$191.38$$

and the corresponding *spr* would be

$$\$88.82 / \$191.38 = 0.46$$

The cost of employing both unskilled and skilled labor in the formal sector exceeded their estimated opportunity costs at efficiency prices. The resulting *sprs* indicate that in both cases only 60 percent of the cost to the employer corresponded to the cost at efficiency prices.

8.8   RESULTS

Shadow price ratios and conversion factors were calculated in the consumption numeraire according to equations (6.7) and (7.13), using the CALPAN program (Londero and Soto, 1998). The values for the *sprfe* (1.18) and the *sprs* for labor were those estimated in sections 8.6 and 8.7, respectively.

Table 8.29 Hourly wages of unskilled workers (in 1984 pesos)

Occupation	Temporary (a)	In small establishments (b)	In medium and large establishments (c)	Relative wages (a)/(c)	(b)/(c)
Manufacturing	61.07	60.64	96.11	0.64	0.63
Painter	71.11	64.53	92.48	0.77	0.70
Construction	74.27	69.58	76.15	0.98	0.91
Machine operator	62.85	53.52	77.43	0.81	0.69
Driver	69.40	73.90	82.42	0.84	0.90
Cleaning staff	89.06	65.60	75.49	1.18	0.87
Laundering, etc.	61.71	43.30	66.17	0.93	0.66

Source: DANE (1987a, Stage 44).

The shadow price ratio for foreign labor was calculated as follows

$$spr(fl) = \beta \; ccf + (1 - \beta) \; sprfe$$

where β is the share of income spent in the country, and *ccf* is the consumption conversion factor. The calculation was carried out for $\beta = 0.50$ and assumes that foreign labor pays no direct taxes (see equation (3.26)).

The shadow price ratios for taxes and normative excess profits were equal to zero, since these are transfers between individuals. Thus:

$spr(tax) = 0$
$spr(b) = 0$

The sectoral gross operating surpluses (*gos*) were valued at shadow prices by means of corresponding sectoral investment conversion factors; that is:

$spr(gos \; industry \; and \; mining) = icf \; manufacturing$
$spr(gos \; services) = icf \; services$
$spr(gos \; transportation) = icf \; transportation$
$spr(gos \; agriculture) = icf \; agriculture$

The shadow price ratio of inputs in fixed supply was set equal to one; that is, $spr(fs) = 1$. Lastly, the shadow price ratio of land was also set equal to one, since it was not possible to obtain an estimate for the opportunity cost attributable to the areas occupied by hydroelectric developments.

A summary of shadow price ratios for nonproduced inputs and transfers is provided in Table 8.30 and the resulting *spr_j* are presented in Table 8.31. In the case of marginally produced goods, the *spr_j* should be interpreted with caution. They do not correspond, and consequently should not be applied to all goods classifiable under these industries, since there could be imports of close substitutes that may be classified under the same group. They rather should only be applied to those goods from these industries that are produced at the margin.

Table 8.30 Shadow price ratios for primary inputs

Primary inputs	spr_{hj}
By-products	1.00
Foreign exchange	1.18
Indirect taxes	0.00
Skilled labor[a]	0.60
Skilled labor, high benefits[b]	0.46
Foreign labor[c]	1.00
Unskilled labor[a]	0.60
Unskilled labor, high benefits[b]	0.46
Administrative labor[a]	0.49
Administrative labor, high benefits[b]	0.41
Professional labor	1.00
Professional labor, high benefits	0.87
Unskilled labor, primary sector	1.00
Gross operating surplus, manufacturing industries	0.87
Gross operating surplus, agriculture	0.91
Gross operating surplus, services	0.80
Gross operating surplus, transport	0.80
Normative excess profits	0.00
Land	1.00

Notes: [a] Includes manufacturing and services excluding industries paying high benefits. [b] Four-digit ISIC industries 3133, 3134, 3411, 3412, 3419, 3511, 3512, 3513, 3551, 3559, 3692, 3710. [c] Note that the value of one was not assumed, but is the result of applying the formula presented at the beginning of this section.

Table 8.31 Shadow price ratios

Code[a]	Description	*spr*
1000-0	Other agricultural products (1-digit ISIC aggregate)	0.91
1000-1	Swine, sheep and other cattle	0.86
1000-2	Poultry farming	0.86
1000-3	Agricultural services, machinery	0.79
1000-4	Agricultural services, plowing animals	0.87
1000-5	Agricultural services, aerial spraying	0.78
1000-6	Agricultural services, irrigation	0.79
1111-1131	Corn	0.90
1111-1157	Sorghum	0.89
1111-1165	Rice	0.90
1111-8208	Bovine cattle	0.90
1112-9200	Fresh milk	0.91
2100-0	Coal mining	0.86
22001124	Natural gas	0.87
2300-0	Iron ore and non-ferrous ore mining	0.90
2900-1	Calcareous tufa quarrying	0.87
2900-2	Sand and gravel	0.91
2900-3	Unpurified sea salt	0.86
2901-3209	Mining and quarrying of other sands for industrial use	0.89
31	Other food products, beverages and tobacco (2-digit ISIC aggregate)	0.76
3111-1	Slaughter of large cattle, with and without refrigeration	0.85
3111-3	Cleaning, and preparation of offal and other by-products of slaughter	0.72
3111-5	Preparation of cold meats, other uncanned cold meats, ham, bacon, sausages, etc.	0.81
3111-6	Meatpacking of preserved meats in sealed containers	0.81
3111-7	Slaughter of farm fowl, and small animals, with or without refrigeration	0.84

Note: [a] Eight-digit codes and those for drinking water, commerce, transport and communications, correspond to ISIC codes used by the DANE. The rest are *ad hoc* codes for this study.

Code[a]	Description	*spr*
3111-8	Extraction and refining of pork lard and other edible animal fats	0.79
3112-1	Pasteurizing, homogenizing, adding vitamins and bottling of fresh milk	0.89
3112-2	Butter and cream	0.85
3112-4	Preserved milk and milk products	0.85
3112-5	Ice-cream, sherbet and milk-based dessert	0.81
3113-7	Dehydration of fruit, legumes and other vegetables	0.88
3114-1	Preparation of edible fish and shellfish, fresh, refrigerated or frozen	0.88
3115-1	Unrefined oils and vegetable fats	0.87
3115-4	Refining of oils and vegetable fats, excluding hydrogenation	0.85
3115-6	Margarine and cooking fats	0.83
3115-7	Hydrogenating of vegetable and animal fats and oils, purified or unpurified	0.85
3116-1	Wheat flour	0.83
3116-2	Corn flour and kernels	0.87
3116-3	Rice mills	0.88
3116-5	Cereal and legume mills n.e.c.	0.82
3116-6	Blended and prepared flour from cereals, legumes and similar products	0.83
3116-8	Coffee husks	0.90
3117-3	Crackers, cookies and biscuits	0.85
3118-1	Sugar manufacturing and refining	0.85
3118-3	Molasses manufacturing	0.83
3119-1	Chocolate and cocoa products	0.80
3119-7	Chewing gum manufacturing	0.81
3121-1	Starches and fecula, including gluten and gluten flour, manufacturing	0.84
3121-2	Coffee grinding and toasting; instant coffee and coffee extracts	0.83
3121-4	Extracts and syrups from fruit, cereals and other vegetables	0.79
3121-8	Yeast and baking powders	0.81

Code[a]	Description	*spr*
3122-1	Livestock feed	0.86
3122-2	Feed for fowls	0.87
3122-3	Pet food for dogs, cats and other animals	0.78
3122-9	Food substances and supplements for animals, including ground oyster shell, bonemeal and fish meal	0.82
3123-1	Baby food formula	0.84
3131-1	Distillation of ethylene alcohol for all uses	0.84
3131-9	Preparation of other similar alcoholic beverages	0.82
3133-2	Malt elaboration	0.78
3134-3	Nonalcoholic beverages, carbonated or otherwise	0.79
3140-1	Preparation of tobacco leaf	0.85
3140-2	Cigarettes	0.84
3140-3	Cigars	0.83
32	Other textile, clothing, and leather industries (2-digit ISIC aggregate)	0.76
3211-2	Preparation and cleaning of cotton for spinning	0.85
3211-4	Preparation and spinning of synthetic fibers	0.82
3211-5	Spinning of animal fibers	0.84
3211-6	Cotton spinning	0.84
3211-7	Spinning and weaving of hard vegetable fibers, including the production of sacks	0.80
3212-1	Curtains and similar ornaments made of textiles and plastic materials	0.79
3212-2	Bed clothing	0.80
3212-6	Canvas articles	0.80
3213-2	Knitted cotton clothes	0.78
3213-3	Knitted wool clothes	0.79
3213-5	Cotton fabric and knitted lace	0.81
3213-6	Synthetic fabric and knitted lace	0.80
3214-2	Carpets and rugs, mainly of cotton	0.79
3215-4	Cordage, rope and twine articles like nets, hammocks, and similar goods	0.82
3216-1	Cotton fabrics, drills, canvases and similar goods	0.81
3216-2	Spongy or felty cotton fabrics	0.82

Code[a]	Description	spr
3216-3	Hammocks of cotton fabrics	0.84
3217-1	Wool fabrics, woolen stuff and cloth	0.84
3217-2	Manufacturing of blankets, ponchos and similar goods	0.79
3218-1	Woven fabrics of artificial and synthetic fibers	0.79
3218-2	Articles of artificial and synthetic fibers	0.77
3219-3	Textile fabrics coated or impregnated with waterproofing materials, including imitation leather	0.83
3219-5	Batting and batting products	0.75
3220-2	Women and girls outer clothing	0.78
3220-4	Women and girls underwear	0.78
3220-6	Shirts	0.76
3220-7	Baby clothes	0.83
3220-8	Working clothes	0.78
3221-1	Swim suits	0.79
3221-2	Hats and hat parts	0.83
3221-5	Leather clothing	0.78
3221-6	Waterproof clothing	0.77
3221-7	Specialized clothing, academic gowns, religious outfits, costumes	0.78
3221-8	Gloves, ties, handkerchiefs, shawls, and similar articles	0.80
3231-1	Leather tanning and preparation	0.76
3233-3	Wallets, bags and other personal leather goods	0.77
3240-2	Leather shoes for men	0.76
3240-2	Women shoes	0.76
3240-4	Leather shoes for children	0.76
3240-5	Sport leather shoes	0.78
3240-6	Cloth shoes, sandals, slippers and similar goods	0.77
3240-8	Shoe ornaments and heels	0.75
3240-9	Other types of shoes n.e.c.	0.76
33	Other wood industries and their products (2-digit ISIC aggregate)	0.77
3311-1	Sawmills	0.84
3311-2	Conservation and treatment of wood	0.82
3311-3	Planing, including the manufacturing of moldings	0.82

Code[a]	Description	*spr*
3311-4	Plywood	0.81
3311-5	Wood-particle board	0.82
3311-6	Doors, windows and their separate parts	0.78
3311-7	Wood structures and on-site facilities for the construction industry	0.81
3312-2	Wood boxes	0.80
3319-1	Cork products	0.76
3319-9	Coffins, funerary urns and wooden articles n.e.c.	0.78
3320-1	Furniture for electrical appliances, sewing machines, etc.	0.79
3320-4	Furniture of cane, bamboo, and similar materials	0.79
34	Other paper, printing and editorial products (2-digit ISIC aggregate)	0.77
3411-1	Manufacturing of wood pulp, sugarcane waste rags and fibers n.e.c.	0.84
3411-2	Paper	0.81
3411-3	Cardboard	0.83
3412-1	Corrugated cardboard and fiberboard boxes	0.80
3412-2	Collapsible cardboard boxes	0.79
3412-4	Paper sacks and bags	0.79
3419-1	Special papers, polished, waxed, laminated and those with hand finishing	0.80
3419-9	Manufacturing of paper and cardboard n.e.c.	0.78
3420-3	Typography and lithography	0.80
3420-4	Engraving, photo-engraving, electrotyping, stereotyping	0.80
3420-5	Library binder	0.78
35	Other chemical substances and chemical products derived from oil, coal, rubber and plastics (2-digit ISIC aggregate)	0.78
3511-1	Organic chemical products, cyclical and acyclical compounds, excluding industrial gases	0.84
3511-2	Organic chemical products n.e.c., excluding industrial gases	0.80
3511-3	Industrial inorganic chemical products, excluding gases that are not of chlorine and other halogen	0.79

Code[a]	Description	*spr*
3511-4	Other inorganic chemical products, excluding radioactive ones	
3511-5	Industrial gases, excluding chlorine and other halogen, natural gas and other untreated hydrocarbons	0.82
3511-7	Organic dyeing products, dyeing extracts and organic tanning materials, synthetic ones, etc.	0.81
3511-8	Pigments and coloring materials n.e.c. for the manufacturing of colors, varnishes, lacquers, enamels, etc.	0.84
3512-1	Nitrogenous, phosphate and potassium fertilizers	0.79
3512-2	Elaboration of mixed organic and natural fertilizers, with dung, vegetable waste and dross	0.77
3512-3	Production and mixing of insecticides, pesticides and physiological regulators	0.83
3513-2	Synthetic materials by polymerization, copolymerization, including synthetic rubber and latex	0.78
3513-3	Regenerated cellulose, its chemical derivatives, vulcanized fiber	0.83
3513-4	Other resins and artificial plastic materials, including those obtained from animal and vegetable materials	0.82
3513-5	Manufacturing of cellulose fibers and other artificial fibers, excluding glass, in the form of monofilament, staples or tows, suitable for use in textile machines	0.81
3521-1	Paints and varnishes for general and industrial use	0.79
3521-2	Lacquers in general	0.81
3522-3	Synthetically-produced, vegetable-based drugs and medicines, excluding antibiotics	0.86
3522-4	Vitamins and provitamins of natural and synthetic substances	0.78
3522-9	Medicines and pharmaceutical products n.e.c.	0.82
3528-2	Compounds for treating metals, soldering compounds, electrode coverings, and similar products	0.84
3529-2	Explosives, ammunition and detonators	0.80
3529-3	Matches	0.79
3529-4	Inks for printing, writing, drawing and other uses	0.80

Code[a]	Description	*spr*
3529-5	Elaboration of essential oils, resins and mixtures, excluding those produced from wood distillation	0.77
3529-6	Photographic film and paper	0.84
3529-7	Glues, adhesives, synthetic cements, plastic starch	0.82
3529-8	Fireworks	0.78
3529-9	Other prepared chemicals n.e.c.	0.83
3530-1	Petroleum derived fuels	0.77
3540-2	Asphalt cement, paving mixtures and asphalt roofing materials	0.82
3540-4	Oils and lubricants not produced by refineries	0.89
3551-1	Rubber tires	0.81
3559-1	Basic rubber forms, plates, tubes and analogous products	0.80
3559-2	Rubber articles for hygienic, laboratory and pharmaceutical use	0.79
3559-4	Rubber shoes and their parts, including rubber/textile shoes	0.77
3559-5	Rubber articles for industrial and mechanical use	0.79
3560-1	Basic plastic forms, sheets, films, bars, tubes	0.82
3560-2	Plastic foam, plastic foam articles	0.79
3560-3	Household plastic articles	0.82
3560-4	Tubular plastic film	0.88
3560-5	Plastic boxes and containers	0.82
3560-6	Plastic spare parts and accessories for industrial use, including furniture for electrical apparatus	0.81
3560-9	Plastic furniture and products n.e.c.	0.81
36	Manufacturing of other nonmetallic mineral products excluding those derived from oil and coal (2-digit ISIC aggregate)	0.80
3610-2	Ceramic sanitary apparatus and accessories for plumbing	0.83
3610-3	Ceramic or porcelain tiles	0.84
3620-1	Glass in primary forms	0.92
3620-2	Safety and hardened glass	0.82
3620-3	Glass containers and articles for industrial use	0.85
3620-4	Glass articles for construction and technical uses	0.89
3620-5	Glass dinnerware and similar utensils	0.83

Code[a]	Description	*spr*
3621-3	Glass fibers	0.77
3621-4	Fiberglass articles	0.83
3691-1	Refractory articles for industry and construction	0.87
3691-2	Clay bricks and tiles	0.82
3691-3	Clay pipes and accessories	0.82
3692-1	Cement	0.79
3692-2	Gypsum and gypsum products	0.80
3692-3	Lime and carbonates	0.77
3699-1	Preparation of concrete	0.81
3699-2	Concrete products, including prefabricated ones	0.79
3699-3	Asbestos-cement products	0.77
3699-4	Stone crushing, cutting and polishing	0.80
3699-5	Marble crushing, cutting and polishing	0.82
3699-7	Asbestos products, threads, materials, felts, etc.	0.80
3699-9	Other nonmetallic mineral products n.e.c.	0.81
37	Other basic metallic industries (2-digit ISIC aggregate)	0.85
3710-1	Iron alloys and their products	0.80
3710-2	Mineral and iron reduction	0.73
3710-3	Steel	0.79
3710-4	Hot rolled steel	0.77
3710-5	Cold rolled steel	0.82
3710-7	Iron and steel products, manufacturing	0.78
3710-8	Forged iron or steel products, manufacturing	0.75
3720-1	Copper recovery and secondary smelting, including copper alloys	0.83
3720-2	Copper rolling and drawing	0.83
3720-3	Rolled and drawn copper and copper alloy products	0.76
3720-6	Plated, stretched and pulled under pressure, excluding aluminum articles and aluminum alloys	0.82
3720-7	Articles of forged aluminum and aluminum alloys	0.79
3721-1	Lead recovery and secondary smelting	0.84
3722-9	Recovery and manufacturing of other nonferrous metals	0.82
3723-2	Gold refining, plating and smelting	0.81

Code[a]	Description	*spr*
38	Other metallic products, machinery and equipment, (2-digit ISIC aggregate)	0.77
3811-2	Hand tools for agricultural, forestry and garden use	0.78
3811-3	Mechanical, carpentry, and construction tools	0.80
3811-9	Hardware articles, including locks and keys n.e.c.	0.79
3812-1	Metal furniture and accessories for offices	0.78
3812-4	Metal furniture and accessories for commerce and services	0.79
3813-1	Metal doors, windows and parts	0.81
3813-2	Metal plated parts	0.81
3813-3	Architectural and ornamental elements	0.81
3813-4	Production of prefabricated houses and parts	0.80
3813-5	Metal structures, including those installed that cannot be declared separately	0.79
3813-6	Items for boiler workshops, even those installed that cannot be declared separately	0.80
3814-1	Sanitary artefacts and metal accessories for plumbing	0.80
3814-3	Metal valves, accessories for pipes, excluding regulating valves, brass plumbing articles	0.79
3819-1	Metal containers, excluding those of large dimensions for use in bales, storage and transportation	0.81
3819-2	Large capacity metal bins and bales for packing, storage and transportation	0.82
3819-3	Safe boxes and bullet-proof containers	0.78
3819-4	Nails and screws	0.81
3819-5	Portable kitchen items and other stamped products	0.81
3819-7	Wire-made goods	0.81
3819-9	Other metal goods	0.79
3821-4	Internal combustion engines, excluding automobile motors	0.79
3822-3	Towing machinery	0.79
3822-5	Machinery and apparatus for poultry farming	0.79
3823-3	Parts and accessories for machine-tools, measuring tools for machinists	0.79

Code[a]	Description	*spr*
3823-7	Machinery for sawmills, and for working timber in general	0.77
3823-9	Special machinery for working with wood	0.74
3824-1	Machinery for food and beverage production	0.79
3824-5	Machinery for the manufacture of wood pulp, paper and cardboard,	0.80
3825-1	Scales and weights, excluding laboratory instruments	0.80
3825-2	Typewriters	0.73
3825-6	Computers, minicomputers, electronic machinery, parts and accessories	0.86
3826-1	Industrial plants, machinery and equipment for the elaboration of chemical products and oil refining	0.82
3826-3	Machinery and equipment for the manufacture of rubber	0.76
3826-8	Special machinery and equipment for the construction industry	0.80
3827-1	Compressors, pumps for water and other liquids	0.80
3827-2	Air-conditioning equipment, excluding pipes and other similar metal-plated items	0.81
3827-8	Equipment for atomization of liquids and powders, excluding domestic ones	0.80
3829-7	Machinery and equipment for services n.e.c.	0.79
3829-9	Ball and roller bearings, pistons, valves, parts for machinery of general use	0.79
3831-1	Electricity generating plants	0.79
3831-2	Electric motors, generators	0.80
3831-3	Electric transformers, convertors and rectifiers excluding those specially designed for radio, TV and communications	0.80
3831-5	Electric soldering equipment, manufacturing	0.80
3831-8	Auxiliary electrical equipment for internal combustion engines, manufacturing	0.78
3831-9	Similar apparatus and equipment n.e.c.	0.80
3832-2	Transmission and reception equipment, radio, television receivers	0.86
3832-3	Transmission and reception equipment for radio, telephony, radiotelephony	0.82

Code[a]	Description	*spr*
3832-4	Systems and principal components for the reproduction, transmission and reception of sound and images, excluding items for communications lines	0.76
3832-6	Telephonic and telegraphic apparatus	0.81
3832-8	Reproduction of records, tapes and videotapes	0.80
3832-9	Apparatus and parts for radio, television and communications not included previously	0.79
3833-2	Electric kitchen apparatus, utensils for food preparation, such as blenders, food processors, etc.	0.79
3833-3	Electrodomestic cleaning and ironing apparatus	0.79
3839-1	Insulated wire and cable	0.81
3839-4	Electric filament, discharge and voltaic arc lamps, flash bulbs	0.80
3839-6	Electrical accessories for lighting in general	0.79
3839-7	Electricity conducting devices such as switches, interrupters, etc.	0.79
3839-8	Nonconducting devices for electrical usage, such as electrical conduits, electric panel boxes, metal accessories for conducting parts	0.80
3839-9	Other electrical apparatus, accessories and articles n.e.c., such as bells, alarms, incubators, and others n.e.c.	0.81
3841-1	Construction and reconstruction of large ships	0.78
3841-2	Ship repair	0.77
3841-3	Construction and reconstruction of boats	0.76
3841-4	Boatyards	0.81
3841-5	Marine engines and boilers	0.79
3842-2	Repair of railway engines and equipment	0.72
3842-9	Parts for railway equipment	0.78
3843-1	Automobiles	0.80
3843-2	Heavy vehicles	0.79
3843-3	Automobile bodies and chassis	0.82
3843-4	Engines, gearboxes for vehicles excluding electrical generators, electric traction motors	0.79
3843-6	Autoparts n.e.c.	0.79

Code[a]	Description	spr
3843-7	Reconstruction of vehicle motors excluding electric equipment	0.79
3844-1	Motorcycles, scooters and similar vehicles with auxiliary motors	0.74
3844-2	Cars, wheelchairs, etc. for the disabled	0.77
3844-3	Bicycles, tricycles, similar vehicles and mopeds	0.77
3844-6	Parts and accessories n.e.c. for bicycles, mopeds, scooters, and similar vehicles	0.80
3845-2	Fabrication and reconstruction of airplane motors	0.88
3845-9	Repair and maintenance of airplanes	0.92
3849-2	Manually operated vehicles, excluding wheelchairs	0.78
3851-1	Medical, surgical, dental and veterinary instruments and apparatus, excluding optical instruments, X-ray and electrotherapy apparatus	0.80
3851-7	Instruments for the regulation and control of industrial operations	0.81
39	Other manufacturing industries (2-digit ISIC aggregate)	0.78
3901-2	Gold, silver and platinum jewelry	0.78
3901-4	State mint	0.80
3902-3	String and bow instruments, excluding electronic ones	0.78
3903-6	Items for billiards, bowling alleys, etc.	0.82
3904-2	Dolls and accessories, puppets, marionettes, etc.	0.79
3904-7	Metal sewing items such as needles, pins, poppers, hooks, etc. n.e.c.	0.79
3909-1	Umbrellas, parasols, walking sticks, and similar articles	0.85
3909-9	Manufacturing industries n.e.c.	0.81
3999-9	Miscellaneous inputs	0.79
4141-0	Electricity, industrial	0.90
4141-1	Electricity, commercial	0.79
4141-2	Electricity, agriculture	1.40
4242-0	Potable water	2.65
5050-0	Industrial construction	0.79
6161-0	Commerce	0.75
7170-0	Gas pipeline transportation	0.78

Code[a]	Description	*spr*
7171-1	Road transportation	0.75
7171-2	Medium-distance road transportation (two axle)	0.75
7171-3	Long-distance road transportation (two axle)	0.79
7171-4	Long-distance road transportation (three axle)	0.71
7171-5	Long-distance road transportation (three axle plus two axle trailer)	0.71
7222-0	Communications	0.76
8140-0	Agricultural machinery	0.78
8282-0	Services and insurance	0.71
8383-1	Accessories and spare parts	0.77
8383-2	Manufacturing services	0.77
8383-3	Industrial machinery and equipment	0.77
8640-0	Office equipment	0.79
8740-0	Transportation equipment	0.79
9000-1	Industrial investment conversion factor	0.87
9000-2	Agricultural investment conversion factor	0.91
9000-3	Transportation investment conversion factor	0.80
9000-4	Services investment conversion factor	0.80
9000-5	Consumption conversion factor	0.82

APPENDIX 8.1   THE PREPARATION OF THE INPUT–OUTPUT TABLE

This appendix provides a brief description of the preparation of the most important columns of the input–output table. Further details are provided in Cervini (1992) and Cervini et al. (1990).

8.A1 MANUFACTURES

The Annual Manufacturing Survey

In 1985, the *Annual Manufacturing Survey* collected data on 6406 establishments, representing 24.8 percent of all industrial firms registered in the *Anuario Empresarial de Colombia* (CONFECAMARAS, 1985) and approximately 75 percent of the gross value of manufacturing production. The *Survey* identifies outputs at an 8-digit ISIC level. The next level of aggregation (5-digit ISIC) is that of an industry; that is, a group of establishments that produce a diversity of products (8-digit level), the most important of which (highest share in total output value) correspond to the same 5-digit ISIC. Thus, the lowest possible level of aggregation for defining an industry was the 5-digit ISIC.

DANE assigns each manufacturing establishment to an industry by identifying the five most important products (eight digits) that correspond to the same 5-digit ISIC, which defines the 'industry' to which the establishment belongs. Hereafter, the 'characteristic product' of an 'industry' refers to all those 8-digit outputs whose first five ISIC digits are equal to those of the 'industry' in question. In a similar fashion, the 'characteristic industry' of a product is that which corresponds to the first five ISIC digits of the product in question. Thus, a product may be produced by various industries. In fact, there were products mainly produced by an industry of which they were not 'characteristic products'.

Manufactured Inputs and Manufacturing Industries

Based on the *Annual Manufacturing Survey*, a proxy of a make matrix U was prepared. Its rows registered the value of inputs consumed, and the columns the consuming industries. A matrix of imported intermediate consumption U^m and another of domestic intermediate consumption U^d were prepared, such that $U = U^d + U^m$. Note that U, U^m and U^d were commodity by industry matrixes. From here on, u_{ij} was the total value of the input i used by industry j, u^d_{ij} the value of the domestic input i used in industry j, and u^m_{ij} the value of the imported input i used by industry j. Therefore, $u_{ij} = u_{ij}^d + u_{ij}^m$ and the total use of input i by all manufacturing industries was the sum of the total domestic and the total imported inputs used

$$u_i = \sum_j u_{ij} = \sum_j u_{ij}^d + \sum_j u_{ij}^m = u_i^d + u_i^m$$

With industries and inputs classified at the 5-digit ISIC level, the resulting matrix was of 461 inputs by 423 industries. The 461 inputs may be grouped as follows:

Manufactured	427
Agriculture, forestry and fishing	16
Mining	12
Others	6
Total	461

Manufactured Inputs

The *Annual Manufacturing Survey* asked each establishment to provide the value of outputs, by-products and manufacturing works performed for others, allowing the total value of each establishment's production (at 5-digit ISIC), to be obtained. The sum of the value of production of each good for all the establishments provided the total value of its production by the subset of establishments represented in the survey. Some of these products were used as inputs by other manufacturing establishments represented in the survey (registered in U^d), others were used by manufacturing establishments not included in the survey, a further share were used as inputs by nonmanufacturing industries, and the remaining products went to final demand. Thus, the survey provided the value of production of i by industry j (X_{ij}), the total value of production of output i (X_i), and the total value of production of industry j (X_j), where $\sum_j X_{ij} = X_i$ and $\sum_i X_{ij} = X_j$.

The first step was to identify those inputs whose 'characteristic industries' did not register production ($X_j = 0$). Eighty manufactured inputs complied with this condition, and four possible causes were found to explain it. First, the input was fully imported, and there was no domestic production. Included in this group were those inputs for which the share declared as of imported origin was high in relation to the total input use ($\sum_j u_{ij}^m / \sum_j u_{ij}$) and for which no industry registered production ($X_i = 0$). Sixteen inputs complied with these characteristics, and at this stage of the study were *preliminarily* classified as imported. This meant that the part of the input that in the survey was declared as of national origin, was also treated as imported under the presumption that there had been a reporting error.

Second, it is possible that the input was, in fact, the by-product of an industry different from the 'characteristic' one; that is no industry in the survey declared it as a characteristic output ($X_{ij} = 0$ for $i = j$), some industries declared it as a noncharacteristic output ($X_{ij} \neq 0$ for some $i \neq j$), and the characteristic industries did not register production ($X_i = 0$). At this level of aggregation (5-digit ISIC) only three inputs were identified with these attributes. The value of the by-product was subtracted from the production value of the industry where it was obtained, so that the resulting cost structure reflects the production conditions of those outputs that were produced at the margin. The value of these by-products was assigned as a demand with a negative sign to a row in matrix $\mathbf{F}$, corresponding to the concept of 'fixed-supply inputs'. Thus, the cost structure reflects the fact that, on producing one more peso of marginally produced outputs, a certain quantity of by-products are *sold* (negative cost).

Third, the input may also have been a 'basket' of unknown composition, and it was therefore impossible to identify, for each industry, the origin of the goods that made it up. Only one 'input' with these characteristics was identified and this was put under the heading of 'other inputs'. A special *ad hoc* cost structure was elaborated for this case by aggregating all manufacturing establishments.

Finally, the input may have been a secondary output of other industries. In these cases, the industry producing the largest share of this product was identified and the row of the secondary input was added to the row of the input corresponding to the industry producing it as secondary. In other words, for each one of these inputs the proportions X_{ij}/X_i, were calculated, selecting as the industry of origin that which corresponded to the maximum value of this ratio.

The initial search allowed most of the inputs to be assigned to their originating industries, except 10 that did not register production in any industry ($X_i = 0$), but declared a high percentage of domestic origin. Presuming that the survey had not captured the data corresponding to the domestic production of these goods, an industry of origin was assigned to each input taking into account the possible alternatives, and the characteristics of the input. Only one input was not assigned, since it was not possible to identify an industry with similar technological characteristics. This input was later added to a group of other 'insignificant' inputs.

Analysis of the Industries

The analysis of the industries (columns) of the matrix began with the identification of those that registered production ($X_j \neq 0$) but whose 'characteristic products' were not inputs of any industry ($u_j = 0$); in other words, identifying industries whose 'characteristic product' was a final good or an input of nonmanufacturing activities. A few were associated with the intermediate demand of one or more secondary products, others were used in agriculture, commerce, construction, communications and transportation. The remaining 65 industries were considered as producers of consumer or capital goods, and given the general denomination of CCG.

These 65 industries made up a separate subsystem, since they used, but did not provide inputs. Thus, the corresponding columns were eliminated from matrixes U^n and U^m. The cost structures of some CCG, however, were taken into account in the calculation of the investment conversion factor, and thus indirectly participated in determining the shadow price ratios of other industries.

Aggregation of Inputs and Industries

The next step was to determine the 'insignificant' inputs by applying the following criteria. First, the share of each input in total manufactured inputs

$$t_i = \sum_j u_{ij} / \sum_i \sum_j u_{ij} = u_i / \sum_i u_i$$

and use coefficients $a_{ij} = u_{ij}/X_j$ were calculated for each input in every industry. Then, an input was defined as 'insignificant' if it simultaneously fulfilled the following conditions

$$a_{ij} < 0.05 \text{ for all } j, \text{ and } t_i < 0.0005$$

Some 'insignificant inputs' were by-products and others were not manufactured, and thus received separate treatment in the matrix. The remaining inputs were aggregated into nine groups or baskets, one for each 2-digit ISIC division. In order to calculate a conversion factor for each group, each basket was associated with a corresponding 'cost structure' (see equation (6.10)). To that effect, these inputs were treated as imported for the part declared as such in the census, and as nontraded for the part declared as of domestic origin. The possible error resulting from this simplification is minimal, since these inputs only represented 1.24 percent of total inputs used by manufacturing industries.

Thus, the remaining inputs presented one of the following characteristics: (1) they were relatively important for at least one of the industries (at least one $a_{ij} > 0.05$); or (2) they were relatively important in total manufactured inputs ($t_i > 0.0005$), that is, inputs of minor importance for each individual industry but widely used in the manufacturing sector.

Classification of Manufactured Inputs

When all establishments in the survey using an input declared it to be foreign, it was classified as imported. When an input was declared as only being of domestic origin, it was classified as nontraded.

A matrix of 1873 inputs and 289 industries called **W** was prepared at the 8-digit level.[18] The corresponding matrixes of imported inputs (8-digit level) **W**^{m} and the matrix of domestic inputs (8-digit level) **W**^{d} were prepared simultaneously, and allowed the imported share of each input (w_i^m/w_i) and the share of each industry in the total (w_{ij}^m/w_{ij}) to be calculated. The data on value of production for each 8-digit input were also available, allowing for the identification of those goods that were used as inputs, but were not produced by any manufacturing industry.

Inputs whose 'characteristic industry' presented an export coefficient greater than one percent were analyzed at 8-digit ISIC level in order to identify potential marginally exported inputs.[19] To that effect, the following criteria were taken into account. First, if the input was not produced domestically ($\delta_i = 0$), the possibility of it being marginally exported was discarded.[20] Second, the ratio of exports of each input in 1985 to the total value of output in the survey was used to obtain an indicator for the exported share.[21] Third, a detailed analysis was conducted on whether the input was the same good being exported; if that was not case, the possibility of being marginally exported was eliminated. Finally, if both goods turned out to be the same, expert opinion was sought on the capacity to expand supply in order to meet an additional domestic demand. In the end, only five inputs produced with high rates of capacity utilization and whose exports represented a high share of their total production were classified as marginally exported.

Thirty-seven inputs were identified as by-products and included in matrix **F** as fixed supply inputs. Inputs derived from oil refining were classified separately due to their importance in total inputs, and to the fact that the information supplied by the survey was insufficient.

---

18. Only those goods actually reported as used as current manufactured inputs were included. Those declared as produced, but not as used by any industry in the survey were considered consumption or capital goods (CCG).

19. In fact, of the group of industries that were excluded and which registered some level of exports, only five exceeded 0.05 percent.

20. For detecting possible omissions, survey production data were compared to those from the Colombian Institute of Foreign Trade (INCOMEX) and the opinion of experts from that Institute. When the INCOMEX data, and the experts' opinion coincided in that domestic production existed, it was assumed that it took place in establishments not covered by the survey.

21. This task required previously establishing, with DANE and INCOMEX sectoral experts, the correspondence between the 8-digit ISIC, used in the *Annual Manufacturing Survey*, and the 8-digit tariff nomenclature (NABANDINA) used to classify trade data.

A simple reading of the data provided by the *Annual Manufacturing Survey* was not considered sufficient for automatically classifying the remaining 1810 inputs, since there could be several sources of error. The respondent could have made a mistake with respect to the imported origin of an input, declaring it to be of domestic origin, simply because it was purchased domestically. The survey may not register the domestic production of an input. Different inputs may have been classified under the same 8-digit ISIC in such a way that the parts declared as imported and domestically produced in reality correspond to different inputs. An input may have been imported, and at the same time produced domestically, in which case it became necessary to check whether it was marginally imported. Finally, the data supplied by the 1985 survey may have been outdated, and no longer represented the current situation. Therefore, it was deemed necessary to consult other sources, such as specialists in each input.

Given the large amout of these inputs, it was also necessary to reduce their number before analyzing them in detail. To that effect, the following criteria were applied: (1) inputs only declared as of domestic origin were classified as nontraded; (2) inputs only declared as being imported were considered to be imported; (3) inputs for which no production data were found in the survey ($\delta_i = 0$) and for which more than 70 percent ($w_i^m/w_i > 0.7$) was declared as of foreign origin were treated as fully imported; that is, it was assumed that either the amount declared as being of domestic origin was the result of a reporting error, or that the input was imported at the margin. A total of 779, 84, and 139 inputs respectively were included under each of these criteria.[22]

In order to classify the remaining 808 inputs the corresponding industry coefficients ($a_{ij} = w_{ij}^m/X_j$) were calculated. Then, inputs were classified as imported for the part declared as such, and as nontraded for the part declared to be of domestic origin, when they fulfilled all of the following conditions: (1) there was domestic production ($\delta_i \neq 0$); (2) their coefficients did not exceed 5 percent ($a_{ij} < 0.05$, for all j); and (3) the imported proportion was greater than 70 percent of all the transactions ($w_i^m/w_i > 0.7$ for all j). These cases included those inputs that were 'insignificant' for all industries that were produced domestically, and a large percentage of which were imported – thus supporting the assumption that the imported goods were different from those reported as being of domestic origin. Also classified as imported for the part declared as such, and as nontraded for the part declared of domestic origin, were those inputs for which the imported share in each transaction was less than 10 percent ($w_{ij}^m/w_{ij} < 0.1$) and whose domestic production was greater than their total use as inputs, both as declared in the survey.

---

22. Initially, inputs were to be considered as imported if there was no domestic production ($\delta_i = 0$) and more than 70 percent was declared imported by all industries ($w_{ij}^m/w_{ij} > 0.7 \, \forall j$). However, no input complied with this criterion.

These criteria allowed for the classification of 41 inputs. The remaining 767 were submitted to a more detailed analysis in order to determine whether those declared as of foreign origin were in fact different goods from those declared as of domestic origin. This was the case for 556 of the 767 inputs in question, which were then classified as imported for the part declared to be of foreign origin, and as nontraded for the part declared to be of domestic origin. The remaining 211 imported inputs were the same as goods produced domestically, and could be grouped into three categories based on the following conditions: (1) the domestic supply was temporarily insufficient, a situation that had been or was expected to be overcome in the short or medium term, in which case the input was classified in its entirety as nontraded (16 inputs); (2) recent manufacturing undertakings had resulted, or would result in the short term, in the substitution of these imports, in which case the input was classified as nontraded in its entirety (14 inputs); (3) the imported input competed with the domestically produced one, in which case it was classified as marginally imported (118 inputs).

Final Inputs and Industries of the Matrix

After classification, inputs were aggregated at the 5-digit ISIC level, and together with those industries classified at five digits as nontraded and those resulting from the groupings at 2-digit ISIC, a total of 209 inputs at five digits was reached. The corresponding columns (cost structures) were prepared from the *Annual Manufacturing Survey*. The column for 'Other inputs' was prepared by simply adding on the columns of all manufacturing industries. It was also necessary to include the cost structures of the 13 industries whose characteristic products were used by nonmanufacturing industries. For this reason, the submatrix for manufactured inputs and manufacturing industries included 209 inputs and 222 industries.

8.A2 OTHER COSTS OF MANUFACTURING INDUSTRIES

Electricity consumption by manufacturing industries was treated in the matrix as an intermediate demand to 'Electricity, manufacturing'. The value of that consumption was calculated as the difference between the value of electricity purchased and that of electricity sold, as declared in the *Annual Manufacturing Survey*.

Accessories and spare parts were not classified according to origin, and were treated as follows. First, a column was prepared by adding on the cost structures of various industries producing 'accessories and spare parts'. Then, the *Annual Manufacturing Survey* was used to obtain the imported share of the 'characteristic products' of these industries, which came to approximately 23 percent. This percentage was then used to break down all elements in the row 'Accessories and spare parts' into 23 percent imported and 77 percent nontraded. The imported part was split into foreign exchange, taxes, transportation and commerce, while that of national origin was treated as an intermediate demand to the industry 'Accessories and spare parts'.

Fuels and lubricants were broken down using the data provided by *Encuesta de Usos en el Sector Industrial* (MINMINAS, 1983).[23] The main limitations of the method used were: (1) it was based upon data on fuels only; (2) it assumed that no technological changes affecting fuel use had occurred since 1982, and that relative fuel prices had remained constant since that year; and (3) it assumed that all fuels bought were consumed during the year.

Expenditures for the renting of property were treated as an intermediate demand to 'Construction'. Those for leasing machinery and equipment were treated as an intermediate demand to 'Industrial machinery and equipment', whose cost structure was prepared by way of adding on the cost structures of the different industries producing these products. Insurance payments and advertisement were considered as an intermediate demand to 'Insurance and services', whose cost structure was prepared on the basis of the input–output matrix (DANE, 1985b). Expenditures on water and sewage, postal services, and telephone were treated as intermediate demands to the 'Drinking water' and 'Communications' sectors, respectively,[24] assuming that 30 percent corresponded to 'postal services, and telephone', and the remaining 70 percent to 'water and sewage'. The column for 'Communications' was also elaborated on the basis of the DANE input–output matrix. The costs of professional services were included in matrix **F** as payments for professional labor. Interest payments, commissions, copyrights and 'other items' remained under the heading of gross operating surplus.

Labor Costs

The *Annual Manufacturing Survey* provided data on employment, and wages and benefits received during the year, divided into seven categories: (1) owners, business partners and unpaid relatives; (2) managers; (3) employees; (4) national technicians; (5) foreign technicians; (6) blue collar workers; and (7) apprentices. In order to match this classification with that resulting from the analysis of the labor markets (section 8.7), it was necessary to regroup wage costs by type into foreign, professional, administrative, skilled and

---

23. It excludes those incorporated directly into the product, as these are included in another section of the survey under the heading of raw materials.

24. It excludes water used as an input as defined in Ch. III of the survey (Consumption of raw materials, materials and packaging).

unskilled workers. To that effect: (1) managers and national technicians, together with payments for professional services, were included under professional labor; (2) payments to apprentices and laborers who work in their homes were included as unskilled labor; (3) payments made for repairs and maintenance were included with those of skilled workers; (4) payments to foreign technicians were classified as skilled foreign labor in matrix F; and (5) wages paid to blue-collar workers were divided into skilled and unskilled, and payments to employees into administrative and unskilled.

Payments to blue collar workers were broken down into skilled and unskilled based on the following assumptions: (1) at least one out of every ten workers in an industry was skilled. In industries were the average wage was equal to the minimum legal wage, the proportion of unskilled workers was assumed to be equal to 90 percent; (2) a maximum of 80 percent of the workers in any industry would be skilled, and the industry with the highest average wage would have 20 percent unskilled workers; (3) between these two hypothetical extremes, the proportion of skilled workers was determined by the ratio between two differences: the average wage in the industry less the legal minimum wage, and the maximum wage less the minimum legal one; and (4) unskilled workers earned the legal minimum wage.

On the basis of these assumptions, the proportion of skilled workers in any industry may be divided into two parts: one that is constant, and equal to 10 percent – assumption (1) – and a variable one determined according to assumption (3), subject to the upper limit imposed by assumption (2). Thus,

$$\frac{L_{si}}{L_i} = 0.1 + \frac{(w_i - w_{min})}{(w_{max} - w_{min})}(0.8 - 0.1)$$

where L_{si} are the skilled workers in industry i, L_i are total workers in industry i, w_i is the average wage in industry i, w_{min} is the minimum legal wage, and w_{max} is the maximum average wage of manufacturing workers. Therefore, the proportion of unskilled workers would be

$$\frac{L_{ui}}{L_i} = 1 - [0.1 + \frac{0.7(w_i - w_{min})}{(w_{max} - w_{min})}]$$

where L_{ui} are the unskilled workers in industry i. Since according to assumption (3) unskilled workers receive the minimum legal wage, it follows that

$$\frac{L_{ui}}{L_i}\frac{w_{min}}{w_i} = \frac{w_{min}}{w_i}[1 - 0.1 + \frac{0.7(w_i - w_{min})}{(w_{max} - w_{min})}]$$

This expression allows for an approximate estimation of the share of the unskilled workers in total payments to blue-collar workers in industry i, and was used in this study to break down the payments to 'workers' in each of the industries found in the *Annual Manufacturing Survey*. The share of salaries corresponding to unskilled employees was estimated according to the same procedure, using the maximum average salary corresponding to the category 'employees'.

Indirect Taxes on Inputs

In the survey, the value of purchases of raw materials, materials and packaging did not include indirect taxes, which had to be assigned. The amount of indirect taxes on all outputs was also added to the total value of the production in each industry.

Gross Value of Production

Gross value of production as reported by the *Annual Manufacturing Survey* had to be adjusted and valued at users' prices. The starting point was identity

$$
\begin{array}{l}
\text{Gross value} \quad\quad\quad \text{value of} \quad\quad \text{changes in} \quad\quad \text{sales} \\
\text{of production} \quad = \quad \text{products} \quad + \quad \text{stock of work} \quad + \quad \text{taxes} \quad + \\
\quad\quad\quad\quad\quad\quad\quad\quad \text{obtained} \quad\quad\quad \text{in process}
\end{array}
$$

$$
\begin{array}{l}
\quad\quad\quad \text{consumption} \quad\quad \text{export} \quad\quad \text{electricity} \\
\quad\quad\quad \text{taxes} \quad\quad + \quad \text{taxes} \quad + \quad \text{sold}
\end{array}
$$

Then, the following adjustments were made. The value of products obtained included revenue from the sales of inputs, even though the cost of acquiring these inputs was not included in the value of the inputs used by the establishment. For this reason, this revenue was deducted from the value of the products obtained. Export taxes were eliminated, since the column was built to supply an additional domestic demand, and electricity sales were deducted from purchases in order to record the net consumption.

Finally, transportation and commerce costs were assigned in order to value output at user prices. Transportation costs were estimated by multiplying the tons produced by each manufacturing industry by the national average cost for the average distance, which underestimates transportation costs for that part of the production that was expressed in units other than weight. Trade margins were calculated on the basis of the DANE input–output table (1985b), which provided trade margins for its 32 industries. These margins were applied to the 5-digit ISIC manufacturing industries. Then, the gross value of production at users' prices was calculated according to the following expression,

Gross value of   Gross value   sales of   trade   transportation
production at   = of production – inputs + margins + margins
users' prices

Gross Operating Surplus at Market Prices

The gross operating surplus at market prices is the difference between the value of the gross production at user prices and the cost of the produced inputs (intermediate demand) and nonproduced ones. It can be demonstrated (section 6.3) that the gross operating surplus at market prices is approximately equal to the capital cost annuity, plus the normative excess profits (positive or negative). In order to break down the gross operating surplus in these two components, the capital cost has to be assigned, something that was not possible in the case of manufactured products. The resulting implicit assumption is that normative excess profits were nil, so that the gross operating surplus at market prices was equal to the capital cost annuity.

8.A3 AGRICULTURE[25]

Selection and Classification

The inputs of agricultural origin represented around 21 percent of total manufacturing inputs. They were initially analyzed at the product level – 101 inputs at 8-digit ISIC – with the aim of selecting and classifying the most important ones, and adding on the remainder. On the basis of the proportion of imported origin, the specific analysis of each product, and data availability, 19 nontraded products were classified as being able to be incorporated individually into the matrix, and as products for which adequate information for preparing their cost structures could be obtained. Of these 19 inputs, swine and ovine livestock were treated together, resulting in a single cost structure called 'Sheep, swine and other livestock'. In a similar fashion, chicken, turkey and egg production were pooled into one cost structure, 'poultry products'.

Some inputs of agricultural origin were classified as marginally imported and treated as other imported inputs. The remaining inputs of agricultural origin represented only 2.85 percent of total manufacturing inputs and were added to a single row called 'Other agricultural products'. The part declared of foreign origin was treated as imported, and the part declared of domestic origin was considered nontraded and associated to a cost structure (column)

---

25. The term 'agriculture' is used broadly in reference to agriculture, livestock, apiary, fishing and forestry activities.

in the matrix.

During the elaboration of these cost structures, four additional columns corresponding to diverse agricultural services were identified as necessary: machine rental, aerial fumigation, contracting of plowing animals, and irrigation.

Cost Structures

Production cost data for temporary crops were obtained from CEGA-ICA (1987). Only two permanent crops – coffee and sugar cane – were incorporated into the matrix due to the difficulty of obtaining data for other permanent crops. In the case of coffee, cost structures were prepared from annual flow data prepared by the *Federación Nacional de Cafeteros*, which include both revenue, investment and operating cost data, including harvesting and replanting. The approach assumed that the increase in coffee production would come from expanding the cultivated land surface. In the case of sugar cane, only the production cost structures for one of the most important regions was used (ASOCAÑA, 1986), since these were the only available ones.

Four columns corresponding to animal products were prepared: bovine livestock; milk; sheep, swine and other livestock; and poultry products (eggs, chicken, turkeys and ducks). The cost structures used were those prepared by CEGA (Balcázar, 1985). For cattle raising, data for an average technological level, as found in the region of Magdalena Medio and Córdoba, were used. It was characterized by the use of management techniques and production methods – such as improved pastures, mineral supplements, and some concentrated foods – and by the regular use of animal husbandry practices and techniques for improving stock, as well as for investment in pastures and fencing. The manure – a by-product of the livestock activity – was assigned with a negative sign to the row of 'fixed supply inputs' in matrix **F**. Milk production data corresponds to farms that were dedicated exclusively to this product, and in which some cattle were sold as a by-product. The value of said by-product was registered in matrix **A** with a negative sign at the intersection with the row corresponding to cattle raising. With regard to 'Sheep, pork and other livestock', pork production was the most important activity, followed by that of sheep. For this reason, a weighted average of the cost structures of these two activities was taken as representative of the group, using the participation in the total value of production as weights.

Given the information available, and little evidence for the use of new techniques in the livestock sector, cost structures were prepared on the basis of average costs of existing farms. This method implies that production increases were expected to originate in increases in land surface using the same production techniques. The cost structures were provided by the Ministry of Agriculture (MINIAGR, 1984) and include only five components: food, veterinary medicines, unskilled labor, new animals and gross operating surplus.

The production of poultry products comprises that of eggs and chicken. Both, however, present very similar cost structures and were treated as a single one. The corresponding cost structure was based on data published by the Ministry of Agriculture (MINIAGR, 1984).

A column for 'Other agricultural products' was included to represent the cost structure for the remaining inputs of agricultural origin. It was prepared using the cost structures of four nontraded inputs of agricultural origin that were not included individually in the matrix, and for which there was sufficiently reliable information: other vegetables, 'caña panelera', banana, and fruit trees. The cost structures of these four crops reflect traditional production processes, no use of machinery, little use of fertilizers and pesticides, and intensive use of unskilled labor.

For those cases were it was possible to calculate some capital cost annuities, input costs included the annuity corresponding to the cost of those capital goods that were identified. The difference between value of production and total production costs (including identified capital costs) was assigned to the gross operating surplus.

8.A4 MINING

In accordance with the criteria used in the case of inputs of manufacturing and agricultural origin, those inputs of mining origin with a significant participation in the costs of other activities – in particular the manufacturing industries – were included separately in the matrix. The remaining inputs, which together only represented 0.3 percent of the total amount of manufactured inputs, were added together into one single group called, 'Other minerals'. This 'basket' of inputs was treated as imported for the part declared as such in the survey, and as nontraded for the part declared to be of national origin.

8.A5 IMPORTED INPUTS

The value of imported inputs was broken down into foreign exchange, taxes, transport and trade margins. The last two were assigned to matrix **A**, while foreign exchange and taxes were assigned to matrix **F**. The data published by DANE (1985c) provided the CIF value for each tariff item (NABANDINA), which was the lowest possible level of aggregation. In the *Annual Manufacturing Survey*, however, imported inputs were classified according to ISIC, making it necessary to establish a NABANDINA–ISIC correlation.

Taxes on Imported Manufactured Inputs

Taxes actually paid for each NABANDINA-specified item were estimated as follows. Tariff and duties under Law 68/83 were taken from the DANE data for the not exempted part of *ad valorem* and other duties. In the case of duties according to Law 50/84, PROEXPO, and the Stamp, the exempted NABANDINA codes were identified, and the amount of each tax was calculated for the remaining codes on the basis of the corresponding rates. Finally, the sales tax was calculated using the rate corresponding to each NABANDINA and applied to the CIF value of the import plus all other charges. With the aim of corroborating the results thus obtained, the resulting average *ad valorem* rates were compared with the implicit rates calculated from revenue collection by the corresponding institutions. The differences at the individual tax level were small and the average total rate was almost the same.

Transportation and Commerce Margins

Transportation costs for imported inputs were calculated by multiplying the tons imported by an average transportation fare estimated from data provided by the Colombian Federation of Freight Transportation, and the Ministry of Transportation and Public Works. Since no detailed information on commerce margins for imports existed, data from the import matrix of Colombia's 1980 national accounts (DANE, 1985b) were used. This matrix provided commerce costs by industry of origin and destination for only 32 industries, resulting in the same trade margin being applied to all NABANDINA codes included in the same industry.

References

ADB (1997), *Guidelines for the Economic Analysis of Projects*, Asian Development Bank.

Ahmad, E. and N. Stern (1989), 'Taxation for Developing Countries', in H. Chenery and T.N. Srinivasan (eds), *Handbook of Development Economics*, Vol. II, Amsterdam: North-Holland.

Ahmad, E. and N. Stern (1991), *The Theory and Practice of Tax Reform in Developing Countries*, Cambridge: Cambridge University Press.

Arrow, K. (1995), 'Intergenerational Equity and the Rate of Discount in Long-term Social Investment', mimeo, presented to the International Economic Association World Congress.

ASOCAÑA (1986), 'Costos de producción de caña de azúcar' (Sugar Cane Production Costs), mimeo, Comité de Costos de Producción, Asociación de Productores de Caña de Azúcar, January–March.

Atkinson, A.B. and N. Stern (1974), 'Pigou, Taxation and Public Goods', *Review of Economic Studies*, **41** (1), 119–28.

Bacha, E. and L. Taylor (1971), 'Foreign Exchange Shadow Prices: A Critical Review of Current Theories', *Quarterly Journal of Economics*, **85** (2), 197–224.

Balassa, B. (1964), 'The Purchasing-Power-Parity Doctrine: A Reappraisal', *Journal of Political Economy*, **72** (6), 584–96.

Balassa, B. (1979), 'A "Stages" Approach to Comparative Advantage', in I. Adelman (ed.), *Economic Growth and Resources*, London: Macmillan.

Balcázar, A. (1985), Costos de producción en la ganadería vacuna (Cattle Raising Production Costs), Centro de Estudios Ganaderos, Bogotá: Banco Ganadero.

Ballard, C., J. Shoven and J. Whalley (1985), 'General Equilibrium Computations of the Marginal Welfare Costs of Taxes in the United States', *American Economic Review*, **75** (1), 128–38.

Banco de la República (1984), 'Indice de la tasa de cambio real del peso colombiano. Métodología y resultados 1975–1984' (The Colombian Peso Real Exchange Rate Index. Methodology and Results 1975–1984), *Ensayos sobre política económica*, (6), 127–48.

Banco de la República (1988), 'Indice de la tasa de cambio real del peso colombiano. Revisión de ponderaciones y cambio de base' (The

Colombian Peso Real Exchange Rate Index. Reviewing the Weights and Changing the Base Year), *Revista del Banco de la República*, **61** (723), 15–18.

Bruce, C. (1976), 'Social Cost-Benefit Analysis: A Guide for Country and Project Economists to the Derivation and Application of Economic and Social Accounting Prices', *World Bank Staff Working Paper* No. 239, Washington, DC: World Bank.

Bulmer-Thomas, V. (1982), *Input–Output Analysis in Developing Countries*, New York: John Wiley.

CEDE (1987), *Encuesta de empleo y vivienda. Cobertura Bogotá (Employment and Housing Survey)*, 1985, 1986 and 1987 tabulations, Centro de Estudios de Desarrollo Económico, Bogotá: Universidad de los Andes.

CEGA-ICA (1987), 'Costos de producción y productividad agrícola en Colombia (Etapa I)' (Agricultural Production Costs and Productivity in Colombia, Stage I), *Coyuntura Agropecuaria*, (16), 35–85.

Cervini, H. (1992), 'Colombia', in Londero (1992).

Cervini, H. et al. (1990), 'Estimación de precios de cuenta para Colombia' (Estimating Accounting Prices for Colombia), working paper, Project BID-DNP, ATN/SF-2879-RE, Washington, DC: Inter-American Development Bank.

Clark, P., L. Bartolini, T. Bayoumi, and S. Symansky (1994), 'Exchange Rates and Economic Fundamentals', *Occasional Paper* 115, Washington, DC: International Monetary Fund.

Clavijo, S. (1982), 'Los depósitos previos de importación' (Import Advance Deposits), *Ensayos sobre política económica*, (1), 53–87.

CONFECAMARAS (1985), *Anuario Empresarial de Colombia* (Colombia Business Yearly Report), Bogotá: Confederación de Cámaras de Comercio.

Curry, S. and J. Weiss (1994), *Project Analysis in Developing Countries*, London: Macmillan.

DANE, *Boletín mensual de estadística* (*Monthly Bulletin of Statistics*), Bogotá: Departamento Administrativo Nacional de Estadística.

DANE (1985a), *Encuesta anual manufacturera* (*Annual Manufacturing Survey*), magnetic tape, Bogotá: Departamento Administrativo Nacional de Estadística.

DANE (1985b), *Cuentas nacionales de Colombia* (*Colombia's National Accounts*), Bogotá: Departamento Administrativo Nacional de Estadística.

DANE (1985c), *Anuario de comercio exterior* (*Foreign Trade Yearly Report*), Bogotá: Departamento Administrativo Nacional de Estadística.

DANE (1987a), *Encuesta de hogares* (*Household Survey*), magnetic tape, Stages 31, 44 and 58, Bogotá: Departamento Administrativo Nacional de Estadística.

DANE (1987b), *Cuentas nacionales de Colombia* (*Colombia's National*

Accounts), Bogotá: Departamento Administrativo Nacional de Estadística.

Dasgupta, P. (1972), 'A Comparative Analysis of the UNIDO Guidelines and the OECD Manual', *Bulletin of the Oxford Institute of Economics and Statistics*, **34** (1), 33–51.

Dinwiddy, C. and F. Teal (1986), 'Project Appraisal Procedures and the Evalution of Foreign Exchange', *Economica*, **53** (29), 97–107.

Dinwiddy, C. and F. Teal (1990), 'Foreign Exchange Equivalence and Project Appraisal Procedures', *Economic Journal*, **100** (401), 567–76.

Dinwiddy, C. and F. Teal (1996), *Principles of Cost–Benefit Analysis for Developing Countries*, Cambridge: Cambridge University Press.

Dobb, M. (1960), *An Essay on Economic Growth and Planning*, London: Routledge.

Dornbusch, R. (1974), 'Tariffs and Non-traded Goods', *Journal of International Economics*, **4** (2), 177–86.

Drèze, J. and N. Stern (1987), 'The theory of cost–benefit analysis', in A. Auerbach and M. Feldstein (eds), *Handbook of Public Economics*, Vol. II, Amsterdam: North-Holland.

Edwards, S. (1988), *Exchange Rate Misalignment in Developing Countries*, World Bank Occasional Paper No. 2 (New Series), Baltimore: Johns Hopkins.

FEDESARROLLO (1984), 'Empleo y salarios' (Employmend and Wages), *Coyuntura Económica*, **14** (4), 70-98.

Feldstein, M. (1978), 'The Inadequacy of Weighted Discount Rates', in Layard (1978b).

Ferguson, C. and J. Gould (1975), *Microeconomic Theory*, 4th edn, Homewood: Irwin.

Fernández Rivas, J., J. Roldán, A. O'Byrne and C. Bello (1985), 'Protección aduanera e incentivos a las exportaciones' (Tariff Protection and Export Incentives), *Revista Planeación Nacional*, **17** (4), 75–150.

Flament, M. (1987), 'Estimación de precios de cuenta para el Uruguay' (Estimating Accounting Prices for Uruguay), mimeo, Washington, DC: Banco Interamericano de Desarrollo and Oficina de Planeamiento y Presupuesto.

Flórez, C., R. Echeverry and R. Méndez (1987), 'Caracterización de la transición demográfica en Colombia' (A Characterization of Colombia's Demographic Transition), in Ocampo and Ramírez (1987), Vol. 1.

Flórez, C., R. Méndez, R. Echeverry, M. Granados, L. García and A. Morales (1988), *Evaluación de la cobertura del censo de 1985 y elaboración de proyecciones de población 1985–2000* (*Evaluating the Coverage of the 1985 Census and Preparing Population Forecasts for 1985–2000*), CEDE, Bogotá: Universidad de los Andes.

Frederick, S., G. Loewenstein and T. O'Donoghue (2002), 'Time Discounting and Time Preference: A Critical Review', *Journal of Economic Literature*,

40 (2), 351–401.

Freeman, A. M. (1993), *The Measurement of Environmental and Resource Values. Theory and Methods*, Washington, DC: Resources for the Future.

Gittinger, J.P. (1982), *Economic Analysis of Agricultural Projects*, Second Edition, Baltimore: John Hopkins.

Grennes, T. (1984), *International Economics*, Englewood Cliffs: Prentice Hall.

Guerrero, P., E. Howard, D. Lal and T. Powers (1977), 'Pilot Study on National Accounting Parameters: Their Estmation and Use in Chile, Costa Rica and Jamaica', *Papers on Project Analysis* No. 6, Washington, DC: Inter-American Development Bank.

Hamilton, C. (1976), 'The Cost of Effort Expended: Examination of Some Arguments for Its Omission and an Illustratiion', *Oxford Economic Papers*, **28** (2), 304–16.

Hamilton, C. (1977), 'On the Social Cost of Individual's Extra Effort', *Journal of Development Studies*, **13** (3), 217–22.

Harberger, A. (1971), 'On Measuring the Social Opportunity Cost of Labor', *International Labor Review*, **103** (6), 559–79.

Harberger, A. (1973), *Project Evaluation: Collected Papers*, Chicago: Markham.

Harberger, A. (1977), 'On the UNIDO Guidelines for Social Project Evaluation', in H. Schwartz and R. Berney (eds), *Social and Economic Dimensions of Project Evaluation*, Washington, DC: Inter-American Development Bank.

Harberger, A. (1986), 'Economic Adjustment and the Real Exchange Rate', in S. Edwards and L. Ahamed (eds), *Economic Adjustment and Exchange Rates in Developing Countries*, Chicago: University of Chicago Press.

Harris, J. and M. Todaro (1970), 'Migration, Unemployment, and Development: A two sector analysis', *American Economic Review*, **60** (1), 126–42.

Haughwout, A. (1997), 'Central City Infrastructure Investment and Suburban House Values', *Regional Science and Urban Economics*, **27** (2), 199–215.

Henderson, J. and R. Quandt (1971), *Microeconomic Theory*, 2nd edn, New York: McGraw Hill.

Hicks, J. (1939), 'The Foundations of Welfare Economics', *Economic Journal*, **49** (196), 696-712. Reprinted in Hicks (1981).

Hicks, J. (1975), 'The Scope and Status of Welfare Economics', *Oxford Economic Papers*, **27** (3), 307–26.

Hicks, J. (1981), *Wealth and Welfare*, Cambridge, MA: Harvard University Press.

Howard, E. (1978), 'Estimation of the National Accounting Parameters at Efficiency Prices for Nicaragua', *Papers on Project Analysis* No. 7, Washington, DC: Inter-American Development Bank.

Hughes, G. (1979a), 'Shadow Prices for Project Appraisal in Morocco', mimeo, World Bank, Washington, DC.

Hughes, G. (1979b), 'Shadow Prices for Indonesia', mimeo, World Bank, Washington, DC.

ILO (1969), *International Standard Classification of Occupations*, revised edn, Geneva: International Labour Office.

ISA (1987), Documento ISA-OPUN 27/10/87 ISSE, Bogotá: Interconexión Eléctrica S.A.

Journal of Economic Perspectives (1994), 'Symposia on Contingent Valuation', *Journal of Economic Perspectives*, **8** (4).

Joshi, V. (1972), 'The Rationale and Relevance of the Little–Mirrlees Criterion', *Bulletin of the Oxford Institute of Economics and Statistics*, **34** (1), 3–32.

Klein, L. (1953), 'On the Interpretation of Professor Leontief's System', *Review of Economics and Statistics*, **20** (2), 131–6.

Krishna, K., R. Erzan and L.H. Tan (1994), 'Rent Sharing in the Multi-Fibre Arrangement: Theory and Evidence from US Apparel Imports from Honk Kong', *Review of International Economics*, **2** (1), 62–73.

Krishna, K., W. Martin and L.H. Tan (1995), 'Imputing License Prices: Limitations of a Cost-based Approach', mimeo, Conference on Empirical Investigations in International Trade, Purdue University, November.

Lal, D. (1973), 'Disutility of Effort, Migration, and the Shadow Wage Rate', *Oxford Economic Papers*, **25** (1), 112–26.

Lanzetta, C. (1986), 'Una nota metodológica sobre las utilidades de los exportadores privados de café colombiano' (A Methodological Note on the Profits of the Private Colombian Coffee Exporters), *Desarrollo y Sociedad*, (17/18), 159–76.

Lary, H. (1968), *Imports of Manufactures from Less Developed Countries*, New York: Columbia University Press.

Layard, R. (1978a), 'Introduction' to Layard (1978b).

Layard, R. (1978b), *Cost–Benefit Analysis*, New York: Penguin.

Little, I. and J. Mirrlees (1969), *Manual of Cost–Benefit Analysis in Developing Countries, Vol. II Social Cost–benefit Analysis*, Paris: OECD.

Little, I. and J. Mirrlees (1974), *Project Appraisal and Planning for Developing Countries*, New York: Basic Books.

Londero, E. (1981), 'El Salvador', in Powers (1981).

Londero, E. (1987), *Benefits and Beneficiaries. An Introduction to Estimating Distributional Effects in Cost–Benefit Analysis*, Washington, DC: Inter-American Development Bank. Second edn, 1996.

Londero, E. (1989), 'Sobre el uso de técnicas de insumo–producto para la estimación de precios de cuenta' (On the use of Input–Output Techniques for Estimating Accounting Prices), *Desarrollo y Sociedad*, (24), 131–58.

Londero, E. (1990), 'On the Treatment of Secondary Products and By-products in the Preparation of Input–Output Tables', *Economic Systems Research*, **2** (3), 321–2.

Londero, E. (1991), 'Los fundamentos del análisis costo beneficio y su reflejo en las principales versiones operativas' (The Foundations of Cost–Benefit Analysis and their Reflection in the Main Operational Versions), *Trimestre Económico*, **58** (229), 73–99.

Londero, E. (1992), *Precios de cuenta. Principios, metodología y estudios de caso* (*Accounting Prices. Principles, Methodology and Case Studies*), Washington, DC: Inter-American Development Bank.

Londero, E. (1994), 'Estimating the Accounting Price of Foreign Exchange: An Input–Output Approach', *Economic Systems Research*, **6** (4), 415–34.

Londero, E. (1996a), 'Reflections on Estimating Distributional Effects' in C. Kirkpatrick and J. Weiss (eds), *Cost Benefit Analysis and Project Appraisal in Developing Countries*, Cheltenham, UK and Brookfield, US: Edward Elgar.

Londero, E. (1996b), 'Shadow Pricing Rules for Partially Traded Goods', *Project Appraisal*, **11** (3), 169–82.

Londero, E. (1997), 'Trade Liberalization with a Fixed Exchange Rate', *International Trade Journal*, **11** (2), 247–76.

Londero, E. (1999), 'Secondary Products, By-products and the Commodity Technology Assumption", *Economic Systems Research*, **11** (2), 195–203.

Londero, E. (2000), 'Poverty Targeting Classifications and Distributional Effects', revised version, originally presented to the *Conference on People, Projects and Poverty*, Development and Project Planning Centre, University of Bradford, May 6–7, 1999.

Londero, E. (2001), 'By-Products', *Economic Systems Research*, **13** (1), 35–45.

Londero, E. and J. Remes (1989), 'Relative Price Changes, Profit Margins, and Expected Rates of Return in Manufacturing Exports: A Simulation for Argentina', unpublished manuscript.

Londero, E., J. Remes and S. Teitel (1998), 'Argentina: Natural Resources and Industrial Policy', in Londero, Teitel et al. (1998).

Londero, E. and R. Soto (1998), *CALPAN: A Microcomputer Model for Calculating Accounting Prices with Input–Output Techniques. User's Manual, Revision 1*, Washington, DC: Inter-American Development Bank.

Londero, E. and S. Teitel (1996), 'Industrialization and the Factor Content of Latin American Exports of Manufactures', *Journal of Development Studies*, **32** (4), 581–601.

Londero, E., S. Teitel et al. (1998), *Resources, Industrialization and Exports in Latin America*, London and New York: Macmillan and St Martin's.

Londoño, J. (1987), 'La dinámica laboral y el ritmo de actividad económica: un repaso empírico de la última década' (Labor Dynamics and Economic Activity Levels: A Review of the Last Decade), in Ocampo and Ramírez

(1987), Vol. 1.

Lucking, R. (1993), 'Technical Problems in the Appraisal of Projects Using the Semi-Input-Output Methdology', *Project Appraisal*, **8** (2), 113-23.

MacArthur, J. (1994), 'Estimating Efficiency Prices Through Semi-Input–Output Methods – A Review of Practice in Available Studies', *Journal of International Development*, **6** (1), 19–43.

McDonald, J. and C. Osuji (1995), 'The Effect of Anticipated Transportation Improvement On Residential Land Values', *Regional Science and Urban Economics*, **25** (3), 261–78.

McKenzie, G. (1983), *Measuring Economic Welfare*, Cambridge: Cambridge University Press.

Maneschi, A. (1990a), 'Project Appraisal Procedures and the Evaluation of Foreign Exchange: A Comment', *Economica*, **57** (226), 263–8.

Maneschi, A. (1990b), 'Income Distribution and Shadow Pricing in Open Economies', *Economic Record*, **66** (192), 23–31.

Marglin, S. (1963a), 'The Social Rate of Discount and the Optimal Rate of Investment', *Quarterly Journal of Economics*, **77** (1), 95–111.

Marglin, S. (1963b), 'The Opportunity Costs of Public Investment', *Quarterly Journal of Economics*, **77** (2), 274–89.

Mazumdar, D. (1976), 'The Rural–Urban Wage Gap, Migration, and the Shadow Wage', *Oxford Economic Papers*, **28** (3), 406–25.

Meade, J. (1972), Review of *Cost Benefit Analysis*, by E. J. Mishan, *Economic Journal*, **82** (325), 244–46.

Mejía, F. (1989), 'Estimación de precios de cuenta para la República Dominicana' (Estimating Accounting Prices for the Dominican Republic), *Monografías de análisis de proyectos* No. 36, Washington, DC: Inter-American Development Bank.

Mejía, F. and P. Roda (1987), 'Razones de precios de cuenta y matrices semi insumo–producto: una aplicación a la economía colombiana' (Accounting Price Ratios and Semi Input–Output Matrices: An Application to the Colombian Economy), *Desarrollo y Sociedad*, (19), 13–66.

MINIAGR (1984), *Diagnóstico de la actividad avícola en Colombia* (*A Diagnosis of the Poultry Activity in Colombia*), Oficina de Publicaciones, Bogotá: Ministerio de Agricultura.

MINMINAS (1983), *Encuesta de usos en el sector industrial* (*Survey of Uses in the Industrial Sector*), Estudio Nacional de Energía, Bogotá: DNP-Ministerio de Minas y Energía.

Mishan, E.J. (1980), 'How Valid Are Economic Evaluations of Allocative Changes', *Journal of Economic Issues*, **14** (1), 143–61.

Mishan, E.J. (1981a), *Economic Efficiency and Social Welfare*, London: Allen and Unwin.

Mishan, E.J. (1981b), *Introduction to Normative Economics*, New York and Oxford: Oxford University Press.

Mishan, E.J. (1988), *Cost–Benefit Analysis*, 4th edn, London: Unwin Hyman.

Misión de Empleo (1986), *Informe final (Final Report)*, Bogotá.

Newbery, D. and N. Stern (eds) (1987), *The Theory of Taxation for Developing Countries*, Oxford: Oxford University Press.

Ocampo, J. (1987), 'Régimen prestacional del sector privado' (The Private Sector Employment Benefit Regime), in Ocampo and Ramírez (1987).

Ocampo, J. and M. Ramírez (1987), *El problema laboral colombiano: informes de la misión Chenery (Colombia's Labor Problems: The Chennery Mission Reports)*, Vol. 1 and 2, Bogotá: Servicio Nacional de Aprendizaje, Departamento Nacional de Planeación and Contraloría General de la República.

Officer, L. (1976), 'The Purchasing-power-parity Theory of Exchange Rates: A Review Article', *IMF Staff Papers*, **23** (1), 1–60.

Parot, R. (1992), 'Venezuela', in Londero (1992).

Parot, R. (1998), 'Venezuela: Natural Resources and Public Enterprises', in Londero, Teitel et al. (1998).

Perfetti, M. (1987), *El impacto macroeconómico de la inversión pública. Un proyecto típico del sector eléctrico (The Macroeconomic Impact of Public Investment: A Typical Electricity Project)*, thesis, Bogotá: Universidad de los Andes.

Potts, D. (1999), 'Forget the Weights, Who Gets the Benefits? How to Bring a Poverty Focus to the Economic Analysis of Projects', *Journal of International Development*, **11** (4), 581–95.

Powers, T. (ed.) (1981), *Estimating Accounting Prices for Project Appraisal*, Washington, DC: Inter-American Development Bank.

Ray, A. (1984), *Cost–Benefit Analysis. Issues and Methodologies*, Baltimore: Johns Hopkins.

Reyes, A. (1987), 'Tendencias del empleo y la distribución del ingreso' (Employment and Income Distribution Trends), in Ocampo and Ramírez (1987), Vol. 2.

Sánchez, M. (1988), 'Una aproximación a la evolución del sector informal' (An Approach to the Evolution of the Informal Sector), thesis, Universidad de los Andes, Bogotá.

Sandmo, A. (1997), 'Redistribution and the Marginal Cost of Public Funds', Discussion Paper 08/97, Norwegian School of Economics and Business Administration.

Schohl, W. (1979), 'Estimating Shadow Prices for Colombia in an Input–Output Table Framework', *World Bank Staff Working Paper* No. 357, Washington, DC: World Bank.

Schwartz, H. and R. Berney (eds) (1977), *Social and Economic Dimensions of Project Evaluation*, Washington, DC: Inter-American Development Bank.

Scott, M., J.D. Macarthur and D.M.G. Newbery (1976), *Project Appraisal in*

Practice, London: Heinemann.

Sen, A.K. (1961), 'On Optimizing the Rate of Saving', *Economic Journal*, **71** (283), 479–96.

Sen, A.K. (1966), 'Peasants and Dualism With or Without Surplus Labor', *Journal of Political Economy*, **74** (5), 425–50.

Sen, A.K. (1972), 'Control Areas and Accounting Prices: An Approach to Economic Evaluation', *Economic Journal*, **82** (325S), 486–501. Also in Layard (1978b) and Sen (1984).

Sen, A.K. (1973) 'Behaviour and the Concept of Preference', *Economica*, **40** (159), 241–59.

Sen, A.K. (1975), *Employment, Technology and Development*, Oxford: Oxford University Press.

Sen, A.K. (1977) 'Rational Fools: A Critique of the Behavioural Foundations of Economic Theory', *Philosophy and Public Affairs*, **6** (4), 317–449.

Sen, A.K. (1979), 'Personal Utilities and Public Judgements: Or What's Wrong with Welfare Economics?', *Economic Journal*, **89** (355), 537–58.

Sen, A.K. (1984), *Resources, Values and Development*, Cambridge, MA: Harvard University Press.

Sen, A.K. (1987), *On Ethics and Economics*, New York: Basil Blackwell.

Sjaastad, L. and D. Wisecarver (1977), 'The Social Cost of Public Finance', *Journal of Political Economy*, **85** (3), 513–47.

Slemrod, J. and S. Yitzhaki (1996), 'The Costs of Taxation and the Marginal Efficiency Cost of Funds', *IMF Staff Papers*, **43** (1), 172–98.

Snow, A. and S. Warren (1996), 'The Marginal Welfare Cost of Public Funds: Theory and Estimates', *Journal of Public Economics*, **61** (2), 289–305.

Squire, L. (1989), 'Project Evaluation in Theory and Practice', in H. Chenery and T.N. Srinivasan (eds), *Handbook of Development Economics*, Vol. II, Amsterdam: North-Holland.

Squire, L., I. Little and M. Durdag (1979), 'Application of Shadow Pricing to Country Economic Analysis with an Illustration from Pakistan', *World Bank Staff Working Paper* No. 330, Washington, DC: World Bank.

Squire, L. and H. van der Tak (1975), *Economic Analysis of Projects*, Washington, DC: World Bank.

Tejada, J. (1980), 'Update of the National Accounting Parameters at Efficiency Prices for Costa Rica', *Papers on Project Analysis* No. 15, Washington, DC: Inter-American Development Bank.

Todaro, M. (1969), 'A Model of Labor Migration and Urban Unemployment in Less Developed Countries', *American Economic Reviw*, **59** (1), 138–48.

Todaro, M. (1976), *International Migration in Developing Countries: A Review of Theory, Evidence, Methodology and Research Priorities*, Geneva: International Labor Office.

Tower, E. and G. Pursell (1987), 'On Shadow Pricing Labour and Foreign Exchange', *Oxford Economic Papers*, **39** (2), 318–32.

UNIDO (1972), *Guidelines for Project Evaluation*, by P. Dasgupta, S. Marglin and A. K. Sen, New York: United Nations.

UNIDO (1980), *Practical Appraisal of Industrial Projects: Application of Social Cost–Benefit Analysis in Pakistan*, prepared by J. Weiss, New York: United Nations.

United Nations (1969), *International Standard Industrial Classification of All Economic Activities*, Department of Economic and Social Affairs, Statistical Office, Statistical Papers, Series M, No. 4, Rev. 2, New York.

Vousden, N. (1990), *The Economics of Trade Protection*, Cambridge: Cambridge University Press.

Weiss, J. (1985), 'National Economic Parameters for Jamaica', *Project Planning Centre Occasional Paper* No. 7, Bradford: University of Bradford.

Wildasin, D. (1988), 'Indirect Distributional Effects in Benefit–Cost Analysis of Small Projects', *Economic Journal*, **98** (392), 801–7.

Winch, D. (1975), *Analytical Welfare Economics*, Harmondsworth: Penguin.

World Bank (1989), 'Commercial Policy Survey', Report No. 7510-CO, Washington, DC.

Author Index

Subject Index